How To Write Successful Business Letters In Just 15 Days

By John P. Riebel

SUNVILLAGE
publications

www.sunvillagepublications.com

How To Write Successful Business Letters In Just 15 Days
By John P. Riebel

Copyright © 2011

www.sunvillagepublications.com

Cover design by www.WebCopyAlchemy.com

DEDICATION
To

Penny, David, Lucy Lee, Mom, and *Dad*— in
fulfillment of a promise made years ago

PREFACE

Anyone smart enough to hold down a responsible job in these highly competitive days of specialization can learn to write successful business letters. And it doesn't take five or ten months to learn how, either. It can be done in just 15 days—in only three weeks of five days each. This book will show you how. If you are the kind of person who doesn't want to waste time—who wants to learn how to improve his correspondence quickly and surely—you are the precise person I'm writing for.

Ordinarily, books on business letters are organized according to "types" of letters, as if a special technique had to be learned to write each different type. That is not true! There are basic, fundamentals that are common to *all* types of letters. Learn them and you will be well on your way toward knowing how to write effectively any "type" of letter.

Before you can hope to *write* a successful letter, you must *think* friendly, forceful thoughts, and you must *develop* friendly, forceful attitudes toward your reader. The first week's study—the first five DAYS—will give you the fundamental attitudes that you need before you can improve your business letters.

Next you will learn how to put your good attitudes or intentions into practice *in your business letters.* You will learn the necessary skills that will enable you to get across to your reader precisely what you intend to say. The second and third weeks' study—the last ten DAYS plus the CONCLUSION—will show you how to write more friendly, forceful—more successful—business letters.

Let me have just three weeks of your time, please. Each day read once, twice, three times, if you will, one day's study. Each day presents just one important new idea summarized by the title of that day's study. Read over and over the examples until these letters become a part of your own thinking and feeling. When you have digested that day's thought, go to the next, and so proceed through the entire book. And try to put into practice in each letter you write every principle you learn. If you will do this, you will, at the end of only 15 days, be writing really successful letters. They will flow so easily and smoothly that you will be surprised.

Included is a nearly complete list of contributors; some names were omitted by request. But this preface would not be complete without special acknowledgment to the following: MARSHALL M. GANS for starting me on the road to writing with his packet of 115 letters on refrigerating and air-conditioning subjects; FRED C. KELLY, editor of *Refrigerating Engineer,* for accepting and publishing my first articles on letter writing; ASHER B. SHAW, my friend and neighbor, for introducing me to the matchless letters of Irving Mack of Chicago; IRVING MACK (and his capable secretary, Vi DANE) for a wealth of material, for friendly encouragement, and for permission to use whatever letters I wanted; L. E. "CY" FRAILEY, my friend and acknowledged master, whose contribution is far more extensive than the few quotations from his excellent book, *Smooth Sailing Letters;* OWEN SERVATTUS, our General Office Manager at California State Polytechnic College; MARJORIE FISCHER of the California Division of Highways, for not only proofreading my manuscript, but also offering many valuable suggestions for improvement; and GLADDING, MCBEAN & Co., largest ceramic manufacturers on the West Coast.

It has been fun writing this book, and I sincerely hope that you will find it the most helpful guide in handling letter-writing problems that you have ever read. I have tried to make you pause and think—and also to pause and laugh a bit. I firmly believe in the salutary effect of well-placed humor, even in the important, serious business of writing business letters.

If you like what I have said, if I have helped you raise the level of your own routine business correspondence, I hope you'll let me hear from you. And if you have any suggestions or good examples, I would like them, too. To repeat a line from Mr. Carl

F. Braun's letter on page 21: "What we're all after is to teach people how to write useful letters." A "useful" letter is one that does the job you intend it to do—it is a successful business letter that will win friends for your company and keep your old customers coming back for more.

JOHN P. RIEBEL

P.O. Box 187
California State Polytechnic College
San Luis Obispo, California

NOTE

For the sake of uniformity, the publisher has felt it best to set all letters except a specified few (the Irving Mack letters in particular) in one style, the indented form. This does NOT mean that the author recommends or teaches this style of paragraphing to the exclusion of all others. There is much to be said for every letter form and style of paragraphing. The author recommends that each letter writer select the form and style that seems best suited to his needs, and that he use this form consistently. If his office or company uses one form, then he should conform to that style. If not, he should choose for himself the one he likes the best.

ACKNOWLEDGMENTS

MARSHALL M. GANZ, J. Herman Co., Inc., Los Angeles, California

ASHER B. SHAW, Manager, Fox-West Coast Theatres, San Luis Obispo, California

IRVING MACK, President, Filmack, Inc., Chicago, Illinois

F. H. ROY, Correspondence Supervisor, Montgomery Ward, Chicago

L. E. "CY" FRAILEY, The Dartnell Corporation, Chicago, Illinois, and Columbus, Ohio

CARL F. BRAUN, President, C. F. Braun & Co., Alhambra, California

W. S. CARPENTER, former President, E. I. du Pont de Nemours & Company, Wilmington, Delaware

R. H. KOCH, The National Cash Register Company, Dayton, Ohio (for permission to use the E. P. Corbett letters)

Printers' Ink, New York

PRENTICE-HALL, INC., New York

GLADDING, MCBEAN & Co., Los Angeles, California
VERNE BOGET, Vice President
M. A. DALY, Manager, Ceramic Veneer Department HAROLD F. SMITH, Manager, Tile Sales Department ALLAN PAUL, Advertising and Promotion Manager, Hermosa Tile Department
L. M. STEVENS, Chief Engineer, Southern Division CHARLOTTE DE ARMOND, formerly Advertising Manager, Dinnerware Division
E. J. FILSINGER, Asst. Mgr., Tile Sales Department J.
K. GIBSON, Ceramic Veneer Department DICK
WHEELER, Tile Sales Department FRANK FERREL, Tile
Sales Department R. P. READ, Tile Sales Department
SAM WILSON, Ceramic Veneer Department

HAROLD L. MAYER, Executive Secretary, Auto Maniacs of America, Stock-bridge, Michigan

J. H. CHAMBERLAIN, Secretary-Treasurer, Crowley, Milner & Company, Detroit

0. M. SCOTT AND SONS COMPANY, Marysville, Ohio

CHARLES W. RIEBEL CO., Louisville, Kentucky

FRANK M. FOLSOM, President, Radio Corporation of America, New York

RALPH PRIESTLEY, formerly Dean of Engineering, California State Polytechnic College, San Luis Obispo, California

WALTER ROTHSCHILD, President, Abraham & Straus, Brooklyn

L. I. KRILOFF, President, Kriloffice, Inc., Chicago

DR. ROBERT R. AXJRNER, Carmel, California, and the Fox River Paper Corporation, Appleton, Wisconsin

HERMAN J. KECK, Educational Director, Fireman's Fund Insurance Group, San Francisco

HARMAN W. NICHOLS, United Press Associates, Washington, D. C, and the Associated Press and the World Wide Photos, Inc., New York

WILLIAM L. BULKLEY, Chicago, Illinois

DEAN E. V. PULLIAS, Pepperdine College, Los Angeles

CAPTAIN JAMES E. MILLER, Armed Forces Blood Donor Program, U. S. Army, Washington, D. C.

ROBERT A. LOVETT, former Secretary of Defense, Washington, D. C.

MRS. JAMES FORRESTAL

MR. CLARENCE DILLON, Dillon, Read & Co., New York

SHERIDAN DOWNEY, former Senator from California, Washington, D. C.

THE BANK OF AMERICA, San Francisco

NORMAN BRUCE, Subscriber Service Bureau, FORBES Magazine of Business, New York

CHARLES KUSHINS, Oakland, California

COMMERCIAL CREDIT PLAN INCORPORATED, affiliated with the Commercial Credit Company, San Francisco

HARRY CASE, Advertising Department, The Trane Company, La Crosse, Wisconsin

C. J. PHILAGE, Advertising & Sales Promotion, The National Radiator Company, Johnstown, Pennsylvania

GEORGE J. LEY, Schwitzer-Cummins Company, Indianapolis, Indiana

FULTON LEWIS, JR., Radio Commentator, Mutual Broadcasting Company, Washington, D. C.

J. M. ARNSTEIN, Circulation Director, Coronet Magazine, Chicago

CORONET INSTRUCTIONAL FILMS, Chicago

K. J. FORSHEE, Division Credit Manager, National Lead Company, Los Angeles

L. L. BLAHNA, Advertising Department, General Mills, Inc., Minneapolis

H. B. RASMUSSEN, Manager of Government Business, Laboratory Chemical Division, J. T. Baker Chemical Co., Phillipsburg, New Jersey

R. J. CHRISMAN, Vice President in Charge of Sales, and L. L. GRASSO, Farmers Insurance Exchange, Los Angeles

R. G. HENRY, Advertising Department, The Goodyear Tire & Rubber Company, Inc., Akron, Ohio

K. W. ROBENSTINE, Kimball Tire Co., San Luis Obispo

ROBERT E. COWIN, Assistant to the Circulation Director, TIME Magazine, New York

CHARLES MASON, Credit Manager, TIME Magazine, New York

ROBERT FISLER, Circulation Promotion Manager, TIME Magazine, New York

K. L. MCKINNEY, J. W. Allen Co., San Francisco

M. E. CAIN, Victor Animatograph Corporation, Davenport, Iowa

ROY LANSING, Product Promotion Manager, Carrier Corporation, Syracuse, New York R. S. YOUNG, Metallurgist, The O.K. Tool Company, Inc., Milford, New
Hampshire
JOHN B. HOGAN, Barnes & Jones, Boston ROGER BROWNE, Assistant Manager, Parts Department, Cadillac Motor Car
Division, Detroit
ART FLOETHE, Parts Department, Cadillac Motor Car Division, Detroit
W. G. MITCHELL, JR., Marblehead, Massachusetts
E. E. Campbell, Kirkwood, Missouri
JOSEPH GARRETSON, Columnist, Cincinnati *Enquirer*
CHARLES E. ARENSTEN, Special Order Desk, Westlake Camera Stores, Inc., Los Angeles
N. UNINI, Assistant Secretary, Circus Foods, Inc., San Francisco EARL WEINSTEIN, California State Polytechnic College, San Luis Obispo G. KREPP, The Heath Company, Benton Harbor, Michigan GRACE BRANSON, Librarian, Public Library, Paso Robles, California GUY MATZINGER, California State Polytechnic College, San Luis Obispo
F. G. VAUGHAN, Vice President, The Grolier Society, Inc., New York
TROY L. DREXLER, President, The Coast Land Club, Los Angeles
DANNY LAWSON, Activities Officer, California State Polytechnic College, San Luis Obispo
MORRIS GARTER, English Department, California State Polytechnic College, San Luis Obispo
IRA METCALF, Application Engineering Department, The Waterman-Water-bury Company, Minneapolis
PAUL R. ANDREWS, Vice President, Prentice-Hall, Inc., New York
T. H. REA, Sales Manager, Armstrong Machine Works, Three Rivers, Michigan
CHARLES MCKENNEY, Supervisor, Southern Division Classified Advertising, Los Angeles *Times,* Los Angeles
D. Q. MILLER, Secretary, United Railroad Operating Crafts, San Luis Obispo Division of the Southern Pacific Railroad Company
MARVIN BARCKLEY, Direct Mail Manager, *Quick* Magazine, Des Moines 4, Iowa
H. L. LINDQUIST, H. L. Lindquist Publications, New York
WARREN LESLIE, Sales Promotion, Nieman-Marcus, Dallas, Texas
The New Yorker Magazine
HERMAN NELSON DIVISION, American Air Filter Company, Inc., Moline, Illinois
DOUG SCOTT, Advertising Services, Ottawa, Canada

T. V. BIHLER, Mail Promotion Manager, McGraw-Hill Publishing Company, Inc., New York

O. F. DEPPERMAN, First Vice President and General Manager, N. 0. Nelson Co., St. Louis, Missouri

GLENDALE MOTOR CAR COMPANY, Glendale, California, and the Pennzoil Company, Oil City, Pennsylvania

MAURICE W. FITZGERALD, San Luis Obispo

JOHN T. SMITHERS, California State Polytechnic College, San Luis Obispo

W. W. PERRY, Chairman, National Engineers' Week Committee, National Society of Professional Engineers, Washington, D. C.

ED MEREDITH, General Manager, Better Homes & Gardens, Des Moines, Iowa

EDWARD JAMES, Beech-Nut Packing Company, San Jose, California J. J. ANDERSON, Manager, Laundry Equipment Department, *Electrical Appliance Division,* Westinghouse Electric Corporation, Mansfield, Ohio

FRED C. KELLY, JR., Editor, *Refrigerating Engineering,* New York City

KATHLEEN M. BURNS, The Odyssey Press, New York City

HENRY HOKE, Publisher, *The Reporter of Direct Mail Advertising,* New York City

THE NATIONAL OFFICE MANAGERS ASSOCIATION, New York City

C. A. BROWN, Chairman, Department of English, General Motors Institute, Flint, Michigan

CONTENTS

xvii

PAGES WHERE YOU'LL FIND LETTERS
FOR THE FOLLOWING SITUATIONS

PUT YOURSELF IN YOUR READER'S PLACE

WELCOME TO THE STUDY of one of the oldest professions known to man—the art of writing letters. May it be as pleasant as it is profitable.

Before we begin our first day's lesson, however, let me quote a few lines from *Letter-Writing in Action.*

NOBLE ANCESTRY Letter writing is very old—much older than most of us realize. When the ancient kings of Egypt extended their areas of influence, they found it necessary to correspond with their vassal-princes. They inscribed letters on moist clay tablets. Then they baked the tablets, and sent them on their way. Thus governing-activities were controlled and tied together. We have many of these tablets today—come down from the fourteenth century BC. Letter-writing is at least 3400 years old![1]

And some so-called modern business letters are still being written in a style, a language, and a tone that must have been popular nearly that long ago. All because their writers failed to do one simple thing—*to put themselves in their readers' place and write the kind of letter they would like to have received.*

That's fine theory, you say. How does it work in practice? Let's take a look at a letter sent by a large store in reply to a very simple request:

---

[1] Braun, Carl F., *Letter-Writing in Action,* p. 17. Alhambra: C. F. Braun & Co., 1947.

1

Dear Mr. Smith:

This will acknowledge your letter of Oct. 21st, and we note your request for a copy of Overstreet's "The Mature Mind" to be sent to James Parks, Room 248, St. Anthony's Hospital.

As we do not accept applications for accounts by mail, it will be necessary for you to arrange to call at our Credit Office to file your credit application. The only other alternative would be for us to send out this book to you c.o.d. and you might deliver it to Mr. Parks.

Should you wish to do this, kindly place your order through our Customer Shopping Service.

Trusting we may have the opportunity to serve you in the near future, we remain,

Yours very truly,

How would *you* like to receive this letter? . . . Smith didn't either! Oh no, it wasn't written by some minor clerk with a bad case of dyspepsia. It was written by none other than the credit manager himself. At least his name and title were typed under the signature.

Let's analyze this letter to see exactly why it is weak, ineffective, and spineless:

1. *It's cold, formal, unfriendly*—"This will acknowledge," "we note your request," "it will be necessary for you to arrange to call."

2. *It's negative, uncooperative, even insulting*—"As we do not accept," "the only other alternative," "we note your request."

3. *It's in trite, old-fashioned, lifeless language*—"kindly place your order," "Trusting we may have," "we remain."

4. *It's wholly from the company point of view with what can be interpreted as a "customer-be-damned" attitude.*

5. *It does not motivate the action desired: the opening of the account.*

Here is a statement that you will hear repeated again and again throughout this book:

IT ISN'T SO MUCH WHAT YOU SAY AS HOW YOU SAY IT!

Read over those words again and again. Let them sink deeply into your mind. Believe them with all your heart, for these twelve short words sum up the whole philosophy of effective business letter-writing.

The immediate problem is: Could this ill-conceived letter have been written in such a way as to *make* Smith really want to dash into the store to open his account? In short, could this letter have motivated positive action on Smith's part? The answer is YES—definitely YES!

Dear Mr. Smith:

Thank you for your letter of October 21 requesting a copy of Over-street's *The Mature Mind* be sent to Mr. James Parks, Room 248, St. Anthony's Hospital. I am glad to do this for you.

I know you are eager to have this book sent promptly, so I shall ask our Customer Shopping Service to have one delivered today. Since we don't open charge accounts by mail, one of our drivers will drop by your office tomorrow to collect $3.09. I hope you don't mind.

The next time you are in town, won't you stop by our Credit Office? We'd like to open an account for you.

Sincerely yours,

There you have a friendly, conversational, modern letter—one sure to win the prospective customer's confidence and make him *want* to stop by and open an account. Now let's compare this revision with the original:

1. *It's warm, cordial, friendly, straightforward*—"Thank you for," "I'm asking our Customer Shopping Service."

2. *It's positive, cooperative, cheerful*—"I am glad to do this for you," "I know you are anxious to have this book sent promptly."

3. *It's in modern, every-day conversational language*—"I hope you don't mind," "won't you stop by."

4. *It's entirely from the reader's point of view.* In this version, the reader is KING!

5. It makes the reader *want* to come in and open an account as soon as he can.

Let me show you some examples of top-notch successful letters. The first two letters were written by that master letter craftsman, Irving Mack, president of Filmack Trailers in Chicago. Filmack makes movie "trailers" and "shorts":

Dear Mr. Shaw:

In these busy days, all of us have troubles of our own, and when someone takes time off to write as nice a letter as you did—without any axe to grind whatsoever—it is just wonderful. It is so unusual I can't help commenting on it. You certainly have been nice about it. I guess the only place you'll ever get your reward is in heaven, because I'll be doggoned if I know of anything I can do to reciprocate.

I can't begin to tell you how pleased I was to hear that Mr. Hudson was so satisfied with the trailer we made for him. You probably know that we do not make negatives of these trailers, but shoot them positive direct. As a matter of fact, we are throwing in animation that the average person would think can't be done—nevertheless, we do it.

I notice that you thank me for the fine service, good work, prompt delivery, etc.—Surely that isn't necessary, Mr. Shaw, because you know that in order to hold an account, we *have* to give good service and give good work—and besides, that's what we're getting paid for! Still, it's nice to know that our efforts are appreciated, because we like to get our flowers while we can still smell them I

I hope that one of these days the mailman will come trotting in with another nice trailer order from you. With the kindest of wishes.

Sincerely yours,

I'm sure you have recognized that as an A-l sales letter. But more of that later when we see how every letter *can* become a sales letter if the writer is only sales-minded. (See Eleventh Day.)

Now I'd like to ask you just one question: How would *you* like to receive a letter like the one Mr. Mack wrote to Mr. Shaw?

In his own way, Mr. Mack puts himself in his reader's place and then writes just the kind of letter that he would like to receive himself. That's why his customer-friends like to get Irving Mack letters. And that's the so-called secret of good customer relations.

Every year, companies spend many millions on "public relations"—which I like to think of as the art of making people like you and what you have to sell. The better your public relations, the more prosperous your business will be.

But why are so many of these companies penny wise and pound foolish? Why are they willing to spend fabulous sums for the showy forms of public relations, but balk at spending anything to improve their cheapest and best form of customer-public relations? By that I mean taking the time and trouble to teach their correspondents how to write Irving Mack-type letters, like this one:

Thank you, Mr. Grist, for telling us why we haven't been serving the Royal Theatre in your city recently.

Naturally, we couldn't expect to sell trailers to a theatre that burned down two years ago—I guess it's a little late for them to run a NO SMOKING trailer explaining that smoking causes fires!

But seriously, it was nice of you to take the time to send us this information, and here's hoping when you're again in need of special trailers for the Bailey Theatre, you'll call on us.

Sincerely,

Throughout this book there will be many Irving Mack letters. Every time you read one, remember that they were written from the heart of a man who *knows* that the most forceful form of public relations is a personal, friendly business letter—one out of the ordinary routine of daily correspondence. That's the kind of letter every businessman should strive to write when he answers an inquiry, writes a personal sales message, or requests payment of an overdue bill.

Here is another letter that is indeed unusual. It is a cordial, sincere, friendly invitation to a man whom the writer has never met, but to whom he feels indirectly indebted because of the actions of someone else.

Note especially the tone of the letter: cordial, sincere, completely devoid of familiarity or condescension—a tone calculated to win the consent of his reader, yet to give him perfect freedom to accept or reject the invitation:

Dear Mr. Lawrence:

You people are probably inundated with invitations, but should you or your wife or any of your party have an idle moment, I should be delighted to place myself and my car at your disposal.

I spent 1949 in your country and can never hope to repay even a part of the boundless hospitality I received at the hands of your countrymen.

You need not feel obliged even to answer this if you are booked up —I myself loathe correspondence and sympathize with others with a like failing. But if you happen to be at loose ends, I should love to help entertain you.

I am a chemical manufacturer. My office address is .¯. . My telephone number is ... and my home telephone ... I shall be in the office until noon and at home part of tomorrow afternoon and in the evening and Sunday. On Monday at the office from 8 a.m. to 5 p.m.

In any case, wishing you all the best of luck and hoping that you enjoy your visit to South America as I did mine to U.S.A.

Yours sincerely,

An excellent letter in spite of the weak, old-fashioned participial ending.

Here is another letter skillfully designed to create the finest kind of relationship between the writer and his reader. This letter was written by Mr. W. S. Carpenter, Jr., then president of E. I. du Pont de Nemours & Company. As a letter from the president of a large company to a new stockholder, it is a masterpiece of good public relations:

Dear Mr. Jones:

It is a pleasure to welcome you as a stockholder of this company.

Naturally you will be interested in the Company's condition and progress, and in order to keep you informed, quarterly statements of earnings and semiannual statements of the Company's financial condition will be mailed to you. You will also receive periodic letters outlining important activities of the Company.

Your Company's principal activities and products are listed on the following pages. Its diversified line of products for individual use is described in the enclosed booklet, "Made by du Pont."

The stockholder is not under obligation either to use or to sell his Company's products. It is natural, nevertheless, for the management to hope that the stockholder, as a partner in the enterprise, will find its products to his liking, that he will wish to buy them for his own use on their merits, and that by example and by appropriate suggestion, he will have opportunity to interest others in their use.

It is inevitable that the cumulative effect of your use of the Company's products and your constructive interest in their use by others will have an appreciable and gratifying effect on its total sales volume with correspondingly favorable effect on the Company's earnings. As a stockholder partner, you will enjoy your proportionate share of benefits accruing from improvements in the Company's prosperity.

Any inquiries or suggestions you may care to make, addressed to the Stockholders' Relations Division, will be given careful attention.

Very truly yours,

Read that letter again and again. It can't be improved upon from the point of view of courtesy, consideration, clearness, and character. "Character?" you ask. Yes, CHARACTER! A letter can have a lot of *character*— "some special thing or quality that makes one person, thing, or group different from others."

Another important point is that friendliness begets friendliness. It's hard not to be friendly with a man who smiles and holds out his hand in friendship.

Don't get the mistaken idea, however, that you can put yourself in your reader's place only in thank-you letters or invitations. Here are three of the most unusual collection letters ever written. They were done many years ago by another master letter writer, E. P. Corbett, for the National Cash Register Company, in an effort to collect money on debts two to five years old.[2]

Letter #1 was sent to 626 customers. It brought in 262 payments:

Dear Mr. Doe:

Yesterday our Treasurer called me into his office and said:

"Mr. Brown, I see that John Doe of Blankville has not yet settled his account. In fact, he hasn't made a payment since November, 19—, though I've written him several times. I did not wish to bring suit, for they've had pretty hard times in that section the past two years. Now, however, conditions are better there. I'd like you to write Mr. Doe and ask him to clear up this account. We've been fair with him, and I think you will find that he will want to be equally fair with us."

1 thought I could do no better than to tell you just what our Treasurer said to me. We have waited a long time, you know. So I am going to ask you to write and let me know what you can do for us.

Yours truly,

No ranting and raving, no shouting and tearing of hair, no

---

[2] Printed through the courtesy of *Printers' Ink* and National Cash Register Company.

name calling and yelling for the law. Just a quiet, dignified, assured "I know you'll do it because you want to be as fair as we have been" attitude. Although it's hard to put yourself in your reader's place when you write a collection letter, E. P. Corbett did the trick!

Letter #2 went to 460 customers, in some cases with minor changes, since these people had sent only a small remittance. There were 165 payments, with 17 replies from others who said that, although they could not pay then, they would do so later on. Their consciences had begun to trouble them!

Dear Mr. Doe:

I know it's the usual thing, when no answer is received from a "Collection" letter, to pretend to believe the matter was overlooked by the other man.

But I'm going to be frank enough to admit that I believe the reason you didn't answer my last letter with a remittance was that you perhaps didn't have the money just then. Am I right?

You see, I'm taking for granted that you feel exactly as we would feel if conditions were reversed. So I'm simply appealing to your sense of fairness. Don't you think it would be only fair to let us have what is due us, after we've waited so long a time?

Think it over, Mr. Doe, and if you cannot possibly send us a check today, let me know when we may look for one. This little courtesy won't take much of your time, and we certainly shall appreciate it. With continued good wishes we remain,

Sincerely yours,

In paragraph three, Corbett comes out boldly and says: "I'm taking for granted that you feel as we would feel if conditions were reversed." In other words, "I'm putting myself in your place and looking at this problem through your eyes." His appeal was sincere enough to get 165 practically "dead" accounts to make some payment. Also, don't forget those 17 conscience-stricken debtors!

Letter #3 was sent to 363 customers: to those who had not responded, to some who had responded without sending money, and to some who had sent insufficient money. This letter brought 165 remittances, also!

Dear Mr. Doe:

If a customer owed you $285, and for two years had paid nothing on it, how would you feel?

But now suppose you knew that that customer had been up against hard conditions all that time. You put yourself in his place and decided not to appeal to the law to collect your money.

Then, when things picked up with the customer, suppose you wrote to him as man to man, asking him to treat you as fairly as you had treated him. Wouldn't you feel certain that, as a businessman and as a gentleman, he would respond? Wouldn't you?

There are laws that regulate business, Mr. Doe. But the biggest thing that keeps business clean and aboveboard is the fact that most men believe in the square deal. Business would go to smash if we couldn't depend upon the sacredness of a commercial agreement.

That's all we ask from you, Mr. Doe—a square deal. You believe in that just as we do, don't you? Then let's settle this thing as between friends and gentlemen. A check from you by return mail would confirm our belief that you do believe in the square deal.

Earnestly yours,

These three masterpieces set a new standard in the writing of all kinds of business letters. The next time you have to write a collection letter, why not pattern yours after one of Corbett's?

In closing the first part of today's lesson, I want to share with you this happy, cheerful letter from the heart of Irving Mack:

Dear Mr. Shaw:

By this time, you have received so many of my flowery acknowledgment letters that you may think they're just a bunch of "hooey."

But I really believe in the stuff I'm handing out ... in the firm I represent . . . and in my ability to make you realize that I appreciate your business.

I get real enjoyment out of the work I'm doing ... I believe in courtesy, kindness, good cheer, friendship, and honest competition . . . and I think there is nothing finer than to have friends who think enough of us to send us their trailer work regularly.

But why say more? If you've read this far, you have probably come to the conclusion that I'm one of the most appreciative cusses in the world!

I only regret that our friendship has been rather one-sided and you are doing all of the giving and I do all the accepting.

However, I really enjoy writing these letters to you . . . maybe more than you enjoy reading them ... So here's hoping I will get a chance very soon to again acknowledge another trailer order from you.

Sincerely yours,

What a beautiful philosophy of life and of business! "I believe in courtesy, kindness, good cheer, friendship, and honest competition." Make this *your* philosophy and you will soon begin to write successful business letters that will win friends for your company and keep your old and trusted customers happy.

Another great letter-writing master, L. E. "Cy" Frailey said the same thing in different words in his delightful *Smooth Sailing Letters:*

Sentiment and sentimentality are horses of different breed. One is a thoroughbred—the other a bag of bones. Genuine goodwill will always be sold at par; imitations are worthless. Get right with the world, think kindly of others, face life and your job as a joyous adventure; then into your letters will come a warm and friendly spirit, winning friends for yourself and favor for your company.[3]

ACCENTUATE THE POSITIVE—ELIMINATE THE NEGATIVE

Now that you know the importance of putting yourself in your reader's place, here is the second important principle of successful business letter writing that I want you to learn today: *Accentuate the Positive—Eliminate the Negative* in every letter you write.

So without further ado, let's plunge into this second important principle by considering the problem of the *tone* of your business letter.

TONE

How would *you* like to receive this letter?

Gentlemen:

This will acknowledge receipt of your letter dated July 16, 1951,

---

[2]Frailey, L. E, *Smooth Sailing Letters,* page 100. New York: Prentice-Hall, Inc., 1938,

regarding order #647196. A copy of this letter has been forwarded to John Smith & Co., Philadelphia, Pa., for their perusal.

Kindly be assured we will abide by the agreement stated in your letter.

Very truly yours,

Brrr! What a stiff, cold, formal, unfriendly letter! Why didn't the writer thaw out a bit, warm up and say, as one human being should to another—

Gentlemen:

Thank you for your letter of July 16 about Order #647196. A copy of this letter has been sent to John Smith & Co. in Philadelphia.

You may be sure that we'll abide by every point in the agreement mentioned in your letter.

Sincerely yours,

That revision will go far toward winning the friendship and confidence of the reader. It's so easy to write letters with a positive tone *if you will only put yourself in your reader's place!*

Here's a good rule to follow: Make the tone of every letter you write positive and friendly, and you'll go a long way toward winning the friendship and confidence of your readers.

POINT OF VIEW

Successful letters are always written from the reader's point of view—with the reader (rather than with the writer) in mind. That means using YOU-words instead of I- or WE-words, as in the following two letters.

Dear Martin:

I know I should have sent you the enclosed catalog long before I did. However, I was hoping I would be able to give you this information in person. Since I was not able to do this and since I am going on my vacation in two weeks, I thought I would send you the information on our products.

After you look over the catalog and decide what you would like to have, I would like to have your list. I promise to take good care of it.

Incidentally, Martin, I should like you to return this book to me when you have finished with it.

I thank you for all the favors you have done for me in the past.

Sincerely yours,

Some people consider 13 an unlucky number. This letter has exactly 13 I's! Let's see how the unpleasant, negative tone could have been eliminated by writing this letter positively—from Martin's point of view, instead of from the writer's:

Dear Martin:

You should have had the enclosed catalog long before this, but I have been waiting to give it to you in person. With my vacation coming up in two weeks, perhaps it is best to send you this information on our products.

After you have looked over the catalog and decided what you want, send me your list. I'll take good care of it. Incidentally, Martin, would you mind returning the catalog when you are through with it?

Many thanks for all your past favors.

Sincerely yours,

This revision has 9 YOU's and only 2 I's—about the right proportion for a forceful, positive letter tone.

Here's a letter that suffers from negative WE-writis:

Dear Sir:

We have your postal card dated March 11, 1952, in which you request we send any information we have available on any air-conditioning equipment we manufacture.

We are sorry to advise we do not have anything we think would be of assistance along this line.

Very truly yours,

There are 6 WE's and only 2 YOU's in that letter. All you see when you read it is we .. we .. WE .. WE .. WE! It can be very forcefully written from the positive YOU point of view:

Dear Mr. Ganz:

Thanks for your inquiry of March 11 asking for information on air-conditioning equipment.

Since we manufacture only boilers and tanks, we won't be of much help to you in your research. It was nice of you to write us, anyway.

Sincerely yours,

Yes, you *can* turn a person down positively, without making him feel like a heel for having asked your help. Just try it and see!

PRESENTING THE FACTS

Just because you can't give a reader what he wants, you need not turn him down coldly and negatively—you need not *accentuate the negative* and *eliminate the positive,* as in the following illustrations. Notice that each negative statement can be rewritten positively:

negative: If you don't let me know the color scheme of this job as soon as you can, this will delay production.

POSITIVE: Let me know the color scheme on this job as soon as possible so that there will be no delay in production.

negative: Although you are not a regular customer of ours, we appreciate the fact that you have given consideration to the use of our products.

POSITIVE: Thanks for your consideration of our products. We hope soon to count you among our regular customers.

negative: Sorry, but we are unable to furnish the tile on this job as you ordered. We have contacted the local office of the Texaco Company, and have received permission to change the order to a single tile check, Light and Dark Olive Textone, cushion edge.

POSITIVE: You will be interested to know that the local Texaco office has approved a change in this order to a single tile check, Light and Dark Olive Textone, cushion edge.

negative: There isn't anything advertised in the A. E. C. that isn't carried or stocked on the West Coast.

POSITIVE: Everything advertised in the A. E. C. is stocked on the West Coast.

negative: We realize your financial condition at the present time is not the best, and that you may require some help in disposing of the parts. Naturally, we would like to clear our books concerning these items.

POSITIVE: If we can be of any help in disposing of the parts, just call on us. That would give both of us a chance to clear our books on these invoices.

negative: We cannot permit you to take this discount 15 days after the legitimate discount period. To do so would obviously be unfair to those who pay their invoices within the allowable period. Therefore we are returning your check for $482.65 and are asking you to please forward to us your check for $492.50 promptly.

POSITIVE: Thanks for your check for $482.65, which we have credited to your account. Your check was dated 15 days after the allowable discount period. Since we know that you would not want an advantage not enjoyed by our other customers, won't you please send us your check for the additional $9.85?

THE LANGUAGE OF THE GAY NINETIES

Here's how you can *accentuate the positive* by *eliminating the negative* language that you may still be using in your letters.— that is, if you use the dull, lifeless, insipid wording of business letters written during the Gay Nineties:

Dear Mr. Riebel:

Pursuant to your recent request at hand, beg to acknowledge receipt of your esteemed communication of the 30th. ult. We take great pleasure in confirming reservations for a room for you and your esteemed family, beginning August 28 and continuing through the 30th, inclusive.

Anticipating with extreme pleasure having you and your family with I us and assuring you of our utmost desire to make your stay in our fair city a most pleasant and memorable occasion, we beg to remain,

Yours very truly,

This letter should have been written in language that businessmen use TODAY:

Dear Mr. Riebel:

Thanks for your letter of July 28. Of course we will reserve a room for you and your family from August 28 to 30, inclusive.

You may be sure, Mr. Riebel, that we'll do our best to make your visit to San Francisco pleasant.

Cordially yours,

How much better that revision is than the stilted, old-fashioned original. It's natural and conversational, the language that the hotel manager would use if he were talking to me on the telephone, or in person. And that leads us directly into our Second Day's lesson: WRITE AS YOU TALK!

But before we start on that lesson, let's turn briefly to the Appendix—OFF WITH THE OLD—ON WITH THE NEW on page 233. There is a list of more than 100 old-fashioned, hackneyed, outworn, meaningless words and phrases that good old Grandpa thought were so necessary in business letter writing—expressions that every unthinking business jargoneer still uses today to befuddle and annoy his readers.

These stale, outworn expressions are listed alphabetically under the most important word; immediately following each negative phrase is the fresh, bright, positive, modern equivalent.

Check them over carefully to see if your pet expressions are included. Then study the revisions to see how easily they can be modernized. Resolve never, Never, NEVER again to allow these weak, hypocritical, mealy-mouthed phrases to creep into and sour your friendly, modern letters.

No letter written in these old-fashioned words and phrases can hope to be successful, for no message can rise above the tone of the language in which it is written. Any modern letter writer who will remember to put himself in his reader's place will always ACCENTUATE THE POSITIVE and ELIMINATE THE NEGATIVE!

WRITE AS YOU TALK

MYSTERY STORIES and "whodunits" always keep their readers in suspense until the very last chapter. Then the cat is let out of the bag—and the only one in the story whom you didn't suspect turns out to be the culprit.

Today I'm going to give you another secret of writing friendly, forceful business letters—and you won't have to wait until the last paragraph, either. Here it is in four simple little words:

WRITE AS YOU TALK!

That's right—if you want to learn to write successful business letters, just learn to write as simply, naturally, and smoothly as you talk.

The trouble with 90 per cent of the business letters mailed to-day is that they are *written,* not *spoken.* And that doesn't mean that "written" letters were not dictated. Most of them were. But they were dictated in the same stiff, unnatural language that most people use when they take pen in hand and start to write their thoughts.

Too many executives, consciously or unconsciously, freeze or stiffen when they have to answer letters or dictate. They become as unnatural and stilted as if they were talking to the top brass in their own organization. They feel that they are on parade and are being blessed or damned by every word they say. Or sometimes they go literary, and the result is very amusing, to say the least.

16

Here is a good example, which the author himself, Mr. Harold L. Mayer, Executive Secretary of Auto Maniacs of America, Detroit 6, Michigan, says is "an ostentatious evincation of aggrandized erudition"—that is, a "tragic example" illustrating the "over-exertion of the English language":

Gentlemen:

Being an object of nation-wide observance, and amounting to one of the largest organizations for young men in the State of Michigan, should habilitate us for such co-operation as is succeedingly requested in this letter.

A goodly portion of the hundreds of young men who are affiliated with the automobile study functions of our clubs have requested that literature with concern of your training school program should be filed in our reference libraries. Factitive to association with our accrescent clubs, most of the boys have thought very seriously of entering into some phase of the automotive industry as a means of life sustentation and luxury provision.

Therefore, we are asking that you send every form available which would furnish information concerning your courses, and any opportunities for men of superlative mechanical or chemical abilities, dealing with.

It would appease much prurience if you would supply us with fifty copies of a folder that would treat the subject in general. We are desiderate of every piece of material of which you can spare a single copy.

First hand information, if our depiction of recognition seems precarious, can be obtained, regarding our clubs, from feasibility unlimited reference sources, which can be supplied in compliance with the asking.

Note the bottom of this letter.

We shall expect your immediate attention to this important matter: some of our members are graduating in two weeks, and they want to know about your course.

Sincerely yours,

THE ROYAL LIONS AUTOMOBILE CLUBS

When I wrote for permission to use this letter, Mr. Mayer graciously agreed, but requested that his authorship be duly acknowledged. Mr. Mayer made this comment in his letter to me:

About that time, I was making an intensive vocabulary study, and attempted to learn by practice; although, you will note, the usages were not always technically accurate.

The point I want to make is that a good business letter must be written in the language familiar to the reader, not in the language of the literary man or the orator.

Here is another good example, not so amusing but far more common:

Dear Sir:

As per your postal card of March 10th last, beg to state we are herewith enclosing one of our No. 021 catalogs. In same you will find complete line of fans and blowers that are of our manufacture and also in same you will find some engineering data in it.

We trust that same is satisfactory.

Yours truly,

There is a "sameness" about this letter that makes it very monotonous. Surely no one would talk like that to a customer, would he? Why didn't that writer just relax, close his eyes, visualize a reader eager to know something about fans and blowers —and then just TALK to that reader in these words:

Dear Mr. Bates:

Thanks for your inquiry of March 10. We are glad to send you a copy of our complete catalog, No. 021.

This catalog lists all of our fans and blowers. In addition, it contains some very interesting and valuable engineering data that should be of much help to you.

If you need more information, just let me know, won't you?

Sincerely yours,

See what I mean by "talking your way to better business letters"? That's what the writer of every successful business letter *must* learn to do sometime in his life. The sooner he learns it, the quicker he will be writing letters that will win friends for his company and keep old customers coming back for more.

Let's take a look at another stiff, awkward letter:

Dear Mr. Baca:

Replying to your card of the 20th inst., enclosed please find suggested specifications for heating and ventilating ducts.

Attached hereto is a copy of our latest catalog, which we trust will be sufficient for your needs.

If we can be of any further service, kindly command. Thanking you for your inquiry, we beg to remain,

Very truly yours,

Shades of old Major Hoople and the pompous language of the dead past! The only difference is that Major Hoople was intended to be funny. Your letter is *not* intended to amuse your reader. But when you write in such unnatural language, laughter is bound to result. It's fun when people laugh *with* us, but very painful when they laugh *at* us.

It's so easy to humanize this stilted expression:

Dear Mr. Baca:

Of course we're glad to send you our suggested specifications for the heating and ventilating ducts you inquired about in your letter of January 20. You will also be interested in the attached catalog, which should be of much help to you.

We are always glad to answer inquiries about our products. So if you need any more information, please let us know.

Sincerely yours,

That's a nicely spoken letter. It's so easy to write that kind of letter every time if you remember that you are merely TALKING TO YOUR READER ON PAPER. That's all there is to it —just visualize your reader sitting across from your desk. Then talk to him in a friendly, natural way.

That isn't hard to remember, is it? Then how about trying this method in the very next letter you dictate? Once you do, you'll never dictate in any other way.

Since it's so easy to "talk your way to better letters," let's look at some letters that really were written in this human, friendly, natural way:

Dear Mr. Wilson:

Whether your letters are long or short, they're always welcome because we're always glad to hear from you.

I'm used to receiving short letters, but I suppose if you ever received a letter from me that didn't take a full page, you'd think I was slipping.

But I think by this time you know that your orders are always appreciated, even though they may not be acknowledged.

Your "Alibi Ike" trailerette is being shipped today!
    Sincerely yours,

By this time you know that Irving Mack is a man who loves to "talk" to his friends in each of the many letters that he writes daily. That's his way of relieving the monotony of answering routine correspondence. But more yet, that's his way of spending a few minutes out of a busy day with a good friend—a sort of one-way conversational visit, but a "conversation," nevertheless.

Here is another splendid illustration of a friendly letter that was "talked" to thousands of customers by the president of Crowley, Milner & Company, a department store in Detroit:

Dear Mrs. Floethe:

Like all good housekeepers, we like to tidy up an extra bit for the holidays. So, with the Easter shopping season at hand, we discovered your Charga-Plate hasn't been used in months. "This," we said to ourselves, "is something we'd better look into right now."

    Have you lost your Crowley Charga-Plate? Do
    we have your correct name and address?

Your Charga-Plate is a friend indeed when it comes to shopping, and we know you'll want to use it especially for Easter. Our exciting, new spring fashions are here for you. Come and see them soon, for it's a good idea to shop early for the largest selection.

Will you give us a minute of your time now and answer the questions on the enclosed postcard? It requires no postage, and if you'll speed it along to us, you'll end our quandary about your Charga-Plate. We shall greatly appreciate hearing from you.

                                        Cordially yours,

On reading this letter, did you realize that it was a "form" letter, one sent to thousands of women in the Detroit area? Don't ever let anyone tell you that form letters can't be friendly, personal, and conversational. That letter was sent to thousands of Crowley customers in an effort to check on their mailing addresses, the spelling of their names, and the whereabouts of their Charga-Plates, which had not been used in some time. The letter did all of that—and much more. It was written in such a way as to appeal to women shoppers; to bring them to Crowley's for their annual Easter shopping. That letter is a masterpiece of feminine psychology, as well as of letter craftsmanship.

While I'm on this subject of talking to your reader, I'd like to show you a letter written by Mr. Carl F. Braun, president of that great West Coast engineering company in Alhambra, C. F. Braun & Co. In the First Day I quoted from Mr. Braun's excellent book, *Letter-Writing in Action.* When I wrote to ask Mr. Braun's permission to quote from his book, I received this reply:

Dear Mr. Riebel:

About your letter of the eighth. Why, certainly you may quote from my book. What we're all after is to teach people how to write useful letters.

I don't need to speak about giving credit for the quotations, for you already cover that point in your letter. All success to you with your book.

Sincerely yours,

I can just visualize Mr. Braun *saying* that to me. That's how I want you to learn to visualize your reader. Then talk to him as Mr. Braun talked to me: simply, naturally, forcefully. You *can* do it if only you will let yourself go, act naturally, cut loose those mental inhibitions that have kept you in a strait-jacket while you dictated your letters.

Once you learn to *talk to your reader* when you dictate a letter, you will enjoy answering your correspondence. You won't mind writing letters any more than you mind picking up a telephone and calling a customer in person. How about trying it on the very next letters you write?

*   *   *   *

I want to show you one more letter—also a form letter, with

none of the conventional salutations or complimentary closings, but one that is natural, personal, and friendly. It is one of the famous John Gaufin letters sent out by O. M. Scott and Sons Company, Marysville, Ohio, manufacturers of Scott's Lawn Care products.

In order for you to appreciate this letter fully, you must see it in its entirety, illustrations and all. It is reproduced below.

Are Tour Lawns Like John Gaufin's?

A stranger came into a certain Michigan town to look up a relative He thought he was in the right neighborhood so entered a small store and asked the proprietor, "How do I find Mr John Gaufin?"

There was a moment's pause, then this. "I'll tell you what to do mister Go down this street to the first traffic light, turn right and keep going until you see the prettiest lawn you ever saw That's where John Gaufin lives "

Had you built this lawn your reputation as a lawn expert would have been established in the community When folks go by they Just can't help stopping, admiring and then asking the proud owner how he ever obtained such a beautiful lawn. Mr Gaufin says Scotts gets most of the credit

Like many well known landscapers he has found that you can't make a silk purse out of a sow's ear - in building beautiful lawns there is no substitute for Scott Quality Year in and year out Scott Lawns prove their superiority You will find one pound of Scotts goes further and does a better job than 3 or 4 pounds of ordinary seed or fertilizer

Check over the enclosed Lawn Care. Save it to explain to prospects why it costs less to fix up lawns in the fall with Scotts. You'll keep clients happy by following the Scott Program. Feed with Scotts Turf Builder Then follow up by sowing Scotts Lawn Seed - 2 to 3 lbs per 1000 sq ft is usually sufficient. Where there is a heavy weed infestation use Scotts Weed 4 Feed instead of Turf Builder

We're in the midst of our fall rush but landscape orders are taken care of daily - just drop yours in the mail today We'll arrange for prompt prepaid delivery

Cordially

O M SCOTT & SONS

LA

DON'T BE A STUFFED SHIRT!

You know what a "stuffed shirt" is, don't you? Did you ever meet one in a business letter? If not, just read the following letter and meet one of the world's prize "stuffed shirts":

Gentlemen:

Pursuant to yours of the 29th, which valued communication has been brought to the writer's attention, beg to state that the writer is cognizant of the urgency of the situation relative to the delay in shipment of the parts for your Model AB-3. However, under the prevailing circumstances and due to the fact that there has been an unfortunate and unavoidable delay in obtaining the requisite steel, it will, in all probability, require the expenditure of an additional amount of time in the amount of seven days, more or less, before we expect to be in a position to initiate shipment. Trusting that this will explain satisfactorily our present position in this matter and assuring you of our sincere and earnest desire to be of whatever assistance we may under the aforesaid circumstances, we beg to remain,

Very truly yours,

Old poker-face himself must have been in an especially stiff and unfriendly mood when he dictated that pompous bit of bombast. Now, why didn't he just relax, tilt back in his chair, close his eyes, visualize his reader—and then just talk to him in a friendly, normal way?

Dear Mr. Basset:

You may be sure that we, too, are disturbed at our inability to ship the parts you need so badly for your Model AB-3. It may not comfort you much to hear me say that the steel shortage is the sole villain this time—but it's the truth.

There is a ray of hope, however. I think that I can ship you these parts within a week, but I won't promise. In any case, I'll ship them just as soon as possible!

Sincerely yours,

Now that's a friendly letter, one designed to win the friendship and confidence of a customer who is already put out and a bit peeved because of the delay.

Here is another unfriendly stuffed-shirt letter:

Dear Madam:

Receipt is acknowledged of your letter of July 27th inquiring about a vacancy at this hospital for an apprentice technician.

Permit me to say that at the present writing there is no foreseeable vacancy that you would be at all interested in in our laboratory. Should such an opening develop in the near future, please be advised that we shall notify you of same.

Very truly yours,

Wouldn't you think that a man intelligent enough to be a doctor would also be intelligent enough to write a more friendly, human letter turning down a hopeful applicant for a job? Surely a doctor, who so often carries the mental and emotional future of his patient in his hands, could do a better psychological job of rejecting an applicant for employment.

Here's what he could have said in a friendly way:

Dear Miss Smith:

Thank you for your letter of July 27 asking about employment as an apprentice technician in our laboratory.

Unfortunately, there is no immediate vacancy in any department. Your qualifications are so good, however, that I should like to keep your application on file. We never know when we will need a young woman with your excellent training and experience.

Sincerely yours,

That may be stretching the original letter a little, but certainly it won't harm Miss Smith's ego, which probably could stand a bit of bolstering at this moment. Although the doctor may never write Miss Smith again, he has given her morale a tremendous boost. Now she can hold her head up high and bravely look for an opening elsewhere, confident of her ability. Moreover, she will have a kind spot in her heart for the doctor who had to turn her application down.

Letters can be tremendous morale builders—or shatterers. I wish I could remember the name of the dean of a Western junior college who always sent back a kindly, sympathetic little note whenever I applied for a job during the great depression from 1930-1935. I think you ought to hear this story, for it did much to keep me in there pitching when the going got tough.

With monotonous regularity I applied for a job teaching in his junior college. Every year, I wrote an application follow-up, hoping that one day there would be a vacancy for me.

There never was. But that dean always wrote such a friendly, personal note thanking me for applying, explaining briefly the situation, and expressing hope that the next time he could be more encouraging. What a lift his letters gave my sagging morale! What a psychologist he was!

Here, as best I can recall it, is one of his letters:

Dear Mr. Riebel:

Thank you very much for sending me your application for a position in the Phoenix Junior College. Unfortunately, the situation has not changed since last year, and we are not taking on any additional teachers for the coming school year.

Don't become discouraged, Mr. Riebel. I enjoy your letters, and who knows, someday when you write there may be the opening you are looking for. You may be sure that I'll keep you in mind if something unexpected develops.

Cordially yours,

I'd like to give that gentleman credit for keeping my head above water during those rough days. He never committed himself to anything more than keeping me in mind if something developed, but oh, what a difference his letters meant to me!

In concluding today's discussion of "writing as you talk," I want to tell you of another little incident that happened to me at Cadillac. One of our service engineers came over to my desk one day with a letter that he was reading. He was laughing uproariously. It seems that an undertaker in my home state of Kentucky had written to the Division asking what he could do to keep the springs on his 1940 Cadillac ambulance-hearse from breaking when the car was driven over rough mountain roads. The service engineer had answered the letter as he would to another engineer. Here, as best I can recall it, was the undertaker's frank reply:

Gentlemen:

I don't know any more about springs—normal load, pounds per

square inch, tension, etc.—than you do about embalming. What the heck do I do to keep these springs from breaking?

Yours truly,

That certainly was not a stuffed-shirt reply. It was in the language of everyday talking. That service engineer failed to "communicate" with his reader because he did not speak his reader's language.

       *   *   *   *

I like to close a day's study with something worth remembering. So here is a very friendly, colloquial letter by a writer who is NOT a stuffed shirt:

Dear Mr. Banning:

I'll bet you thought I was going to forget to thank you for your order on "The Band Played On,"—which was shipped the very same day the order arrived.

I can just see you pacing back and forth in your office wondering where my "Thank you" is ...

But a policy is a policy ... It is our intention always to acknowledge an order, so once again, please consider yourself thanked!

By the way, Mr. Banning, I guess I'll have to admit I'm not on the job because we had nothing made up on this subject. We made the items specially for you. So although I'm charging you for the cards, I'm not charging you for the photostat.

I think you're to be congratulated for having enough courage to advertise this short subject. Business would be a whole lot better if other managers paid as much attention to shorts as you do ... More power to you 1

My very best wishes to you, Mr. Banning 1
    Sincerely yours,

DON'T HAVE I-TROUBLE!

TODAY YOU ARE GOING to learn about an old but common disease of letter-writers and letter-dictators—a malady that has afflicted them for centuries and still crops up in too many modern business letters. This disease is called, medically, I believe, *scribus egocentripus*. Translated into very loose English, it means writing with yourself as the center of attraction—having I-trouble, in short.

The odd thing about I-trouble is that it doesn't bother the letter-writer, but acutely pains his reader, for all he sees or reads in such letters are *I's*. He is completely surrounded by first-person pronouns—so much so that it often gives him an acute inferiority complex. Take the following letter, for example:

Dear Mr. Jones:

I was very glad to hear from you and to have your kind reassurance that you will be able to make use of the copies of the September issue of *Blank's Magazine* that I recently sent you.

I am returning your exercises enclosed, and I can sincerely assure you that I am profoundly impressed with them. I wish I knew a publisher who might be interested in doing the sort of workbook which you outlined. I have asked one of our editors who has been with a textbook publishing house, but he could suggest no publisher to me. I can't help thinking that the *Literary Digest* might be interested, but I do not know.

I shall be wishing you every success in your project. Please call on me any time I can be of any assistance to you.

Cordially yours,

There's no question about that's being a friendly letter. Anyone will admit that. In some ways, it is even a forceful letter. That's why I have hidden the identity of the writer, for he was cordial, sincere, and helpful. In such a letter, much can be overlooked, but his letter does suffer from I-trouble.

Let's analyze this letter to see why:

1. Each of his three paragraphs begins with I.

2. Six out of his seven sentences begin with I.

3. Fifteen I-words (*I, me, our, ours*) are used in this 138-word letter. That means more than 10 per cent are I-words!

4. Only eight YOU-words are used *(you, your, yours).*

5. Only his last sentence starts with a YOU-word understood —the subject of the verb "call."

Unfortunately, this letter suffers needlessly from I-trouble. The writer's thoughts so easily could have been written from his reader's point of view (YOU) rather than from his own (I).

Maybe I can hammer my point home by saying that

when you write		*your reader reads*
I	....	YOU
MY, MINE	....	YOUR, YOURS
ME	....	YOU

Psychologists tell us that the little word "my" is the most important one in any language. Consciously or unconsciously, people are inherently selfish—egocentric, self-centered, interested primarily in themselves. They are like that Hollywood actress who, after talking for three hours about herself, finally said to her long-suffering companion: "But enough about me, darling. Let's talk about you. What did you think of my latest picture?"

Since people are egocentric or self-centered, they like to read words that inflate their egos—words that glorify them—words that make them the center of attraction. They are really not interested in the other fellow. That's the reason why you deflate your reader's ego when you fill your letters with I-words. What you really should do if you want his favor is to *inflate* his ego—make him the center of attraction in this little drama that you're writing for his sole benefit.

And it's really so very, very easy to write your letters from your reader's point of view if you will think about him and then use a liberal number of YOU-words in your letters, and soft pedal the I-words. Remember:

when you write	*your reader reads*
YOU	I *or* WE
YOUR, YOURS	MY, MINE *or* OUR, OURS
YOU	ME *or* US

Now let's put this fundamental psychological principle to work in rewriting our original letter from the YOU or reader's point of view. It's so easy to do. So that you can easily spot them, I have capitalized each YOU-word:

Dear Mr. Jones:

Thank YOU for YOUR assurance that YOU will be able to make good use of the copies of the September issue of *Blank's Magazine* recently sent YOU.

YOUR exercises, which are enclosed, profoundly interest me, Mr. Jones. Some publisher would probably be glad to publish the sort of workbook YOU outlined. Neither I nor any one of our editors to whom I spoke about YOUR work knows of any, unfortunately. Perhaps YOU might try the *Literary Digest.*

May YOU have every success with YOUR project. Please call on me at any time that I can be of assistance to YOU.

Cordially yours,

See, there wasn't any trick to it—just doing what comes naturally, talking to your invisible reader as if he were right there in person. That's putting into practice what we learned yesterday.

Let's look at this revision critically. It says exactly what the original did, no more, no less. But this time it has been written exclusively from Jones's point of view and in words that will attract Jones's attention and appeal to him:

1. Each of the three paragraphs begins with a big YOU, not with I. *That makes the openings forceful and strong.*

2. Five of the seven sentences also begin with YOU, only one with I. *That is an excellent proportion.*

3. There are eleven YOU-words plus one friendly use of the reader's own name. *That is quite important,* for your reader will like to see his name used once or twice throughout your letter. That makes the letter much more personal.

4. There are only six I-words in this 99-word revision. *Excellent!*

5. The entire letter has been rewritten with the reader (YOU) in mind. It has been dictated with a BIG YOU and a little I.

6. Notice also that the revision requires only 99 words as com--

pared with 138 in the original. That's a saving of 39 words, or 28.3 per cent. More of this important matter another day.

WE-WRITIS

An even commoner disease is WE-writis. It is more common than I-trouble because most writers use "we" rather than "I" when writing on company business. (See page 35) Regardless of which pronoun is used, letters filled with I- and WE-words are equally annoying to your readers. Here's a representative sample of this type of bad letter—and it came from a fairly large company, too:

Dear Mr. Hart:

WE wish to thank you for your recent inquiry regarding OUR refrigeration equipment.

WE are enclosing current literature containing essential data for OUR refrigeration units.

Should you desire additional information, WE would be very glad to hear from you.

Very truly yours,

Here is a running post-mortem on this ill-conceived letter:

1. Two of the three paragraphs begin with WE. Notice how these WE's stick out like sore thumbs.

2. WE is the subject of each of the three sentences.

3. WE-words have been used five times in the 40-word letter.

4. YOU-words have been used only four times.

5. This letter is entirely from the company point of view, not from the reader's.

How easily this letter could have been written with the reader in mind:

Dear Mr. Hart:

Thank YOU for YOUR recent inquiry about our refrigerating equipment.

YOU will be interested in the enclosed literature, which gives YOU helpful data on [use your trade name] units.

If YOU want more information, just drop us a line, won't YOU?

Sincerely yours,

Why is this revision more forceful and friendly than the original?

1. It's conversational—just plain, every-day talking to the reader.

2. It's written *to* the reader, not *from* the company.

3. YOU-words are prominent in every sentence—six as com pared with only two WE-words.

4. The second paragraph gets in a bit of free advertising by using the trade name of the unit. That's good psychology.

5. It didn't cost one word more to be friendly and forceful— each letter is exactly forty words long, but what a difference.

Here's another example of how *not* to win friends by ignoring your reader and blithely writing solely from your company point of view:

Dear Mr. Lawrence:

WE thank you for your reply to OURS of December 29, 195-.

WE suggest that you return the alarm clock to US and upon receipt of same WE will credit your account for the purchase price.

WE hope this is satisfactory and WE regret exceedingly any inconvenience WE have caused you.

Assuring you it is a pleasure to serve you and thanking you for your patronage, WE are,

Very truly yours,

It's hard to believe that this letter was written by the credit manager of a large department store. Shades of the nineteenth century! That chap must have learned his "business" English before the turn of the century, when men wore long beards or sideburns, and women wore bustles and mutton-chop sleeves.

This is as good a time as any to disillusion you about so-called "business" English. There just isn't any such language. The only language of successful, modern business letters is the language of successful modern conversation—in other words, just plain *talking your way to more successful letters.* Here is a magic formula, if you are looking for one: just learn to be a good conversationalist in your letters, and you will write good, forceful letters.

You are probably wondering how a correspondent can breathe life into such a routine letter as the one to Mr. Lawrence. The answer is simple: by being friendly, human, sympathetic—by looking at every problem through the customer's eyes:

Dear Mr. Lawrence:
Thank YOU for YOUR reply to our letter of December 29.

We are very sorry for any inconvenience this alarm clock has caused YOU. Just pack it up and ship it back. We'll be glad to credit YOUR account.

YOU may be sure, Mr. Lawrence, that we are always glad to serve YOU in any way.

Sincerely yours,

There's no trick to it at all. Just as easy and simple as talking to Mr. Lawrence over the telephone.

Here is something that will surprise you: THE ORIGINAL LETTER HAD MORE YOU-WORDS THAN WE-WORDS! That's hard to believe, but count them: nine YOU-words and only eight WE-words. But six of those WE-words were "WE" itself. The revision had six YOU-words and only four WE-words.

Is there any significance in this? What does it mean? The original has more YOU-words than WE-words, but still it is not a good letter. Just what *is* the score?

Here is the answer: It isn't just the *number* of YOU-words *vs.* WE-words—it's their position in each sentence that really counts. YOU-words at the beginning and ending of a sentence or paragraph are far more forceful and impressive than YOU-words smothered within the sentence.

And the same applies to WE-words. When you use WE-words (and no modern business letter can be written without them, I assure you) then place them in the most inconspicuous position possible—*within your sentence,* not at the beginning or ending.

Here's another point to consider: Don't use as many WE's as you do OUR's, OURS's, and US's; and the same applies to I *vs.* MY, MINE, ME.

This next letter is a real prize of some sort—a letter in which the writer used nineteen WE-words and *not a single YOU-word!* It's hard to believe, but here it is:

Dear Sir:

WE manufacture heating, ventilating and air conditioning equipment, operating a job shop in which WE build equipment to specifications.

OUR Standard lines of equipment include OUR blank line of unit heaters for use where steam or hot water is available. OUR Standard unit heaters are built to withstand a working pressure of 125 p.s.i.; however, they are just as efficient and are frequently used on vapor, low pressure, etc., steam and forced circulation hot water.

WE also, build gas fired unit heaters; and in the air conditioning field, WE build air conditioning units for any of the following services: Filtration, Cooling, Dehumidifying; Filtration, Heating, and Humidifying.

OUR Blank line of Evaporative Condensers are used in conjunction with air conditioning and diesel engine installations and other applications where it is necessary to cool water or reuse same.

WE have nothing in the way of a complete catalog of OUR various products giving performance data on various standard size units. Since WE are not a production shop, WE have not thought it expedient to prepare such a catalog.

If there is any way WE can cooperate or be of further service, WE shall be pleased to do so.

Yours very truly,

Have you ever read another letter in which the reader was so completely ignored? He was not even mentioned by name in the salutation, much less in the body of the letter! Nor is he referred to even once by a YOU-word. The writer surely missed a good chance in his last sentence: "If there is any way we can cooperate or be of service to YOU. . . ."

That's bad enough, but this is even worse: not until the fifth paragraph does this writer actually get down to answering the inquiry. I know, for I got this letter from a friend, who wrote merely for a catalog. Instead, he received this terrific "sales" letter.

Since this letter is really not an answer to the inquiry, I am not going to try to revise it from the YOU point of view. This letter should be scrapped and rewritten from beginning to end *from the reader's point of view.*

Just one more letter that suffers from acute WE-writis:

Gentlemen:

WE are, indeed, sorry that all material had been made up as covered by OUR original order, and you may consider this letter your authority to bill US for the items all made by you and cancelled by OUR revised order and OUR letter of May 1. Please send US a separate invoice, however, for these items as listed on page two of your letter, which WE have checked and find to be correct. The first four items on your list are standard shapes, and the 4302-8, 4302-13 and 4302-17 can by cutting be made into standard shape 4301-1. WE, therefore, do not want you to grog these, but at the same time, WE do not want you to ship them on the subject order. Since WE have authorized you to bill US for these shapes, will you kindly arrange to hold them in stock as WE feel confident WE can use them on future orders.

WE would appreciate your checking to see whether or not it would be possible for you to cut 4302-8, 4302-13, and 4302-17 to make tile 4301-1. However, do not do this cutting until WE advise you, which will probably not be until WE are in a position to place an order with you covering 4301-1 tile.

WE sincerely regret the inconvenience caused you by the necessity of OUR revising OUR original order and do appreciate your checking so thoroughly with US as you have done in your letter of May 7.

Very truly yours,

There you have a 254-word letter with twenty WE-words and fifteen YOU-words. WE has been used fifteen times. Now let's see how this letter can be rewritten to eliminate some objectionable WE-words and also to trim the letter down to reasonable size:

Gentlemen:

Since you have manufactured all the items on our original order, just bill us for them, including those cancelled. Please send a separate invoice for those listed on page 2 of your letter. They are correct.

Will you check to see whether 4302-8, 4302-13, and 4302-17 can be cut into shape 4301-1? Don't cut them until we request it, however.

We are sorry to cause you so much inconvenience by revising our original order. Your careful checking with us through your letter of May 7 is sincerely appreciated.

Very truly yours,

How do you like this streamlined 88-word letter? It's certainly an improvement over the original—and at what a saving in time and words!

*   *   *   *

Don't get the idea that *all* I- and WE-words are tabu in friendly, forceful modern business letters—that you must *not* use any I- or WE-words under any circumstances. That isn't true. Use I- or WE-words in your letters whenever the occasion demands, when your use of these words will make your letters more friendly and forceful, and when you want your reader to know exactly how YOU feel.

Probably you are wondering when you should use *I* and when you should use *We* in business letters. It is customary for the writer of a business letter to use the plural *We* whenever he speaks for the company or the organization as a whole. When he is voicing his own opinion or promising to do something, the usual pronoun to be used is *I*. The writer himself must use good, common sense in interpreting the oft-stated rule that *We* should always be used. As Cy Frailey so aptly puts it:

The use of *We* instead of *I,* which in many companies is a law that must be obeyed, is another queer custom we seem to have inherited from earlier writers. When a business writer speaks wholly for the company, as in telling a customer "We will ship your order tomorrow," obviously he should not speak for himself. On the other hand, if he means to see personally that the order is shipped, why shouldn't he say, "I will personally look after this order, and you can be sure we will ship it tomorrow"? Thus, in the same sentence, both *I* and *We* properly appear, and logically there is no reason why they shouldn't. The idea that a business writer must always speak in the sense of "We, the King," seems utter nonsense. Certainly, the insistence on *We* to the exclusion of *I* in all cases, is a barrier to the goal of "writing as you talk"; no writer can be his natural self if he must forever conceal his presence as an individual person.[1]

In a letter of condolence, I- or WE-words are absolutely necessary. You can't write a sincere one without using them, for you want your reader to know how you feel personally. Here is a fine letter written by Mr. Verne Boget, Vice President of Gladding, McBean & Co. in Los Angeles:

Dear Mrs. Miller:

I want to extend you my sincere sympathy, and that of my associates here at Gladding, McBean. Although there isn't much that we can say that will comfort you at a time like this, we do want you to know that Walter's passing has made us feel that we have lost a very close friend whom we shall never forget.

If there is anything we can do to be of help to you, won't you please call on us?

Sincerely,

That is a good example of a really difficult letter to write. That kind of letter must be sincere and genuine in tone; it must not be sentimental or maudlin.

Here is another letter which uses many I-words, but the writer felt that they were necessary to explain his request:

Gentlemen:

Although we out in California are a bit off your beaten path, I wonder if you would do me a favor—a very great favor.

A number of years ago I was teaching at General Motors Institute in Flint, Michigan. While I was there, your Detroit representative let me have several of those excellent SUNOCO booklets on hydraulic oils and on lubrication.

---

[1]Frailey, L. E., *Handbook of Business Letters* (Copyright 1948 by Prentice-Hall, Inc., New York), page 537. Reprinted by permission of the publisher.

When I left the Institute I left these booklets for the use of those who taught my courses in reports and technical writing. I did not expect to be teaching again. Now, however, I again am teaching courses in reports and technical writing, and my thoughts keep running back to your excellent technical bulletins.

I hope that I have been able to identify them so that you will know which ones I mean. If so, would you send me one copy of each for use in my classes here at Cal Poly? Any additional material available to college teachers interested in practical industrial material will also be appreciated.

Although you don't have any SUNOCO stations out here in California, I can promise you that each of my students will know of your company and its various products through your excellent bulletins.

Sincerely yours,

The company responded by sending the two booklets requested, plus quite a large assortment of other technical reports and literature. But to get back to the letter itself: How could such a letter have been written from the YOU point of view? It had to be largely from the writer's point of view.

Here is another good letter. After you read it, I'll tell you how many I-words there are as compared with YOU-words:

Dear Mr. Shaw:

Should I ... or shouldn't I ... acknowledge your cross-plug trailer order that we received today? . . .

My associates here in the office tell me, "What's the use of wasting so much time acknowledging each individual order? Send just a printed post-card and let it go at that!"

I know that's one way of acknowledging an order . . . but it's not my way. If you came in here personally I'd go out of my way to thank you for bringing in the trailer order.

Just because you sent it through Uncle Sam is no reason why we shouldn't be any less enthusiastic or appreciative.

I want you to know that we appreciate your orders, and even if we didn't thank you, our appreciation would be just as great. Sincerely yours,

Well, there were thirteen I-words and only seven YOU-words, but when you read this letter, you knew that Mr. Mack was just *talking* to Mr. Shaw as if the latter were standing at his side.

DICTATE WITH A BIG YOU

The secret of writing letters with the right point of view is in writing with a big YOU. I borrowed those five words from another master of the art of writing effective business letters, Dr. Robert R. Aurner of Carmel, California, who is Director of the Fox River Better Letters Division. The title of a little booklet Dr. Aurner did for the Fox River Paper Corporation in Appleton, Wisconsin, is "Dictate with a Big YOU!"

And now the big question is: How can anyone dictate his letters with this all-important "big YOU"? That's easy—simply by thinking your letters through in terms of your reader, what he wants and what he would like to hear. Then tell him these things in a simple, natural, friendly way.

Another way of dictating with a big YOU is by starting as many sentences as possible with YOU—and by ending as many with YOU, particularly the last sentences in your letters. When you do this, you invariably focus your attention on your reader. Then you just talk to him; you quit talking *about* or *from* your company or your own point of view.

Enough of this preaching. I want to close this day's work with two more letters written by my friends at Gladding, McBean. The first is from the pen of Mr. Boget, and the second from Mr. Daly. Both are written with a great big YOU:

Dear Mr. Riley:

YOUR application was brought up at this morning's meeting of our department executives. Unfortunately, there is no immediate opening in any of our departments.

Sometimes, however, vacancies occur unexpectedly. YOU may be sure that we will keep YOU in mind the next time anything of interest turns up. It will be a pleasure to let YOU know if something does.

Best personal regards.

Cordially yours,

Dear Fritz:

Enclosed are our usual Terra Cotta Contract forms in duplicate for the Ceramic Veneer on the Pickwick Hotel job. Just sign and return both copies. One will be signed by an official of the company and returned to YOU.

The work is being sent to the shop today, and we are asking the factory to rush this to YOU with all possible speed.

Have YOU heard if they intend to finish the jewelry store and the Front Street alteration? If so, now would be the time to order the Ceramic Veneer so that the colors will not vary too much by being manufactured later. We can't always control the matching colors, especially now when some pigments are so hard to get.

Would YOU mind letting me know if they plan to go ahead with this alteration?

Sincerely yours,

Truly, there is *no* substitute for dictating with a great big YOU!

SUCCESSFUL BUSINESS LETTERS
ARE PLANNED

NOTHING REALLY GOOD ever just happened—it was planned that way! That's the most important lesson that you are going to learn today, and perhaps any day.

Now I know what you may be thinking: "Abe Lincoln wrote his famous Gettysburg Address on the back of an old envelope while he was traveling on a train going to the battlefield. I know it's so, for I read it. And Lincoln's address is good, isn't it?"

Yes indeed it's good; it's one of the greatest pieces of writing. But Lincoln certainly didn't write his immortal piece of only 266 carefully chosen words (about the same number as in the average full-page letter, like the excellent John Gaufin letter on page 22) on the back of any envelope. Far from it!

According to an Associated Press story dated Chicago, November 11, 1950, Lincoln carefully wrote his first draft several days before he left Washington. He wrote his second draft at the house of David Wills in Gettysburg on the morning of the dedication. This draft, according to the AP story, was the paper Lincoln held in his hand when he spoke.

But Lincoln was a perfectionist, something that every good letter-writer must strive to be. He knew that only by carefully revising and rewriting could he improve his address. As a result of this desire to perfect his words, Lincoln wrote in his own hand no fewer than five copies. On November 19, 1950—the day on

40

which the address was "four-score and seven years" old—the Chicago Historical Society displayed these five copies in Lincoln's own handwriting.

According to Paul Angle, a noted Lincoln authority, ". . . one purpose of the exhibit is to show the public that Lincoln did not deliver this speech spontaneously with little or no preparation as is commonly believed. . . . These revisions, along with occasional crossed-out and changed words, are further evidence of the care Lincoln took with the address that is a treasured part of the American Heritage."[1]

The ability to stir the souls of many of those who heard him speak and of all who read his immortal words today; the ability to be brief without being curt; the ability to say what he meant and mean what he said; the ability to plan and re-plan, to write and rewrite—these skills were not inborn with Lincoln. They were acquired the hard way, *by writing and rewriting,* again and again, until he achieved the precise effect he wanted.

Now, there are very few, if any, Lincolns living and writing today. But here is something that should encourage each of us: Lincoln's ability to do a better job of writing forcefully can be acquired by anyone who is willing to pay the price of hard work, of careful planning.

1. ALL SUCCESSFUL BUSINESS LETTERS HAVE THREE PARTS

About 2,300 years ago, Aristotle said that all good literature (by which he meant writing and speaking) must have a *beginning,* a *middle,* and an *ending.* There you have the perfect formula for the plan of a successful business letter—and it's just that simple:

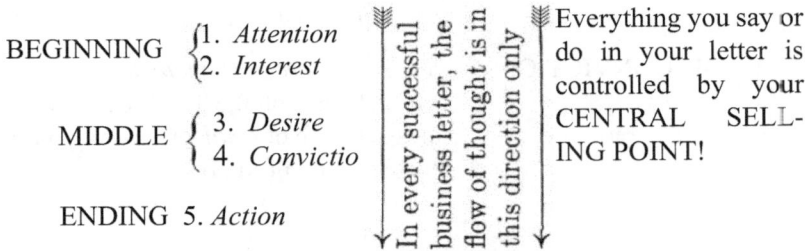

BEGINNING { 1. *Attention* 2. *Interest*

MIDDLE { 3. *Desire* 4. *Convictio*

ENDING 5. *Action*

In every successful business letter, the flow of thought is in this direction only

Everything you say or do in your letter is controlled by your CENTRAL SELLING POINT!

---

[1] Quoted by permission of World Wide Photos, Inc., New York.

Don't get me wrong. I didn't say that every letter you write must have five separate parts. That's not true. For example:

Dear Mr. Duenas:

Attached is a letter from M. A. Sanabia Ortega, Republica Dominicana.

Will you please answer this for us? Thank them for their inquiry, and handle the matter from there on.

Yours very truly,

Although this excellent letter has only three sentences, it very definitely has a beginning, a middle, and an ending. It also has a central selling point: "Thank them for their inquiry, and handle the matter from there on." This letter of only thirty words was as carefully planned as a letter ten times as long could be.

Now let's take a closer look at those five points I have just mentioned:

1. ATTENTION   —*The opening sentence in your business letter must capture your reader's attention.* Unless it does, he is not likely to be interested in what you have to say.

2. INTEREST   —*You can't possibly be interested in something before your attention has been called to it.* Often, however, your attention can be attracted and your interest aroused in one simultaneous action, as in the first paragraph of the letter just given. This is often true in well-planned short letters.

3. DESIRE   —*Here's where you put forth your greatest selling effort.* The more desirable you make your sales talk, the more likely you will be to break through your reader's wall of sales resistance: CONVICTION.

4. CONVICTION   —*Here's your greatest obstacle to success.* As you will learn on the Tenth Day, every letter is a sales letter. Not *until* or *unless* you are able to muster enough forceful argu-

ments to break down your reader's resistance—not until you can *convince* him that he should buy your product, service, plan of action, or whatever you have to sell —can you hope to make that sale.

5. ACTION   —*Action will come automatically, once you convince your reader that he should or must do what you suggest.* But don't make the mistake so often made by careless letter-planners: THEY FAIL TO MAKE CLEAR THE ACTION THEY WANT! Some even fail to ask for any action whatsoever! I have seen many an application for employment fail because the writer failed to ask for an interview.

Notice that the flow chart on page 41 shows the arrow pointing downward only. There is only one direction of flow in a carefully planned business letter—from *beginning* to *ending.* Here, then, is your basic formula for writing a successful well-planned business letter:

1. You *attract attention,* then

2. You *arouse interest,* then

3. You *quicken desire,* then

4. You *establish conviction* by overcoming sales resistance, then

5. You *get the action* you planned for.

This is what the chemist calls a one-way reaction: the flow is swiftly and surely in one direction only, from the beginning of your letter to your ending. That, of course, is the formula for a well-planned letter.

2. CENTRAL SELLING POINT

Everything that you include (that is, say) in your letter is controlled by one thing, your CENTRAL SELLING POINT. *Every letter,* no matter how long or how short, *must have a central selling point.* There is no exception to this rule. Any letter without a central selling point, either actually expressed in the letter or implied beyond any shadow of a doubt, will inevitably be poor, weak, ineffective, forceless.

Without a central selling point, your letter is like an automobile without a steering wheel, a ship without a rudder, a book without a title. The reader is muddled and confused; he doesn't know where to go or what to do. The CENTRAL SELLING POINT is the one idea that you had in mind even before you began to write or dictate your letter. It is, in brief, the real reason why you wrote your letter!

Often the central selling point is best expressed by some sentence taken directly from the letter itself. In the following letter, the central selling point is given in the fifth paragraph: "Now here's something that will interest you—every job that is now being done with your old-fashioned, leaky air gun can be done with an economical, leak-proof 'Hermiticus'—" That is the central idea around which the entire letter was written:

Dear Mr. Jones:

Attention   You have heard it said: "Money talks!" To a businessman, it usually shouts out loud!

Interest   That's why we know we have something to shout about —a promise that "HERMITICUS" leak-proof air guns *can* and *will* save YOU money—lots of money—on compressed air, a mighty costly foundry expense, especially when it's wasted through leaky air guns.

You wouldn't keep an employee who worked only part time yet drew full wages, would you? Or one who could do only half as much useful work? Of course not! That's why we know you won't continue to use inefficient, leaky, old-fashioned air guns that give you only half their useful work—not when you can so easily and inexpensively replace them with guaranteed leak-proof "HERMITICUS" air guns. Will you?

Just look at Figure 2 in the attached booklet. Notice the leaking air bubbles? Costly little air bubbles boiling away your hard-earned profits. Not a very pretty picture, is it? Now look at the other side of the page! No air bubbles in Figure 3, are there? There can't be. *This* air gun is a leak-proof "HERMITICUS"! *Not one single air bubble can escape!*

C ⎫
S ⎬   Now here's something that will interest you—every job
P ⎭   that is now being done with your old-fashioned, leaky air
        gun can be done with an economical, leak-proof "HER-
        MITICUS"—

1. Cleaning drags, patterns, castings, cores, and core boxes.
2. Spraying dried molds, cores, and large vertical mold walls.
3. Moistening molds and cores too dry to use.
4. Blowing oil on molds, plates, and machines.
5. Cleaning machines and typewriters with compressed air.
6. Blowing sand out of deep and narrow cavities and holes.
7. Doing many other cleaning jobs around your foundry, plant, office.

Conviction   There's an old saying that the only way to tell how good a biscuit is, is to eat it. We know that the only way to tell how good "HERMITICUS" is, is to use it.

Action   So ... just look over the attached booklet—send us your order for the numbers and sizes you want, and for whatever attachments you will need. Try modern leak-proof "HERMITICUS" air guns and convince yourself that they *can* and *will* save YOU money. Send us your order today!

                                        Sincerely yours,

The next letter is one that did a remarkably fine job of persuading busy architects to leave their offices for a few days and travel often hundreds of miles to accept this invitation—an excellent public-relations gesture coupled with a very carefully worded, thoughtfully planned letter by Mr. Ralph Priestly, then Head of the Department of Architectural Engineering at California State Polytechnic College.

Dear Mr. Holdridge:

Attention-   One hundred selected West Coast architects are being *Interest* invited to a dinner and preview of an exhibit designed to portray Cal Poly's program of architectural education— and YOU are one of those invited.

Desire

C ⎫
S ⎬
P ⎭

This is not a typical exhibit of student work, but an extensive portrayal of *our* solution to the problem of closing the gap between architectural education and actual practice. We believe that a student's college training should equip him, upon graduation, to be of immediate value to his profession. For this reason the entire presentation will be of vital interest to architects who are constantly confronted with the problem of obtaining properly trained young men.

Conviction   The Student Architectural Club at Cal Poly, through its president, Mr. Cletus Fenel, has asked me to send you the attached invitation to attend an informal dinner preceding the exhibit. We believe that the entire two-day program of Poly Royal is so packed with interesting events that you will want to bring your family along to combine a bit of pleasure with the more serious aspects of this important professional problem.

Action   We have been fortunate in obtaining a limited number of hotel reservations. At Poly Royal time, hotel reservations are at a premium. How many would you like us to hold for you?

Cordially yours,

The following short, one-paragraph letter was just as thoughtfully planned as any I have given you. Why write more when this much does such an adequate, forceful job?

Dear Mr. Peterson:

Attached is our reply to Mr. Roll's letter of February 24. The CSP—leather pad for his new desk was shipped from the factory on Order P-3635. Your cooperation in seeing that this pad is delivered to Mr. Roll's office will be greatly appreciated.

Sincerely yours,

This letter opened with the central selling point, and the following letter closes with it. Both are perfectly O.K. if the occasion dictates:

Dear Mr. Steneck:

Your letter of June 18 was received too late for us to get an authorization to you by mail. So I left your summer certificate in the Recorder's Office.

CSP—   Please report there to complete your registration.

Sincerely yours,

By this time I am sure that you know that it doesn't matter where you put your central selling point, *as long as you have one.* That *is* important!

3. HOW TO PLAN SUCCESSFUL LETTERS

Here is a very brief but workable formula for helping you to write successful business letters:

1. Use a BEGINNING or opening that attracts your reader's *attention* and arouses his *interest.*

2. In the MIDDLE of your letter, create within him a *desire* to do what you want, and then *convince* him he should do it.

3. Select your ENDING so that you will get the *action* you are striving for done easily, quickly, and finally. AVOID WISHY-WASHY ENDINGS!

Now let's translate this general formula into an easy-to-follow plan that outlines, step by step, the procedure for planning more successful business letters. For the next two weeks, dictate or write every letter according to one of these two plans. After that, successful business letter-planning will have become a habit.

Plan I

IF YOU ARE STARTING OR INITIATING THE CORRESPONDENCE

A.   *Your OPENING sentence or paragraph should*

  1. *Identify yourself:*

  a. *Tell who you are*—Give your name and tell something about yourself:
    My name is John Smith and I am a senior student at California State Polytechnic College in San Luis Obispo.
OR
  b. *Give your reason for writing this letter*—Tell *what* you want and *why:*

One of the requirements for a B.S. in air conditioning and refrigeration engineering is the writing of a thesis. The topic I have chosen is refrigerants used in domestic electric refrigerators. Any information you may have available for distribution for refrigerants that you manufacture will be most helpful to me in the preparation of this thesis.

OR

c. *Mention your point of contact*—Tell who told you to write and why:

Mr. John E. Jones has suggested that I write to you about the position of refrigerating engineer which you now have vacant.

OR

2. *Identify your letter*—People like to know immediately just what kind of letter they are reading: a request for information, an invitation, a job application, a request for adjustment, an application for credit, and so forth:

As president of the Young Businessmen's Club I want to invite you to be our guest speaker at our March 21 meeting.

....

In the December 31 Fresno *Bee* you advertised for a used car salesman. I believe you will be very much interested in my qualifications.

....

The refrigerator that we purchased from you on April 1 has developed a noticeable crack in the upper right-hand corner of the inner door.

OR

3. *Start right off with your first main point*—This is especially forceful when you open with the subject of your letter:

The specifications that you requested are enclosed.

....

There will be no price increase before the first of October.

....

Here are four questions that I have concerning the servicing of your X3 rectifier:

OR

4. *Open your letter so as to attract your reader's attention, arouse his interest, and make him want to read the rest of your letter:*

May I have a moment of your time, please?

....

Thanks very much for your courtesy to our representative, Bill White.

....

Effective October 14, there will be a 10 per cent increase in the salaries of all non-supervisory employees.

B. *The BOD Y or MIDDLE of your letter should:*

1. *Start with your first main point* (unless, of course, you opened your letter with it) *and complete this point before going to your next one.*
2. *Present your second main point and complete it*—in a separate paragraph.
3. *Present your third main point and complete it*—in a separate paragraph, also.

   NOTE: Don't try to include too many main points in your letter unless you tabulate them (with or without identifying numbers).

C. *The ENDING of your letter may be one sentence or one short paragraph.* It must:

1. *Be clear*—Unless your reader knows exactly *what* you want him to do, *when, where, how,* and sometimes *why,* he is not likely to do anything—that is, anything you want him to do: As soon as your check is received, this machine will be shipped to you.

....

Some of our members are graduating in two weeks, and they want to know about your course.

....

May I have an appointment on Monday, July 27, between 9 and 10, if that is convenient for you?

2. *Be courteous*—You'll get much, much more *with* courtesy than *without* it!

   The next time you are out our way, please drop in, won't you?

   _____

   It was mighty nice of you to bring this matter to our attention.

   _____

   You certainly deserve a pat on the back for sending me all these letters, Marshall. Here it is!

3. *Be concise*—Don't be a babbling brook, especially at the end of your letter. But also, don't be curt!

   WORDY —Again I want to assure you that we are always glad to be of service to you and yours, and all you have to do is to call on us, for our engineers are always at your disposal.

   CONCISE—You may be sure that our engineers and facilities are always at your disposal. *Or* Call on us whenever you need any help.

   CURT   —Your application will be filed.

   CONCISE—We'll be glad to keep your application on file.

4. *Be complete*—Make your ending complete and final. Don't just stop, leaving your reader wondering whether you have actually finished. Readers don't like to be disappointed or teased:

   VAGUE   —I owe you many thanks.

   BETTER   —Many thanks for your advice.

   INCOMPLETE—Here is an addressed, stamped envelope.

   COMPLETE —The addressed, stamped envelope is for your convenience in answering promptly.

VAGUE   —Thanks for the opportunity of serving
                        you in this instance.

CLEAR   —Thanks for your nice order.

5. *Be modern*—By all means, your ending must avoid those meaningless, old-time, conventional expressions, such as Hoping to hear from you soon, we beg to remain *Instead, say:* We hope to hear from you soon.

(NOTE: See also Ninth Day, pages 114-115.)

And now I'd like to show you how letters can be organized according to this plan. Here are several letters that show careful organization. To help you follow the organization, the opening, middle, and ending have been marked A, B, C:

Dear Frank:

A—   You will recall that I promised to forward the article on the Utah State Prison, which was given in LIFE magazine a few

B— weeks ago. Here it is, Frank. The article is not very long, but it C—   may interest you.

Cordially yours,

Dear John:

A—   I have just talked with Joe Kerr about his visit with you last week. He mentioned in particular your order for the Smith residence.

B—   A check with our Shipping Department showed that you had cancelled this order. A revised shipping date of October 13 had been put on this order, and we understood that this date was satisfactory to you. Do you want this order reinstated with the revised shipping date?

C—   Please let us know as soon as possible, John.

Cordially yours,

Dear Professor Cruikshanks:

A—   Many people, both in and out of government, do not appreciate the extent to which small business firms are participating in production for defense; nor are they aware of the splendid contribution these companies are making to our defense effort.

Both as a procurement officer in World War II and as president of a company engaged in war production work, I have been close to this situation.

It occurred to me, therefore, that you might be interested in seeing an example of our own company's effort to give the public some idea of the fine work small business firms are doing.

B—   While the enclosed advertisement, which is scheduled for publication next week, deals with the accomplishment of one particular small businessman, it is actually typical of the contribution being made by thousands of firms classified by our government as "small business."

CSP—   We at RCA rely heavily on our thousands of suppliers, and

C—   it gives us great pleasure to give public recognition to the important part they play on America's industrial team.

Sincerely,

That is a carefully planned letter by Mr. Frank M. Folsom, president of the Radio Corporation of America, explaining his company's policy toward the importance of "small business" in the present economic setup, and calling Professor Cruikshanks' attention to his company's advertisement.

I'd like to close this section by showing you one of the finest public-relations letters I have ever read. It was written by Mr. Walter Rothschild, president of Abraham & Straus, of Brooklyn, New York:

Dear Mrs. Gertz:

For ten years, this month, you have been a valued charge customer of Abraham & Straus. During that time we have sent you many communications—bills, catalogs and advertisements—but this particular letter is different. It is written with no other purpose than to express our thanks for your friendship and continued confidence.

When the store was much smaller, it was the custom of my grandfather, Abraham Abraham, the founder, to greet our customers in person. This neighborly gesture helped to establish the spirit of friendliness which, I believe, is characteristic of Abraham & Straus.

During recent years the store has grown by great strides, and 1948 saw the opening of still more new departments—notably the Rose Room for couturier fashions, and the beautiful Junior Size Center. Our expansion program will continue, bringing you even greater shopping conveniences. But I hope you will always find the same friendly spirit that, in earlier days, was symbolized by the founder's personal greeting.

Because old friends know us best, we will particularly welcome your comments and suggestions. It is through your confidence that Abraham & Straus has prospered, until now, in its 85th year, it is one of America's truly great stores.

Sincerely,

Plan II

IF YOU ARE ANSWERING A LETTER A.

Your OPENING sentence or paragraph should

1. *Tie in with the letter you are answering:*
   Thank you for your letter of January 15.

   _____

   The information contained in your letter of May 4 was very helpful.

   _____

   It was mighty nice of you to send me those pictures in your last letter, Mr. Lawson.

   _____

   Your letter of July 27 contained just the material I needed to complete my report. Thanks very much for sending it.
   OR

2. *Mention your point of contact:*
   Mr. Jones, our president, has asked me to thank you for your letter of December 31.

   _____

   Attached is a note from Mr. Grant about the number of departmental meetings to be held during March.

   _____

   Your recent letter to Mr. Wroble has been referred to me for answering.

   _____

   "Take Your Letter Out of the Freezer" looks O.K. to me.
   OR

3. *Begin with your first main point*—Although this is not used

too frequently when you are answering another letter, there may be occasions when it is just the kind of opening you will want to use:

> The local representative for "HERMITICUS" leak-proof air guns is the Chas. W. Riebel Co., 209 West Main Street, Louisville, Kentucky.

———————

> The attached bulletin will give you complete information on the scholarships which are available to agricultural students at California State Polytechnic College.

B. *The BODY or MIDDLE of your letter should:*
  1. *Start with your first main point* (unless, of course, you opened with it) *and complete this point before going on to the next one.*
  2. *Present your second main point*—in a separate paragraph.
  3. *Present your third main point*—in a separate paragraph, also.

> NOTE: After the letter is started, there is no difference between answering a letter and initiating a new one unless, of course, you keep referring to or answering points brought up in the letter you are answering. Each point is taken up, one at a time and in some sequence. The important thing is to ANSWER the letter courteously, clearly, concisely, completely.

C. *Your ENDING or closing sentence or paragraph should:*

  1. *Be clear*
  2. *Be courteous*
  3. *Be concise*
  4. *Be complete and final*
  5. *Be modern*

  (There is little difference between the ending of a letter in answer to another and of a letter you are initiating. The main thing to remember is the purpose of your ending—the action ending to motivate the action You want from your reader!)

One thing that the letter-writer must learn to do is to be able to terminate correspondence without hurting the feelings of his reader. He must learn how to close the correspondence gently but forcefully—NOT ABRUPTLY—especially if there is no reason for continuing. Every needless letter costs your company money, as you will learn tomorrow. But please remember that letters are your best and most personal form of public-customer relations, and your cheapest, too.

Here are excellent examples of the two types of letter endings:

TERMINATING ENDINGS

Thank you very much for your nice order, Bill.

A copy of this letter is being mailed to Mr. Smith, so that he will know of your request.

We are moving along rapidly with the work, as you requested.

Your wholehearted cooperation is very much appreciated.

NONTERMINATING ENDINGS

After you've seen this film, we'd like to know what you think of it.

As soon as you know how much time you will need, please let us know.

Any suggestions that you may have to offer will be very much appreciated, Joe.

Will you please have someone determine exactly what will be needed for this office, and then let me know?

NOTE: Question and challenging endings are always non-terminating.

Here are some letters that show careful organization according to Plan II:

Dear Mr. Jones:

A — Attached are copies of some correspondence between Mr. G.
Y. James of Sacramento and the factory on the servicing of his B
—Model 353-B. We shall be glad to help you obtain any necessary
parts that are available. As you can see, we have assured Mr. C
—James that you will do your best to take care of his needs.

Cordially yours,

How do you do, Mr. Blank . . .

A — Thank you' for your "First-Time" Order!

Now that we've gotten started we are sure you will find that
CSP—our aim is to PLEASE YOU . . . ALWAYS! You will always get the
kind of service and treatment that folks like.

B — We sure would like to have you become a REGULAR CUSTOMER . . .
and call on us often.

C — "KRILOFFICE" is always on the job to please you! We don't want to
merely 'deliver the goods' and forget you . . . but want to take care of
your every office need ... for continued satisfaction always!
"YOUR BUSINESS IS INVITED"

Quite a delightful thank-you letter from the friendly pen of Mr.
L. I. Krilofio, president of Kriloffice, Inc., in Chicago.

I'd like to close today's discussion by showing you a very
well-written, carefully planned "sales" answer by Harold Smith,
Manager of the Tile Sales Department at Gladding, McBean:

Dear Jeff:

A — I am delighted to answer your request for information on Hermosa tile
Dura-Glazes.

Hermosa Dura-Glazes were developed more than 15 years ago to
meet the demand for a sanitary, easy-to-clean bathroom floor and
drainboard deck tile that would retain the beauty of regular ceramic
wall tile finishes. Dura-Glazes come in eight popular colors.

CSP— Dura-Glaze finish gives a very tough, long-wearing, scratch-resistant
surface. It is also resistant to food acids.

B — There is a very small additional charge for Dura-Glaze— only $5¢$ a square
foot for the standard grade and $2¢$ a square foot for the commercial
grade. This would amount to only $80¢$ for the average 40-square-foot
bathroom—and only from $36¢$

to 56¢ for the average 10-foot-long drainboard! You see, Jeff, anyone can afford to specify Dura-Glaze, the additional charge is so very slight.

C — I certainly hope that I have pointed out to you the great advantage in using Dura-Glaze. Just let me know if you want any more information.

Sincerely yours,

Fifth Day

BUSINESS LETTERS ARE COSTLY

LETTER-WRITING is really BIG business, no matter how you look at it. Here are some statistics that I learned from the *Annual Report of the Postmaster General* for the fiscal year ending June 30, 1951: The United States Post Office handled a grand total of 28,564,780,000 first-class, airmail, and free (government) pieces of mail in one year. That total will startle, if not surprise, you.

Obviously, not all of those 28½ billion pieces of mail were personally dictated business letters. Let's assume that only one-fourth of them were. That will give us approximately 7 billion personally dictated letters per year. Quite a staggering figure, isn't it?

Now what do you think it costs your company to process a business letter? What would you guess: 25 cents? 50 cents? 75 cents? $1.00? more? Pause a moment in your reading and jot down some of the costs involved, and you will soon realize that letter-writing is really BIG business.

In his delightful *Smooth Sailing Letters,* Cy Frailey estimated the cost of a business letter to be about 50 cents. But that was back in 1938. In 1948, Dr. Robert R. Aurner of Carmel, California, estimated the average cost of a business letter at approximately 75 cents.[1] On March 31, 1952, in an article written for

---

[1] Quoted from Dr. Aurner¾ booklet, *Money-Making Mail,* printed and distributed by the Fox River Paper Corporation in Appleton, Wisconsin. Dr. Aurner *is* the Director of the Fox River Better Letters Division.

the United Press Associations, Harman W. Nichols quoted a figure of $1,003 per letter.[2] Mr. Nichols obtained this cost from John M. Breen, educational director for the Correspondence Improvement Division of the Kemper Insurance group.

If you think that either Mr. Nichols or Mr. Breen is overestimating the cost of business letters, just read carefully the following letter, which I received from Herman J. Keck, Educational Director for the Fireman's Fund Group in San Francisco: [8]

Dear Mr. Riebel:

When we speak of the average cost of letters sent out by Fireman's Fund Insurance Company, we get into a research problem that can be endless. Our most recent survey was made using one hundred dictators who use our Central Typing service for transcribing letters. These persons are at the minimum salary for those whose duties include letter writing. For the control group, the average cost of each letter is *89.47¢*.

While this survey reveals that the minimum cost of a letter at Fireman's Fund is *89¢,* if we include the cost of another control group of one hundred dictators who are compensated at a much higher rate, the average cost of a letter is $1.11. Of course, if a secretary rather than the Voicewriter and the Ediphone operators is used to transcribe the letter, the cost rises materially. You certainly may use the figure of 89¢ as a minimum cost.

The $1.03 cost mentioned at the Association meeting in Berkeley was based on a survey made in May 1951. Two hundred dictators were used in this study. Without doing a complete research on all salary levels, I should hazard a very conservative estimate of $1.75—$2.00 as an average cost of *all* letters sent out from our Home Office. Since it is not practical to make a complete survey, I cannot statistically substantiate this estimate.

Sincerely yours,

Let's do some simple multiplying, using these seven sets of figures:

Cy Frailey's estimate of *50¢*   × 7 billion = $3,500,000,000
Dr. Aurner's estimate of 75¢   × 7 billion = $5,250,000,000
Mr. Keek's estimate of 89¢   X 7 billion = $5,930,000,000
Mr. Breen's estimate of $1,003 × 7 billion = $7,021,000,000

---

[2] Quoted through the kind permission of the United Press Associations.
[8] These figures are for the San Francisco office only, according to Mr. Keck.

Mr. Keek's estimate of $1.03 × 7 billion = $7,210,000,000 Mr. Keek's estimate of $1.75 × 7 billion = $12,250,000,000 Mr. Keek's estimate of $2.00 × 7 billion = $14,000,000,000

No matter which estimate we take, we must admit: FIRST-CLASS, PERSONALLY DICTATED BUSINESS LETTERS ARE COSTLY! It might be a good idea for you to start figuring up all the expenses that go into the cost of your business letters. Then you will know how true this statement is: *Every time you reduce either the number of letters that you have to write or the number of words in those letters,* YOU ARE SAVING YOUR COMPANY MONEY.

WORDY LETTERS WASTE MONEY, AS WELL AS TIME

If a letter is clear, concise, and courteous, what more can you expect it to be? The answer is simple and obvious: CHEAP— that is, reasonable in cost.

Well, what *is* the answer to this rising cost of business letter-writing? What *are* we going to do about it? What *can* we do about it? Cut out writing so many letters, just as we cut out smoking so many cigars or packs of cigarettes every day, or reducing the number of sodas or candy bars we eat? NO! *Of course not!*

A business letter that needs to be written MUST BE WRITTEN! We would indeed be penny wise and pound foolish if we failed to write a necessary business letter. But there is very definitely one practical way that almost any letter-writer can cut the cost of his letters, and that is by eliminating the unnecessary wordage. But before I get into this subject, I want to quote another passage from Mr. Carl F. Braun¾ excellent book, *Letter-Writing in Action:*

THE GREAT BINDING-MEDIUM Letters are still our most reliable form of communication. They are the chief means of tying our great present-day organizations together. It is our letters, reports, and other writings, that keep our cooperative groups working in reasonable harmony—in harmony of aim, in harmony of method, in harmony of spirit. And this is true of government, of science, of the professions, or industry, of all those things where men must pool their efforts.[4]

[4]Braun, Carl F., *Letter-Writing in Action,* pp. 17-18. Alhambra, California: C. F. Braun & Co., 1947.

Business letters that should be written *must be written*. They are not only our best but also our cheapest medium of communication, and if they are written properly, they can become our best medium of public-customer relations. And now back to the art of reducing the cost of our letters by eliminating the number of unnecessary words.

Don't get the wrong impression: eliminating half the words in any given letter won't automatically cut the cost of that letter by 50 per cent—but it will reduce the cost by at least 25 per cent, and perhaps more, if the letter is a long one. What office manager wouldn't be overjoyed if he could reduce by 25 per cent his costs on *any* item?

The illustrations given on pages 23, 33 and 34 show what can be done to padded letters by reducing them 30 to 60 per cent, and at the same time making them far more friendly.

Often letters can be shortened by eliminating unnecessary words in only one sentence or even one paragraph. Here are some good examples of this kind of shortening:

I am sorry that I was not at home on the other evening when you phoned me, and I should say, in the future, on
61 words any long distance calls, you would have a much better chance of catching me at home around 8:00 or 9:00 in the evening, rather than at the time of day when you actually did call me.

I am sorry I was not home when you called the other eve-
25 words ning. The next time, try calling me between 8 and 9 P.M., won't you?

The latest information that we have had is to the effect that our car will be ready on or about August 1st. If this information happens to be in error, or if perchance you can give
77 words us a little more accurate date as to just when we may take delivery on said car, I assure you it would be most sincerely appreciated. Thank you very much for your kind cooperation in this very important matter to us.

21 words Our latest information is that our car will be ready about August 1. Can you give us a more definite date?

A very favorable, not to say even flattering, review of the
31 words new sales management motion picture which your concern had produced recently has been brought to the attention of the undersigned.

14 words   I have just read a very favorable review of your new sales management movie.

BE BRIEF, BUT NOT CURT

Now, in your desire to eliminate unnecessary words, please don't go to the opposite extreme and write curt, telegraphic letters. Your letters should be brief, concise, condensed—BUT THEY MUST NOT BE CURT, ABRUPT, TELEGRAPHIC. There is a vast difference between brevity and curtness.

Note the curt abruptness of the following letters:

Dear Sir:

Here is the bulletin you asked for. If you want further information, please write us.

Yours very truly,

That is about as cold and unfriendly a reply as one could receive without its being downright insulting. Yes, the letter is brief—it saves the company money in that respect—but it loses the good will of the customer. And from that angle, it loses money. It defeats the purpose of every business letter: to win friends and influence customers. Here's how he could have written his reply:

Dear Mr. Weston:

We are pleased to send you the attached bulletin, which you requested. If we can be of any more help, just let us know.

Sincerely yours,

Yes, it's true that the revision does have seven more words than the original—24 as against 17—but those extra seven words put more smiles and friendliness and warmth into that letter, and this makes them well worth the added cost. It's fine to save money on letters by reducing the excess wordage, but cutting out vital parts of your letter is the wrong way to save.

Here is another of the same breed:

Dear Sir:

Y'rs of the 1st. inst rec'd. Beg to state we have no parts for your

BM-34 on hand. Don't know when we will have any. So can't be of help to you.

Y'rs resp.,

Not only is that letter cold and lifeless, but it's very, very old-fashioned. What it needs is a good shot of modernizing:

Dear Mr. Johnson:

Thank you for your letter of October 1. Unfortunately, we don't have any parts for your BM-34, and we don't know when any will come in. I'm afraid we aren't of much help at this time. You might try the Blank Company in Fresno. They try to carry a complete stock of Daisy Tractor parts.

Sincerely yours,

When you can't fill a customer's order, as in this case, why not be good enough to suggest some other place where he might get what he needs? Yes, you lose this sale, but you have lost it anyway because you did not have the parts in stock. If you are merely temporarily out of them, you could answer in this way:

Dear Mr. Johnson:

Thank you for your letter of October 1. We are temporarily out of the parts you need for your BM-34, but we have them on order, and are expecting them any day now. I'd like to book your order for shipment the day our car arrives from the factory. Will that be O.K. with you?

That, of course, changes the meaning of the original curt, discourteous letter. But it does give you a good idea of how *you* can stall off a customer and still keep your strings tied to him.

SAY WHAT YOU MEAN—BUT MEAN WHAT YOU SAY!

Robert Louis Stevenson once said something like this: *you must write not merely so that you can be understood, but so that you cannot possibly be misunderstood.* This is a modern echo of what John Dryden said over 250 years ago: "The first duty of an author is to be understood." In other words, what both Dryden and Stevenson meant was:

Say what you mean—but mean what you say!

Failing to say what you mean can be costly in several ways. It usually will result in the writing of two additional letters: one asking what the first letter meant, and one in reply telling what the original writer meant to say but didn't. Here is an excellent example of such a letter: [5]

Gentlemen:

I want recordings of Meet Me at the Corner, Sad Sally, and Blue Blues. Can you send them to me?

Sincerely yours,

The answer is, of course, an unqualified NO! Such an order is not tillable. It is so vague and incomplete that the only thing the company that received it could do was to write back asking whose recordings were wanted, when they were needed, and how they would be paid for. Then the original inquirer had to write back and answer these three questions, as in this admirable revision:

Gentlemen:

Will you please send me the Swing Sisters' recording of "Meet Me at the Corner/[7] "Sad Sally," and "Blue Blues"? These are Regal Record numbers 3890, 3751, and 3808, priced at 85 cents each.

I enclose a money order for $2.55 for the three records. I understand you will pay postage on this order.

I need these records by July 28, and since I have always received prompt and helpful service in the past, I feel sure that you can fill this order by this time.

Sincerely yours,

Although this revision is not a perfect letter—it suffers from I-trouble, needlessly—it at least is answerable. It will get the writer *what* he wants *when* he wants it. Here's how paragraphs two and three could be improved:

Enclosed is a money order for $2.55 for the three records. I understand you will pay postage on this order.

These records are needed by July 28, and since you have always given prompt and helpful service in the past, I am sure you can fill my order by this time.

---

[5] Letters reprinted by permission of Coronet Instructional Films.

But losses are not limited to money only. Vague, incomplete, unanswerable letters cause frayed patience, loss of time, and loss of customer good will. All of these may be much more important than the additional expense of needless letters.

See if you can figure this one out. Frankly, I can't:

Since you told me what has happened while this administration was questionable, I hope that men, interested in quality, will be appointed to fill the vacancies.

The only thing I'm sure of is that the writer wasn't talking about the Administration in Washington, or else he would have used a capital A!

This sentence sounds inconsistent to me. What do *you* think?

We have added the 120 units to your shipment, but did not have any of them in stock for immediate shipment.

Did they ship the 120 units or not? If they shipped them, how could they, since they didn't have any in stock? I'm confused. To what did they "add" the units? There seems to be a definite lack of communication—a lack of careful, thoughtful planning—in these examples. The same thing can be said of this sentence:

Do you know whether or not the plans have been completed for the new high school at Great Bend, out of Jones and Williams' office?

That sounds like a racehorse pedigree. You know the lingo: Nancy Banks, by Happy Medium out of Stardust. What this dictator probably meant to say was:

Do you know whether Jones and Williams have completed their plans for the new high school at Great Bend?

I can understand that question.

There is no room for guessing in a carefully planned business letter. The reader should never have to guess what the writer meant to say.

FLOW SWIFTLY, SWEET LETTER!

Have you noticed a definite "flow of thought" in all the good letters I have shown you in this book? From the time you begin reading a letter until you finish it, there should be a steady progression or flow of thought from the opening sentence to the closing words. Forceful business letters just don't start and stop, jerk and twist, meander and hesitate, wind and turn like a tortuous mountain road. Everything is smooth and easy, so that your reader can sail right through your letter as swiftly and easily as he skims along a modern super-highway.

Here are some dandy illustrations of swiftly flowing, friendly, letters:

Dear Mr. Gold:

Your interior decorator, Mr. McInerny, has asked me to write you about the delivery of the Hermosa tile for your lovely new home.

Our shipping Department is confident that this tile will be shipped in ample time to meet your building needs.

Thank you, Mr. Gold, for your prompt approval of the color selection.

Sincerely yours,

Dear Tom:

There isn't much that anyone can say that will comfort you in your great loss, but I do want you to know that you have our heartfelt sympathy.

I have known and worked with your father for over thirty years. He was always grand to me and a bulwark of the business. His passing is a terrific loss to all of us.

Sincerely,

Dear Mr. Riebel:

Your articles in the most recent issue of "Refrigerating Engineering" are an excellent presentation of a most important subject. I have found them most interesting and believe they will be very helpful in eliminating some of the common misuses of the English language in business organizations.

If you have reprints available, I should like to have a copy for ready reference.

Very truly yours,

Dear Bert:

Thanks for the information on the Sisters' residence in San Pozo.

We are getting right to work on this order, and will have the color selection ready for you soon.

Sincerely,

Dear Mr. Paul:

Thank you very much for your letter and the enclosed clipping. We shall be glad to add this to your file which we are keeping here in our office.

Best wishes for the coming school year.

Sincerely yours,

Each of these swiftly flowing letters not only saved the company money by having a point and coming to it quickly, but each also created a tremendous amount of customer good will through friendliness and conciseness.

Here are two more letters which say exactly what is meant to be said in a swift, friendly flow of carefully planned words:

Dear Fred:

Enclosed is a copy of a drawing showing the Glazed Structural Unit Panels which we built and tested at our Glendale Plant.

This drawing is to be attached to the Osborn Laboratory report I left with you yesterday.

Many thanks for helping to get this type of construction approved.

Best regards,

The second is the best letter report I have ever read:

Mr. R. C. Conover Los
Angeles Office

EQUIPMENT OFFERED FOR SALE AT THE BLANKVILLE MINE—BLANKVILLE, CALIF.

Ben Taylor and I drove to Needles Thursday evening, July 19, proceeded to Blankville Friday morning to inspect the mining equipment and mills, and returned to Glendale Saturday morning.

The only equipment that appeared to be in first-class condition was three Allis-Chalmers ball mills with drives, feeders, etc. The mills are driven through herringbone gears by direct-connected slow-speed electrie motors. The ball mills are 6' x 6', 5' x 5', and 5' x 6' in size. The 6' x 6' mill appeared to be in the best condition, and was located in a position where removal from the plant would not be extremely difficult.

The Robinson Company, liquidators, has reduced the price on the 6' x 6' mill from $16,000 to $9,000.

We offered $7,500 for the 6' x 6' mill complete with motor, starters, apron feeder, and miscellaneous spare parts loaded on our truck at the mill site. Mr. Henry Schwab, the Head Company representative, is to call us July 25 with their decision relative to acceptance of our offer.

It's almost unbelievable, the amount of information that Mr. Stevens, Chief Engineer, Southern Division, Gladding, McBean & Co., was able to put into his 175-word letter. But he did, and this took careful, thoughtful planning that gave his superior officer exactly the amount of information that he needed just as inexpensively as possible.

Truly, ANY WELL-PLANNED LETTER IS GOING TO BE AN INEXPENSIVE LETTER IN THE LONG RUN!

GET OFF TO A FLYING START

TODAY WE START the sixth day in your 15-day program of learning to write more friendly, forceful business letters. Last week we built that solid foundation of modern attitudes and points of view which determine the degree of success you will have in applying the skills you will learn this week.

You have made an excellent start, but you have much to learn about the details of writing letters that will win friends for your company and keep your customers happy and satisfied. So today let's start with the most trying problem facing the modern business letter-writer: how to get off to a flying start in your opening sentence.

There's an old German proverb that a good beginning is half the battle. And that applies doubly when it comes to writing successful business letters. I have never read a really successful letter that stumbled and fumbled at the beginning. Every really good letter got off to a flying start—it zoomed into the subject like a jet plane taking off.

More pencils have been chewed to pieces by dictators and secretaries alike at the beginning than at any other place in the letter. Once the letter has been planned; once the writer knows *what* he is going to put into his letter in the way of facts, information, and so on; once the dictator gets started—he usually has little trouble keeping his message rolling along smoothly and swiftly. IT'S THE OPENING SENTENCE THAT'S THE BIG BOGIE TO MOST LETTER-WRITERS!

Now, there's really no trick to getting started, if you'll just quit thinking of starting your letters with those moth-eaten, meaningless opening phrases that dear old great-grandpapa loved to use.

Don't Start Your Letters This Way:

1. I have before me your letter of the 25th, which I am now answering.

2. Yrs. of the 10th inst. rec'd. Beg to state ....

3. Replying to yours of the 5th, would say ....

4. Your letter of the 7th to hand and wish to say ....

5. Receipt is acknowledged of yours of the 8th.

6. This is to inform you that we are pleased to send you a catalog.

7. In compliance with yours of the 20th, permit me to say ....

8. This will acknowledge and thank you for your card of the 13th.

9. Pursuant to your recent request, wish to state that ....

10. Complying with your inquiry of the 10th ult., beg to state we are in a position to be definitely interested in your proposition re parts.

I'll have to admit that these opening sentences aren't the worst I have ever seen, but they are typical of stumbling, fumbling starts.

Instead of using such weak openings, why not start with something fresh, meaningful, and appropriate that will get your letter off to a flying start. Here's what I mean:

Instead, Start Them This Way:

1. Thank you for your letter of January 25.

2. I am glad to have the information contained in your letter of May 10.

3. Enclosed are the ten folders you requested on June 5.

4. The order you inquired about in your letter of October 7 will be shipped on October 20.

5. Thanks for your letter of the 8th.

6. We are pleased to send you a copy of our latest catalog.

7. As you requested in your letter of February 20, we are glad to confirm our asking price for the pneumatic conveyor: $4,520.00 f.o.b. our plant at 2901 Los Feliz Boulevard, Los An geles, California.

8. It is a pleasure to have your card of November 13.

9. As you requested, we are glad to send you our ....

10. Thanks for your inquiry. We are definitely interested in ....

These ten openings get you off to a flying start. They *say* something. They don't just wildly fan the air with words in hopes of getting up enough power to take off. They zoom right into the heart of the letter itself.

Here is a formula that you can remember so that you will always be sure of getting your letters off to a flying start:

1. Mention your reader either by name or through the use of a YOU-word. This is always a high-gear start, for it gives your letter that much-sought-for YOU, or reader, point of view.

2. Give the date of the letter you are answering. This isn't always necessary, but it often helps make contact. THIS YOU MUST DO!

3. Say something worth while.

4. Scatter a little sunshine over your reader. Don't chill him with a shower of frigid, futile, and frustrating phrases.

Of course, your opening sentence isn't supposed to do everything. It can't, any more than one gear can do everything when you drive your car. But your opening sentence can easily do one or more of these four important things without overcrowding. For example:

It was thoughtful of you to send me those prints in your letter of May 4.

There's a short opening sentence (only 16 words) that does all four! Behold:

1. Mention your reader: ". . . of you . . ."

2. Give the date: ". . . letter of May 4."

3. Say something worth while: ".. . send me those prints . . "

4. Scatter a little sunshine: "It was thoughtful of you . . ." Now, that wasn't hard to do, was it? Of course not. BUT IT DOES TAKE PRACTICE AND THINKING! There are really only two kinds of openings—good and bad. I like to call them green-light and red-light openings. Today I'm going to show you SEVENTEEN good, friendly, forceful ways of getting started in your business letters. And every one will be generously illustrated with forceful openings taken from actual letters.

GREEN-LIGHT OPENINGS

Modern city driving has taught us the meaning of stop-and-go driving. The RED light stops us cold in our tracks; the AMBER light means to take it easy, be cautious; but the GREEN light is our signal to sail straight ahead at whatever speed is permitted.

Here are some excellent ways in which you can *always* be sure of getting your letters off to a flying start with a green-light opening:

1. *Open with a reference to time—*

   a. The parts you ordered will be delivered Monday.
   b. For the past ten years you have been a valued charge customer of Abraham & Straus.
   c. Last April I placed an order for a right rear fender for my 41/61 Cadillac.
   d. In reply to your letter of May 15, I want you to know how very sorry I am that you had such unfortunate experiences at our Blankville office.
   e. Some time has passed since your last letter, but I am still looking forward to hearing further from you about the way you have used LOST FORTUNES in your classes.
   f. Let's take a moment to analyze the efforts and accomplishments that our Chamber of Commerce has made.

   NOTE: It is often a good idea to tie your letter in with the one you are answering by referring to the date of the other letter. Since time is important in all business transactions, a time or "date" opening is always forceful.

2. *Begin with the subject of your letter—*

a. Your order of the eleventh was shipped today, com plete.
b. The local representative for Jackson tubes is the Jones-White Company, 4091 Santa Ana Avenue—phone TRinity 7411.
c. The specifications you requested are enclosed.
d. There will be no immediate price increase for any item in our line.
e. Some problems encountered in the use of our refrac tories have made it desirable to set up equipment for testing resistance to carbon monoxide disintegration.
f. Your articles in the most recent issue of *Geography* are an excellent presentation of a most important subject.
g. The prices of our February 13 list are still in effect, Mr. Jones.

> NOTE: If you just can't think of any other opening, you can always begin your letter with the subject about which you are writing. This isn't always the *best* way, but it is always a *sure* way of getting your letter off to a flying start.

3. *Use the YOU point of view, either through the use of your reader's name or with the pronoun "YOU"—*

a. Your courtesy in sending us this information is very much appreciated.
b. You will be delighted to hear the news that I have to tell you, Mr. Jones.
c. Your copy of "Color Combinations" is enclosed with our compliments.
d. You will, I know, be as pleasantly surprised to read the enclosed copy of Mr. O'Brien's letter as I was to receive the original.
e. If only you were a little closer, I could drop in to se« you, instead of having to write you.

> **NOTE:** The **YOU** opening is *always* forceful. It calls the reader's attention immediately to the most important person in this two-way communication: YOUR READER. *Never forget him!*

4. *Ask a pertinent question—about your reader, about some information, about an order, about the weather, about any thing that will catch his attention—*

   a. Do you have an inventory of the items being held in the Receiving Department? If so, may I have a copy? (NOTE: That's a double-barrelled opening!)

   b. What is your earliest delivery date on 10,000 standard silica brick?

   c. When may we expect shipping instructions on your Order #3625?

   d. How much discount will you allow us if we purchase 500 sets?

   e. Who is in charge of your San Francisco office?

   f. Under what conditions would you consider giving us exclusive sales rights for your HERMITICUS leak-proof air guns?

   g. If a customer owed you $285, and for two years had paid nothing on it, how would you feel?

   > NOTE: The question opening is really double-barrelled: it not only *asks* a question, but also *stresses* the YOU point of view. No one feels comfortable ignoring a question directed at him in person, over the telephone, or in a letter. From early childhood, we have been "conditioned" to answer questions. We just can't ignore them without embarrassment. That's why the question opening is so forceful. Start using more question openings, and you'll start writing more successful business letters!

5. *Make a specific or definite statement of fact—*

   a. Thirty of our sales personnel are operating leased motor vehicles.

    b. Modern processes and production are constantly re
       quiring more precise controls and instrumentation.
       That is why ....

    c. Non-scale has given very satisfactory service in many
       boilers in California. It can prove a very valuable ma
       terial to you, also.

    d. A purchase order has been issued for the fabrication
       of a blanking die as described on the enclosed drawing
       B #651.

    e. The subject of sight screening was discussed at our Ex
       ecutive Safety Committee meeting on Wednesday of
       this week.

    f. This is a very brief reply to your interesting letter of
       October 14 requesting an evaluation of carbide tools as
       compared to similar tools made of steel.

       NOTE: As you probably have noticed, often the "defi-
             nite statement" opening and the "subject of
             your letter"[7] opening are one and the same.
             Both focus your reader's attention on some-
             thing positive and concrete. Both openings get
             you off to a flying start!

6. *Use a thank-you opening or one of the many variations of*
   this appreciation opener—

    a. Thank you for your interest in Brown equipment.

    b. Thanks, Ray, for including me as one of your guests at
       the Town Hall meeting today.

    c. We certainly enjoyed the basket of fruit you sent up
       to our hotel room yesterday, Mr. Howes.

    d. I am delighted to have your application for member
       ship in the Chamber of Commerce, John.

    e. Your continued use of our products means a great deal
       to us, Mr. Dow.

    f. What a pleasant surprise I received this afternoon when
       the mail came in—a nice letter and a dandy order from
       our good friend, Joe Schwarz!

    g. Just a word to let you know how pleased I am to have
       such a fine letter about you from, Mr. Long.

    h. It is always very gratifying to us here at the factory to get such letters as the one Mr. Harned sent us.

> NOTE: There is really no end to the possibilities of such a business-letter opening. The only limitation that I can see lies in the imagination of the dictator, or in his degree of friendliness. This opening reminds me of that beautiful song, "The Sunshine of Your Smile." An appreciative opening scatters the sunshine of the writer's smile over the reader at the very outset. And that bright sunshine is very likely to go through the entire letter, from the opening sentence to the closing words. THAT IS EXACTLY WHAT SHOULD HAPPEN.

7. *Make a courteous request or command*—

    a. May I have a moment of your time, please?

    b. Come over to my office just as soon as you can, Bill. I have something really important to show you.

    c. Hold everything, Mr. Jones! Here's an idea that can save you many thousands of dollars every year in main tenance costs!

    d. Please furnish me with parts lists, parts-list drawings, descriptive literature, and suggested operating instruc tions for your #214 standard disc grinder.

> NOTE: Admittedly, this opening is much more limited in its use than some of the others. However, it has a definite use in certain types of sales letters, and it can be very effective when used judiciously. Try it once in a while.

8. *Open with a big name or with a name that means something to your reader*—

    a. Mr. George has asked me to thank you for your letter of application for a position in our Engineering De partment.

    b. Bill Jones has suggested that I write you about the change in delivery date on your Order #45891.

c. *Heating and Ventilating* magazine has sent us your re quest for information on Blank cooling towers.

d. Your interior decorator, Mr. Hastings Smith, has asked me to write you about the delivery of Hermosa tile for your new home.

e. Attached is our reply to Mr. Reed's letter of February 24.

f. "Take Your Letters Out of the Freezer" looks okay to me.

> NOTE: What is more natural than to use the name of some mutual friend or acquaintance as your "point of contact"? Be sure, however, that the person to whom you are writing will get the significance of the name you are using, or else your opening will confuse him. Don't go over-board and start all your letters with names.

9. *Open with a bit of friendly sentiment, but don't get senti-mental!—*

a. May I extend my very best wishes for your continued success in your new associations with Smith & Smith!

b. Welcome to the Commercial Credit Family!

c. My very best wishes for your continued success, Joe.

d. It was a real pleasure to receive your letter of July 27 telling us of your acceptance of an engineering position with our company.

e. Congratulations on your appointment as Western Cor respondent for *Ceramic Industry!*

f. Good for you, Ben! It couldn't have happened to a nicer fellow!

g. I think it was mighty fair of you to put through the invoice for four of the six "cross-pluggers" when you originally wanted only two.

h. Whether your letters are long or short—they're always welcome because we're always glad to hear from you.

i. I remember pleasantly the short visit we had together when you were at Grand Rapids.

NOTE: Although definitely limited in scope, this type of opening is extremely effective when used at the psychological moment. There is always room for sentiment in business relations, but there is absolutely no room for sentimentality, as Cy Frailey told us in an earlier quotation. Particularly cordial relations between you and your reader really do call for a special type of opening, don't you agree? In other words, suit your words to your feelings for your reader. If you are really good friends, for heaven's sake, don't open your letter with a frigid stereotype. Be friendly, natural, human —just as you would be if you greeted him in person!

10. *Use a split opening for eye appeal—*

a. If you had $5,000 to invest today . . .

. . . just what would *you* do?

b. For prompt, dependable service ...

. . . call Service, Incorporated!

c. When things go wrong . . .

. . . just think of Bill Jones, the Fixit-Man!

d. We of the Fox West Coast Theatres are pleased and proud to present to our many friends in the San Luis Obispo area one of the greatest stories of all times—

OLIVER TWIST
_____

NOTE: Although not used very often, the split opening offers the clever, forceful business letter-writer an unusual opportunity to catch the eye of his reader, to arouse his interest and attract his attention, and to intrigue him into reading more of his letter. There is nothing in the books that says you can't or shouldn't open your letter in an interesting, attention-getting way as long as you don't just hoodwink your reader into reading your letter. NEVER UNDERESTIMATE THE POWER OF EYE

APPEAL IN ANY PART OF YOUR BUSINESS LETTER!

11. *Challenge your reader—*

   a. If you are completely satisfied with your personal appearance, just drop this letter into the nearest wastebasket.
      (NOTE: This would make a dandy split opening.)
   b. Would *you* like to save 25 per cent of your compressed air costs? If so, just try a leak-proof HERMITICUS air gun *for only one week!* If HERMITICUS doesn't save you 25 per cent of your compressed air cost, the gun is yours—without cost!
   c. Would you like to be the lucky winner of a brand new Cadillac convertible, with all the accessories that go with America's finest car? If so, ...

   > NOTE: Limited though it obviously is, this opening can be very forceful in starting certain types of letters on their way, particularly sales letters. It's perfectly O.K. to pique your reader's interest or curiosity with a startling statement or a challenge *provided that it leads directly into your sales pitch!* There must be a definite tie-in with your sales message.

12. *Tell a story that has a point—*

   a. Once we saw the desk of a teacher of English piled so high on three sides that it looked like a bomb-proof shelter. The chances that your copy of McCloskey and Dow's READING AND THINKING is buried beneath such a pile is no more than one to twenty. Yet that one chance has us worried.[1]
   b. Like all good housekeepers, we like to tidy up an extra bit for the holidays. So, with the Easter shopping season at hand, we got to looking around at this and that and discovered your Charga-Plate hasn't been used in

---

[1] Used by permission of The Odyssey Press, Inc.

months. "This," we said to ourselves, "is something we'd better look into right now. ..."

> NOTE: Once in a blue moon there comes an opportunity to start your letter with a good story that has a definite point. There's the rub— YOUR STORY MUST HAVE A POINT IN YOUR MESSAGE THAT FOLLOWS. Whenever you have an opportunity to use a story opening, by all means take advantage of it, for story openings can be tremendously forceful and effective.

13. *Accentuate the positive—*

   a. Increase your word-power and you will increase your earning power!
   b. Your order will be shipped on Monday, for sure.
   c. Our answer to your request is an enthusiastic YES!
   d. Of course we are glad to send you the information you requested in your recent letter.
   e. HERMITICUS all-brass air guns are leak-proof, eco nomical, and mighty easy to operate.
   f. Just as soon as our new catalog is received from the printer, I'll send you your personal copy.
   g. My favorite subject is better business letters. Before you finish reading this letter, I hope to make it yours, too.
   h. Nothing is too much trouble to do for a good customer like you, Jim.

   > NOTE: I could go on and on showing you positive openings—the very best way to begin your business letters. Too many writers open negatively and then slip in their positive points almost unnoticed. That's bad. Tomorrow you'll see how this has been done—and how it can so easily be undone, too!

14. *Make an offer, or give a gift—*

 a. The attached coupon entitles you to a free gift at Bloke's any day next week.

 b. Here are two tickets to the Builders' Show to be held during the week of December 23-29. Please accept them with our compliments.

 c. This is a special invitation for you to attend a sneak prevue of our latest picture, *For Now and Forever,* to be held at our plant, 2901 Los Feliz Boulevard, Los Angeles, at 1:30 Thursday afternoon, December 6.

  NOTE: Although generally limited to sales letters, this opening has certain possibilities in such routine letters as invitations.

15. *When the occasion permits, use a novelty opening—*

 a. This acknowledgment is really a double-header!

 b. Should I ... or shouldn't I ... acknowledge your cross-plug trailer order that we received today? . . .

 c. Do *you* know that in California—
  FIVE NEW SCHOOLS ARE NEEDED EVERY MONDAY FOR THE NEXT TEN YEARS?

 d. AKHTN OYU!
  No, it's not Russian, or even Turkish. Just my usual "Thank you" with the letters jumbled up a bit.

 e.   So long,
     dear friend,
    we'll have to part,
 Although it almost breaks my heart! (See page 133 for entire letter.)

  NOTE: Since I am listing as many different kinds of letter openings as I can think of at the moment, I felt that some of these novelty beginnings should be included, although I am fully aware of their limited use, particularly in the writing of routine correspondence. However, there are times when a novelty opening is most appropriate. When such occasions arise, use them, but don't use them indiscriminately. Remember, *there is no substitute for good, common sense in the writing of business letters!*

16. *Express sorrow or regret if the occasion demands such an opening expression—*

   a. I am very sorry about the delay in sending you the re vised specifications.
   b. I was indeed distressed to learn that you have not re ceived any copies of our monthly lists since last April.
   c. Much as I hate to admit it, I must confess defeat in my efforts to get you a Volume 2 of the 1938 printing of *The Book of Knowledge.*
   d. All of us here at the office are very sorry to hear of your illness, Joe.

   > NOTE: Some companies do not believe in apologizing, even when they are in the wrong. To my way of thinking, there are times when the only decent thing you can do is to say, in person or in your letter, that you are sincerely sorry that something amiss happened. You may be sure that your reader will think all the more of you for having acknowledged your error and made amends by saying you are sorry. BUT BE SURE YOU HAVE SOMETHING TO APOLOGIZE FOR. Don't be a Uriah Heep, forever apologizing and being humble for something you didn't commit. Such a person is simply playing the part of the fool—and he fools no one but himself.

17. *Start with an apt quotation—*

   a. There's an old saying: "Money talks." To a business man, it usually shouts out loud!
   b. The remark, "I'd stand on my head to hear from you again," may be just a flip remark to some people . . .
   c. Sam Goldwyn's most famous remark was "Include me

out!" The only reason we are bringing this up is that we are afraid we are being "included out" of consideration for your parts replacements.

> NOTE: Again, this is an opening used only occasionally. That's why it can be so forceful if used wisely. If you can attract your reader's attention and arouse his interest with an apt bit of dialogue or an appropriate quotation, you have one of the best means of getting off to a flying start. There is no law against attracting attention legitimately, but if you merely trick your reader into giving you his attention, you will pay the penalty of having him drop your letter into his circular file—his wastebasket!

That's the story on forceful letter openings. Of course, it's not the whole story. Nobody could ever tell you that, for tomorrow or the day afterward, someone will come along with a brand new way of getting the favorable attention of his reader. Then a new section will have to be added to this chapter. And more power to anyone who can think up a new and forceful way of getting his letter started!

After all, these seventeen different ways—some of which overlap, of course—are simply thought-starters. If they have *started* YOU thinking about YOUR letter openings and ways that YOU can improve them, today's study has done all that I hoped it would do. Don't slavishly copy any one of these openings, or limit yourself to any single type. Try all of them. Develop your own, and you'll find that your own ingenuity will send your letters merrily on their way toward winning new friends for your company, and keeping your old and valued customers happy and contented.

DON'T STUMBLE WHEN YOU START

YESTERDAY YOU LEARNED to get your letters off to a flying start. Today you are going to learn how to avoid or eliminate stumbling starts—weak, puny, ineffective beginnings that simply annoy your reader and get your letter off to a limping, stumbling opening.

So without further comment, let's take a look at ten different breeds of bad beginnings. At the same time, let's also see what can be done to strengthen each one so that a stumbling opening can become a really flying start.

In parentheses immediately following the weak opening is a really forceful rewrite. Remember that this is only *one* of a number of forceful ways in which this letter could have been started. Time and space do not permit my exhausting the possibilities, interesting though they may be. For several, however, I have listed two or three equally forceful beginnings.

RED-LIGHT OPENINGS

1. *Don't start your letter with trite, moss-covered, old-fashioned language that great-grandpa thought so elegant and necessary—*

    a. Pursuant to your request, we enclose herewith copy of our latest price list.

       (This correspondent learned his "business English"

in the gay nineties! Why didn't he talk in modern, every-day English:

Enclosed is a copy of our latest price list.

Or

,

Here is your copy of our latest price list. Don't be afraid to be friendly, human. Your reader will like you and your company all the more when he sees that you are flesh and blood, not a dictating robot.)

b. Further to my April 11th letter, we take great pleasure in enclosing herewith glossy print photographs of Messrs. Jones & Brown, together with brief captions describing the activities shown thereon.

(This writer got lost in a welter of words. Why didn't he say:

It is a pleasure to enclose glossy prints of Messrs. Jones and Brown, together with brief descriptions of their activities. Cheaper, too—20 words *vs.* 30 in the original!)

c. As per your request, enclosed please find copy of our latest bulletin.

(Here's old "as per" rearing his ugly head again! Also, this writer makes his reader hunt to "find" the bulletin! no! No! NO! Say:

Enclosed is a copy of our latest bulletin you re quested.   *Or,*

The latest bulletin you requested is enclosed.

These openings are short, simple, direct, natural.)

d. We anticipate we will be in a position to ship your or der the latter part of November.

(How stiff, stuffy, and supercilious can language get? That just isn't a normal, natural way for one person to talk or write to another.

We expect to ship your order late in November. Not only better but also less expensive and clearer, too.)

e. In response to your favor of the 28th, attached please find price sheets.

(Just *when* is a letter a "favor"? When it brings you an order? Try:

Here are the price sheets you requested in your letter of May 28.

It's often a good idea to include the date of the letter you are answering, but that isn't always necessary.)

f. We are forwarding under separate cover four samples in green.

(If the samples aren't enclosed or included, obviously they are being sent separately. How about:

Today we sent you by Parcel Post four samples of our green shades.)

g. The subject job was inspected today.

(Here the word "subject" refers to the subject line in the letter heading. Although there is much to recommend the use of subject lines in communications, they should not be referred to in the body of the letter in this manner. Such is the lazy man's approach. This is better:

The Los Angeles Safeway #475 job was inspected today.

This is clear and unmistakable.)

h. We take pleasure in sending you herewith and attached hereto an 11" x 14" enlargement of one of your graduates now in our employ.

(Just how *does* one "take" pleasure? Say your piece simply, naturally:

We are glad to enclose an 11" x 14" enlargement of Jimmy James, one of your graduates now working for us.)

i. In reply to yours of March 19th, 1949, please be advised that at this time we are not in a position to furnish you with one of our catalogs.

(Stiff, pompous, negative. Thoroughly bad from beginning to end. This wet-blanket opening will dampen the enthusiasm of any reader. Try: Just now our stock of catalogs is depleted.   *Or,*
Unfortunately, we are just out of catalogs. If you wish, follow this up with: "We'll be glad to send you one as soon as our supply is replenished.")

    j. Beg to advise are pleased to enclose herewith prices re-
       quested in letter of recent date.

          (Clipped, hackneyed, curt—cold and lifeless. *Don't
          beg!* And be very chary about giving advice. Most
          people won't appreciate it. Say:
          We are glad to send you the prices you recently re
          quested.   *Or,*

             Here are the prices requested in your letter of
             March 4.)

2. *Don't open your letter with a participle. Participles are weak
verb forms—*

    a. Complying with yours of May 4th, we are enclosing
       herewith our latest bulletin for your information.

          (This language was in high style when the
          Spanish-American War broke out. It dropped out of
          friendly, forceful business letter-writing over 30
          years ago. Unfortunately, not everyone knows that.
          Write:
             We are glad to send you our latest bulletin, as you
             requested.
          That's probably what you would say to him face to
          face.)

    b. Referring to yours of the 5th, the parts will be shipped
       next week.

          (Not only old-fashioned and weak, but illogical. This
          sentence says that the parts are referring to your
          letter. Impossible! He meant:
             The parts referred to in your letter of June 5 will
             be shipped next week.
          That's honest, plain, straight-from-the-shoulder talk-
          ing.)

    c. Enclosing your policy and trusting you find same in
       order.

          (It's hard to believe, but I have the letter with this
          absurd opening. This isn't even a complete thought.
          These revisions are better:
             I am sure the enclosed policy is complete and cor
             rect.   *Or,*

The enclosed policy should be complete and correct.

d. Confirming our telegram of today, formal proposal is herewith enclosed.

(Stiff, stuffy, and sheer nonsense. Loosen it up a bit: The formal proposal enclosed confirms our telegram today, Mr. Dye.

The use of the reader's name does wonders to loosen up an otherwise stiff opening.)

e. Being an object of nation wide observance, and amounting to one of the largest organizations for young men in the State of Michigan, should habilitate us for such co-operation as is succeedingly requested in this letter.

(This revision is clearer:

The Royal Lions Automobile Clubs have gained nation-wide recognition as one of the largest young men's organizations in the state of Michigan. We'd like your cooperation in a project we have undertaken.)

3. *Don't beat around the bush. Have a point and come to it quickly and forcefully. Wordy, repetitious, long-winded openings are weak and wasteful—*

a. In reply to your kind letter requesting delivery information on the above-mentioned order, we are pleased to be able to inform you that this order will in all probability be ready and awaiting shipment on or about September 27, 1948.

(This writer hates to let go of his sentences, once he has them under way. This 40-word long-winded sentence should be streamlined:

Your order #46416 will probably be shipped September 27.   *Or,*

On September 27 your order #46416 will probably be shipped.   *Or,*

You will be glad to know that your order #46416 will probably be shipped September 27. Any one of these three openings is more forceful and less expensive than the original. LEARN TO SAY MUCH IN FEW WORDS!)

b. Last week I went over to Flint and there I took meas urements of your existing building and have had them approved by our Mr. Fischer.

   (This sentence is stringy, as well as wordy and repetitious. Cut it down:

   Last week I took measurements of your Flint building, and have had them approved by Mr. Fischer.   *Or,*

   The measurements I took of your Flint building last week have been approved by Mr. Fischer. These revisions are both natural and readable.)

c. We received a letter from you dated August 30 in which you told us that your books agreed with ours, and on the strength of that information we have pre pared our refund check No. 17727 in the amount of $1,616.41, which check we have sent directly to you on September 21.

   (Wordiness compounded and doubled! This reminds me of Hamlet's famous reply to the inquisitive Polonius, who asked: "What read ye, my lord?" To which the wily Hamlet replied, enigmatically: "Words! Words! Words!" Try:

   We were glad to know from your letter of August 30 that your books agreed with ours. Therefore, on September 21 we sent you our refund check No. 17727 for $1,616.41.

   Don't be afraid to chop a long, unwieldy, tortuous sentence into two or even three shorter ones. A 51-word sentence is 10 times as hard to read and understand as two 14- to 17-word sentences.)

d. In response to your request of recent date, we regret to inform you that the Graduate School at the University of Blank has no provision for offering major work to ward an advanced degree in the field of Aeronautical Engineering and we are, therefore, unable to serve your interest in this instance.

   (How would you like to go to a college whose officers

wrote such stiff letters? Maybe that's what's wrong with our educational system today: there is such a discrepancy between what the schools and colleges teach and what is good business practice. But then, I may be wrong. How do you like this revision: Thank you for your letter of April 15. Unfortunately, the Graduate School at the University of Blank does not offer work toward an advanced degree in aeronautical engineering. Don't try to say everything in one sentence, especially in your opening sentence. LEARN TO WRITE SHORT, CLEAR, READABLE SENTENCES. See also the Fifteenth Day, pages 206 ff.)

e. In accordance with your suggestion during our telephone conversation yesterday, we are enclosing a duplicate copy of our proposal which was submitted on May 24, 1951.

> (People just don't talk that way today. Here's what they would say:
>
> As you suggested over the telephone yesterday, here is a duplicate copy of our proposal of May 24. Use the year only when necessary to a clear understanding of the date in question—during December and January, at most.)

4. *Don't be curt or abrupt. In your desire to avoid wordiness or repetitions, don't clip your sentences. Don't write incomplete, fragmentary thoughts—*

a. Your postcard of the 13th, will state are pleased to enclose bulletins for your perusal. Also catalog of same. (It's hard to realize that this is an actual opening from a letter from a fairly large company. This is much better:

> It is a pleasure to send you some literature and our catalog.
> NEVER OVERLOOK THE VALUE OF FREE ADVERTISING IN THE BODY OF YOUR LETTER—YOUR TRADE NAMES! Wherever possible, include the names of your products. As Mr. F.

H. Roy of Montgomery Ward would say: "Don't have merehandise-itis!")

b. Vermiculite plaster is used in place of sand. The pro portions depend upon whether it is used on board or metal lath.

(This writer jumps right into the middle of things without adequately preparing his reader. This letter has a middle and an ending, *but no beginning.* That's very poor letter organization. (See Fourth Day.) Try:

I am glad to answer your inquiry. When Vermiculite is used instead of sand for plaster, the proportion depends upon whether the plaster is to be laid on board or on metal lath.

Then proceed to give the proportions for each mix. Although this revision is longer than the original, it is much clearer and not at all abrupt. Curtness and abruptness are as undesirable as long-windedness and wordiness.)

c. Your letter of the 26th to hand and contents noted.

(THAT'S AN INSULT. Don't ever brag about having received and read a customer's letter. That is the least you can do. It's expected of you. This opening is what is often called a "platform" beginning. Why not say:

Thank you for your letter of June 26. This gets you off to a flying start, for it tells him three important things: 1. You received his letter; 2. You have read it; 3. You appreciate his having written you. That's good psychology.)

d. Referring to yours of Sept. 24th regarding your order No. 7691 for 24 6" tees. Expect this material in in about three days.

(This writer probably prides himself on being a man of few words. He is—*too few!* He cuts his reader off in nothing flat. But how much good has he done himself or his company? He could have said:

The twenty-four 6" tees referred to in your letter of September 24 will be here in about 3 days.

Whenever you have two consecutive numbers, as in the original sentence—24 6" tees—always write one out.)

e. Reference my letter of April 6th re the photos of Mr. John Smith.

(Do you *really* know what he wants or means? I don't. Without the rest of his letter, you would have to guess at what he meant to say. That is very bad letter-writing practice. Your opening sentence must stand alone, logically as well as grammatically. This is clearer:

Please refer to my letter of April 6 about the photographs of Mr. John Smith.

That is clear, but is it what he meant to say? Could be. Your guess is as good as mine. Business letters are poor places for playing guessing games.)

f. I'd suggest that you address a letter to Mr. Samuel Mintner, Associate Director, National Letter Writer's Association, 201 West Main Street, Louisville 15, Kentucky, and ask him to send you copies of "Punctuation Made Easy" and "There's a Better Way of Doing It," and any other literature pertaining to the writing of better business letters.

(This sentence suffers from two usually opposing faults: it is not only wordy and long-winded, but as the first sentence in a letter to a total stranger, very abrupt. How about:

Thank you for your inquiry about better letter writing. May I suggest that you write to Mr. Samuel Mintner, Associate Director, National Letter Writer's Association, 201 West Main Street. Ask Mr. Mintner to send you copies of PUNCTUATION MADE EASY, THERE'S A BETTER WAY OF DOING IT, and any other available material on the art of writing successful business letters. (Longer, but less abrupt and easier to read.)

g. In reply to your letter of October 20th requesting information on Carbide and High Speed Tools.

(So what? This is supposed to be an opening *sentence.* Make it complete:
Thanks for your letter of October 20 asking for information on carbide and high speed tools. This sentence really says something. After all, that's just what your opener should do—SAY SOMETHING!)

5. *Don't have I-trouble or WE-writis—*

   (The WE-words have been capitalized on purpose.)
   a. WE have your request for information on OUR products which WE note you wish to obtain for reference in your refrigerating engineering course at California State Polytechnic College.

   (They actually sent some material. And after such a stuffy opening, too. Try:
   Thanks for your request for information on our products. It is a pleasure to send you material which should be helpful in your refrigerating engineering courses at California State Polytechnic College.)

   b. I checked into the order for the Triple job and it looks as though WE should be able to complete at least 90% of it by Monday of next week, and WE have arranged to ship that portion of this order by that time.

   (This sentence suffers from wordiness and clumsiness, as well as WE- and I-trouble:
   It looks as if 90% of the Triple order can be completed by next Monday or Tuesday. Whatever is ready will be shipped then.
   That is a better opening—one sentence cut into two. Also there are only 24 words as compared with 46 in the original—a saving well worth while in these days of rising costs.)

6. *Don't use the internal revenue or stiff-collar opening—*

   a. This is to inform you that we are happy to send you our latest catalog.

(He probably cracked his face when he forced that thank-you smile. Be human, natural, friendly: It is a pleasure to send you our latest catalog.   *Or,* We are glad to send you our latest catalog.   *Or,* Of course we'll send you our latest catalog.)

b. This will acknowledge your letter of March 1st answering ours of January 18th and we have cancelled the items that you specify.

(Wordy, vague, illogical, and frigidly stiff and formal. Here are five much better revisions:

The items specified in your letter of March 1 have been cancelled, as you requested.   *Or,*

As you requested, the items specified in your letter of March 1 have been cancelled.   *Or,*

The following items specified in your letter of March 1 have been cancelled: [then list them]   *Or,*

As requested in your letter of March 1, we have cancelled the items you specified.   *Or,*

We have cancelled the items specified in your letter of March 1.)

c. We wish to advise you that we can supply you with bright, semi-bright, or dull immediately upon receipt of your order.

(Don't let your opening stiffen up. Relax! Be natural and loosen up:

As soon as you send us your order, we can ship you bright, semi-bright, or dull.)

d. It would be appreciated if you would bring us up to date on the equipment that would be needed to expand our manufacturing facilities.

(Round and round he goes, and where he stops, nobody knows. How's this:

What equipment do we need to expand our manufacturing facilities?   *Or,*

What additional equipment is needed to expand our manufacturing facilities?

Shorter, sweeter, stronger than the awkward, round-

about "it would be appreciated if" phraseology. See
Appendix, page 235.)

  e. Application is hereby made for permit to install a dust
collector in accordance with your notice #817.
> (Letters to, or even *from,* governmental agencies—
> national, state, or local—should be friendly and
> human, not stiff and formal, like this one:
> > As you requested in Notice #817, we wish to apply
> > for a permit to install a dust collector.)

  f. This is in answer to your request for information about
Cart College.
> (Unfortunately, college administrators are not im-
> mune to icy openings:
> > We are glad to send you information about Cart
> > College. At least they can *say* they are glad, can't
> they?)

7. *Don't open negatively if you can avoid it. Wherever you can,
accentuate the positive and eliminate the negative—*

  a. We cannot ship your order this week, but will send it
next week for sure.
> (Don't waste time telling him what you can't do;
> spend your time telling him what you *can:*
> > Your order will be shipped next week, for sure.
> This tells the reader the one thing he wanted to know:
> when his order can be shipped!)

  b. On your first order, dated July 7, you neglected to take
your trade discount.
> (This starts off like a notice from the Internal Reve-
> nue Department. Such openings frighten your reader
> stiff, so that he really can't enjoy or appreciate the
> welcome news you have for him. Just a slight change
> in wording can make a tremendous difference in the
> tone of your letter:
> > On your order of July 7, you overlooked your trade
> > discount, which comes to the tidy sum of $57.93. We
> > have credited this to your account. Like manna from
> > Heaven, and just as welcome, too.

This revision not only tells him what he has done, but also tells him what *you* have done to correct his oversight. He'll love you for that.)

c. We cannot permit you to take your discount after the discount period has passed. To do this would be grossly unfair to our other customers who pay their bills within the allotted time. For that reason we are returning your check #456 for $764.40 and are asking you to send us promptly one for the correct amount, $780.

(What a warped conception of service that fellow had. He has the disposition of a bilious rattlesnake. Why didn't he say:

Thank you for check #456 for $764.40, which we have deposited to your credit. This check was received 15 days after the discount period had expired. Since we know you would not want us to make an exception in your case, please send us your check for $15.60 to cover the amount still due on this invoice.

About the same number of words, but what a difference the positive approach makes. It is also not a good idea to return a check or money sent you. If the check is short, credit the account with the amount of the check, which you deposit, of course, and then politely ask for the *additional* amount still due. If the customer has sent too much, deposit his check and send him a refund.)

d. We regret that we cannot comply with your request regarding literature because we are in the process of revising all our published articles on heaters.

(This is the first, last, and only sentence in this letter. It's short, but *not* sweet. Of course he cannot send what he doesn't have, but why not say he is putting the reader on a mailing list for future releases? Say:

Thanks for your request for information on our heaters. Just now we are revising all our articles.

They should be ready in about four weeks. As soon as they are published, you'll get copies of each one. This gives your reader something to look forward to.) e. We are very sorry but we cannot allow your claims #46475 for $7.20 and #46476 for $9.33, as this merchandise was delivered in July and we should have been notified before this if the shortage was our fault. (For a mere $16.53 the writer risks losing this customer. It may be far better to allow his claim and keep him happy and contented. But if you still won't allow it, try writing this way: I am sorry that there evidently has been a misunderstanding about when the shortage must be reported in order to be allowed. Then proceed with your decision in this case.)

8. *Don't be silly—*

    a. We have received your postcard of March 4 asking for details on our equipment.

       (Of course you have received it. How else could you be answering his request? Wasting your reader's valuable time and patience telling him what he re quested is being downright silly. Why not write: Thanks for your request for details on our equip ment.   *Or,*
We are glad to send you details on our equipment.
    Or,
Enclosed are the details you requested on our equipment. Any of these openings gets you off to a flying start.)

    b. Kindly inform us of the availability and cost of secur ing 1,000 or 2,000 copies of this article on plain white stock, similar to your magazine.

       (You wouldn't inform him gruffly or unkindly, would you? Forget that word "kindly" and your letters will be more friendly. How about:
How much would it cost for 1,000 or 2,000 copies

of this article on plain white stock like that used in your magazine? Shorter and better.)

c. We checked into the two orders that Kunz and Schwarz did not receive acknowledgments on HB-13417 and 13418, and find that both orders were set up for shipment on November 24. I am unable to explain what happened to the acknowledgments for these orders, but will make up duplicate copies and will mail them right away.

(This writer is trying to cover his confusion with words. What he meant was:

The two unacknowledged Kunz and Schwarz orders, HB-13417 and -13418, were ready for shipment November 24. Duplicate acknowledgments will be mailed immediately.

22 words *vs.* 60—a worth-while saving of 65 per cent.)

d. I am glad you were able to visit Bay City and had a touch of manufacture of pumps, condensers, radar, etc.

(Something like catching the flu or a cold, eh? Here's what he probably meant:

I am glad you were able to visit Bay City and see how pumps, condensers, and other things are manufactured here.

I suppose that's what he meant to say. Your guess is as good as mine. Reduce reader guessing to a minimum in forceful business letters.)

e. In reference to your letter of August 15, 1951, we would like to thank you for your application for employment.

(He doesn't actually thank him—he only "would like to." Say:

Thank you for your application letter of August 15.

Shorter, sweeter, friendlier. Cheaper and more sensible, too.)

9. *Don't be pompous, unfriendly, testy, or peevish—*

    a. The writer wishes to say that we are giving serious consideration to your application.

         (Is this modesty? If so, it's certainly false modesty. Don't be afraid to use "I" or "We" whenever the occasion demands. Use common sense and just don't overwork I-words. This is much more sensible: We are seriously considering your application.)

    b. It would be much appreciated if you would be kind enough to bring us up to date on the equipment necessary to bring our manufacturing facilities into maxi mum production.

         (He probably doesn't mean to sound peevish, but he certainly does—and quite uppity, too. Why not phrase it in question form:

             Would you please bring us up to date on the equipment necessary to get maximum production in our foundry?

         Although I usually try to avoid "please," this time it seems O.K. Too often "please" sounds commanding, demanding.)

    c. I regret to announce that it will not be possible for me to attend the meeting of the Promotion Committee on December 12. It so happens we are having a general meeting here that week.

         (Stiff, stuffy, pompous, supercilious—and the salutation was "Dear Joe"! This bit of peevishness could be humanized so very easily:

             Sorry, but I can't attend the Promotion Committee meeting on December 12. We're having a general meeting here that week.)

    d. Concerning the above subject, either you are in a mood to do business or not.

         (At least he writes to the point, although his point is quite sharp and it may prick deeply. He could have softened it so easily:

How about getting together on this matter soon? At least give him the benefit of any doubt.)

e. You stated that you expected to be in Los Angeles sometime in June.

(Sounds as if you didn't believe him. You wouldn't call him a liar, would you? How about this version: We are glad to know that you will be in Los Angeles sometime in June. That he will be glad to hear.)

f. We feel you are in a better position than we to judge the results of these tests; therefore we are sending you them under separate cover for evaluation at your earli est convenience.

(Keep your hands to yourself. Consider the implication of your words. Say:

Since you are better equipped to evaluate the results of these tests, we are sending you all the data we have collected.)

g. As I believe we informed you before, we do not regularly handle body parts, but we will obtain these for you if you wish.

(This puts the reader in his place, all right. But how much good has this letter done the writer or his company? Be friendly, cooperative, helpful:

Although we do not regularly carry them in stock, we can get body parts whenever you need any. This will win his friendship and reaffirm his faith in your company.)

10. *Don't be clumsy or awkward—*

a. Your letter, referring to waste paper, to the Universal Paper Company, Denver, has been forwarded to this office for answering.

(This sentence is badly muddled. The parts are improperly put together:

The Universal Paper Company in Denver has asked us to answer your letter about waste paper.)

b. In talking with the office today, they advised that the

water pump which they shipped you on December 28
has not been picked up as yet.

(Sounds as if the people at the office are talking to
themselves. Could be. Most unlikely, however. This
is better:

Today Mr. McCorkle at the office telephoned us
that the water pump shipped you on December 28
has not been picked up yet.)

*   *   *   *

There they are—10 different kinds of RED-LIGHTS, with 54
examples showing what must be avoided. Of course, this list is
incomplete. Almost every week I run across a new kind or species
of RED-LIGHT.

Now here is a most important question, which only *you* can
answer:

WHAT CAN / DO ABOUT *MY* BUSINESS LETTER OPENINGS?

The answer is quite simple. Here are some concrete suggestions
that will help you transform your RED-LIGHTS into friendly,
forceful GREEN-LIGHTS:

1. Check through every letter you have written during the
past week or two.

2. Make two lists, one of your own RED-LIGHTS and one of
your GREEN-LIGHTS.

3. Rewrite every RED-LIGHT until it has become a good,
friendly, forceful GREEN-LIGHT.

4. Watch for any pet or stock openings that you use frequently. Copy down each one, and make as many variants as you
can. Whenever you think of another way of saying it, add it to
your list.

5. From what you have learned in the past two days, make up
your own list of GREEN-LIGHTS.

6. Start using GREEN-LIGHTS in the next letters you dictate or write. The only way to make GREEN-LIGHTS a part of
your daily thinking is to start using them immediately, and to
continue using them in every letter you write.

7. Criticize the opening of every business letter you receive—and then read critically through the entire letter. If it has a RED-LIGHT, rewrite that opening until it is a good GREEN-LIGHT. If it contains some letter-writing techniques worth remembering, jot them down and put them to immediate use in your own letters.

8. PRACTICE MAKES PERFECT! That's a trite statement, but it's true. Unless you start practicing friendly, forceful business-letter techniques, you will probably continue in the same old-fashioned, ineffective way. So, PRACTICE ONE OR MORE BETTER-LETTER TECHNIQUES EVERY DAY. In a month or two you'll be amazed at the improvement in your own business letters. That's no idle promise.

END WITH A BANG!

LIKE A PERFECT DAY, every letter must come to a close. Some just stop. Others really end. For many, however, that stopping or ending is as final as the tomb. These are "dead" endings.

Remember Aristotle, whom we talked about on our Fourth Day, page 41? He's the fellow who said that all good writing should have a beginning, a middle, and an ending. That's the part we're concerned about today: the various ways you can always be sure of closing your letters in a friendly but forceful way.

Just a few preliminary comments about letter endings in general before we read some sure-fire rules for always writing successful letter endings:

1. Your letter ending must motivate the action you want from your reader.

2. Your ending must be natural and logical. It must be the inevitable result of what you have previously said in your letter. It must not be abrupt, unexpected, artificial.

3. Your ending must be final and complete. When you end your letter, end completely, finally. Don't leave your reader help lessly, hopelessly looking for more—wondering whether this is all you have to say, or whether there is more to follow.

4. Your ending must be gentle but firm. It must be friendly but forceful. It must either terminate the correspondence, or be a cordial invitation to your reader to answer, whichever you wish.

Some people begin and end their letters as they drive their cars, particularly when they start or stop their cars. You know what I mean: a series of bone-shaking jerks when starting; sudden and unexpected weaving and turning, with bursts of speed and unexplainable fits of dawdling along aimlessly; and finally a head-bumping, spine-snapping jolt when they slam on their brakes for a stop.

All too many people write business letters in the same haphazard way. They fumble around getting started, wasting time and patience. Suddenly, without any previous warning, they zoom into their message with lightning-like speed. And then, without any warning whatsoever, they jam on their brakes, mumble some meaningless complimentary close, and are off to the next race. For example:

Dear Mr. George:

We beg to acknowledge receipt of yours of the first inst. requesting information concerning our products.

The literature in the attached envelope explains our offering.

We will be glad to have your orders for immediate shipment and it is not necessary for you to sign any franchise now unless you prefer to do so.

Yours very truly,

That, word for word, is a reply received from a postcard requesting information about refrigerating equipment—not a dealership. That letter-writer was certainly an eager beaver. But his overzealousness really scared the reader off. He did not send that company any more inquiries. He was afraid he would end up having to buy some of their equipment.

You probably dislike going into certain stores in your community because the clerks are so persistent in their sales approach. They make you feel that you just can't get out without buying. And if you don't, they make you feel cheap and small. Remember, you can become one of those obnoxious eager beavers in your letters, as well as in your personal actions. DON'T!

Enough of talking *about* letter endings. Now let's look *at* some friendly ways of bringing your letter to a safe, gentle landing. As with letter openings, I have divided them into GREEN-

LIGHT ENDINGS and RED-LIGHT ENDINGS. As usual, my emphasis will be on how to make the RED LIGHTS into good, safe, forceful GREEN LIGHTS.

GREEN-LIGHT ENDINGS

1. *Stress the YOU point of view—*

    a. Your splendid cooperation is sincerely appreciated by all of us, Jack.
    b. After you have seen this film, let us know what you think of it.
    c. The next time you are out our way, please drop in, won't you?
    d. You will always find Mr. Smith and his entire organiza tion ready to serve you.
    e. Your usual prompt attention will be appreciated.
    f. Your recommendations will help us come to a prompt de cision in this matter.
    g. It was thoughtful of you to bring this to our attention,
    h. If you think we should allow this claim, Joe, we'll go along with you.

    (NOTE: If you open your letter with a big YOU and close it with a big YOU also, your letter will give the impression of being entirely from your reader's point of view. Nowhere in your letter is it more important to use the YOU attitude than at your ending. Last impressions are lasting impressions. Lasting impressions are strong, forceful. Talk *to* your reader when you close your letter, and you will leave him a happier person than if you talked about yourself. The ending of your letter is a poor place for I-trouble or WE-writis.)

2. *Use some variation of the thank-you or appreciation clos ing—*

    a. Thank you very much for handling this request for us, Mr. Jackson.

   b. Your fine cooperation is much appreciated.
   c. I am very grateful for your assistance in helping me get
      these parts.
   d. We look forward to entering your name among our satis
      fied subscribers.
   e. Thanks for your part in keeping Mr. Jones a satisfied
      customer.
   f. It is certainly good to know that you are using Terra-Lite
      in your own bath house and like it so much.
   g. Keep up the good work—others appreciate it, and so do
      we.
   h. Believe me when I say that I am tremendously indebted to
      you for writing me as you did, Mr. Shepherd.
   i. It will be a real pleasure to let Mr. Jones know how sat-
      isfied you are with the work his department did on your
      tractor.

   (NOTE: Shakespeare once wrote:
                  Blow, blow, thou winter wind!
                  Thou art not so unkind As
                  man's ingratitude.
   That's a good thing to remember. Few things
   hurt worse than ingratitude. Failure to thank a
   person for a favor, or failure to show some
   appreciation comes pretty close to ingratitude.
   But let me throw out a warning: If you start a
   letter with "Thank you," don't close it with
   "Thank you again." Thanking your reader once
   is fine. Doing it twice or three times in the same
   letter smacks of insincerity. Above all, *your
   appreciation must be sincere and genuine.*)

3. *Close with a pertinent or important statement—*

   a. For the small cost, this paper is well worth while.
   b. Your letter will be kept in our active files for future ref
      erence.
   c. I am sure that anything we develop here will be taken
      up by other manufacturers.

    d. I'd like to come in and talk with you tomorrow.

    e. As soon as we receive this information, well send you a new contract and get started on our shop drawings.

    f. As you can see, this *is* an ambitious program.

    g. Many of the improvements we are making now will not show up in the record until next year.

    h. We at RCA rely heavily on our thousands of suppliers, and it gives us great pleasure to give public recognition to the important part they play on America's industrial team. (NOTE: A double-barrelled closing!)

    i. A copy of this selection is being mailed to the Horan Hanger Company.

    j. I am already looking forward to the Seventh Annual Conference!

        (NOTE: If you close with something important, your reader is much more likely to remember what you said. The ending of your letter is the worst possible place for something trivial or inconsequential—*never forget that.* And it is the very best place for a significant statement. That kind of ending is bound to be forceful.)

4. *Close with a question—*

    a. May I call for an interview on Thursday between 9 and 12?

    b. Don't you think it bad policy to circulate anything not completely up to date?

    c. What do you think, Joe?

    d. How much education will YOU help us buy for San Luis Obispo children?

    e. Would you like to see our program?

    f. Won't you let me call in person to tell you why I am sure that the Blank Agency can find good use for a young, ambitious fellow like me?

    g. "How are our chances of getting to bat soon again?" asks
                             Irving Mack.

(NOTE: Like the question opening, the question closing can be very effective. I once saw a letter that opened with a question, and closed with the same question. But what a difference in that question at the ending. The opening was a real question. The closing was a rhetorical question that answered itself. I wish I had a copy of that letter to show you.)

5. *Make a courteous command or request—*

    a. Remember, the pictures you'll enjoy tomorrow *must be taken today!*

    b. Please let us know at once if you approve this model.

    c. If you need more information, just let me know.

    d. Won't you send me an extra copy of your letter?

    e. Best of all, talk to your printer or binder—he'll be glad to help you.

    f. Report to the Recorder's Office to claim your certificate, please.

    g. Just write to me whenever you believe our service is not living up to the high standards which your purchase of your new car entitles you.

(NOTE: This is a very forceful closing. It focuses your reader's final attention on something important—something you want him to remember in your letter. This type of ending is always safe to use.)

6. *Accentuate the positive—*

    a. Your letter of application will be kept in our active files for future reference.

    b. The carpenters are making good progress on the form work, and it looks as if we will be ready to pour concrete on Monday.

    c. Our usual charge for this manual is $1.00, but we are sending it to you with our compliments.

    d. Expressions such as yours are a real help in making de cisions on future designs.

e. You are to be complimented on selecting this novel way of advertising B. F. Goodrich tires.

f. You may be sure that we are always glad to cooperate in every possible way.

g. I am certain that you will like it!

(NOTE: One of the best places in your letter to be POS-ITIVE is your ending. Here you want to make a lasting impression on your reader. Make your final sentence a positive one—a direct hit, not a miss.)

7. *Close with a strong sales appeal—*

a. Take advantage of our delivery service. It will mean a BIG saving to you.

b. We look forward to entering your name among our happy REFRIGERATING ENGINEERING subscribers.

c. If you will fill out and mail the enclosed card, our repre sentative will be glad to demonstrate this instrument in your own plant.

d. Mail it today, and I will reserve your seat for fifty-two Friday nights for the greatest show on earth!

e. The appointment of Mr. Jones brings to the New Haven area a man rich in experience and in the tradition of Blank service—a man who has the interest of every Blank owner at heart and knows the importance of *good* service.

(NOTE: Although much longer than is generally recom-mended, this ending is strong, friendly, force-ful, confidence-creating.)

f. Whenever your Blank is in need of expert care and atten tion, just take it to our nearest authorized dealer. He has the men and equipment necessary to perform any service operation on any Blank we have built.

g. For prompt service, simply present the enclosed card at our office.

h. So let this be a friendly little reminder that when you need any special trailers, just send your order to

Irving Mack

(NOTE: Never lose sight of the fact that your closing sentence is important because of its position. It is your parting shot at your reader—your last chance to make your sales pitch. Don't muff this grand opportunity to get in another good plug for your company and its products. This may well be the central selling point in your letter. But don't forget the "Dear Mr. George" letter that started us off today. YOUR SALES CLOSING IS FORCEFUL *ONLY* IF YOU HAVE ADEQUATELY PREPARED YOUR READER FOR SUCH AN ENDING. This you must do from your opening sentence on.)

8. *Close with a friendly, personal note of good will—*

   a. Keep up the good work, John!
   b. You are certainly doing a fine job of guidance with your college students.
   c. Please accept our best wishes for the preparation of a successful thesis.
   d. Kindest personal regards to all of you.
   e. Good luck and best wishes!
   f. My best wishes for your success in your chosen field.
   g. It is always a pleasure to serve you, Mr. Wright,
   h. Good luck to you in your fight for better letters.

   (NOTE: Every forceful closing has a bit of the personal in it. As I come to discussing each type of closing, that type seems the most important at that particular time. So it is with this personal ending. Given the right occasion, you will have to hunt far and wide before you will find a better way of ending your letter. There is plenty of room in every letter for sentiment—GOOD WILL—especially at the ending.)

9. *Close with your reader's name—*

   a. Any inquiries or suggestions you care to make, addressed

to me, personally, will be given careful consideration, Mrs. Williston.

b. When I come, I'll bring all the records with me, Miss Howe.

c. If there is any cost involved, please let me know so that I can reimburse you when I see you next Monday, Mr. Shaw.

d. The next time I go north, I'll try to arrange an interview with you, Mr. Norton.

e. We hope that this arrangement is completely satisfactory to you, Mr. Larsen.

(NOTE: Closing with a person's own name gives your endings an air of friendliness that just cannot be beat. But don't drag his name in for effect. Your use of his name must be a natural and logical outcome of the message your letter is conveying. Don't use a person's name too often in a letter, for that smacks of familiar-

ity·)

10. *Close with an expression of time—*

a. Mr. Jones said that our complete system will be installed and operating by late August.

b. As soon as your check is received, we shall forward the machine to you.

c. I can be at your office by 9 A.M., as you suggested.

d. Just fill in and return the enclosed card promptly.

e. I'll drop in to see you on my next trip out your way.

f. See you Saturday!

g. We'll look forward to seeing you in our office on Monday, October 14.

h. I shall look forward to hearing from you whenever a vacancy develops.

(NOTE: A time ending is usually something definite and specific for the reader to take hold of. It can be used very forcefully upon occasion.)

11. *Use a seasonal close whenever appropriate—*

    a. Merry Christmas!

    b. Happy birthday, Lucy Lee!

    c. May the New Year be a happy and prosperous one for you and yours.

    d. In the meantime, all best wishes for the New Year, and kindest personal regards.

    e. The average individual very seldom has an opportunity to congratulate a couple on their 50th wedding anniversary. Since I have not yet had this privilege, I wish to take advantage of this opportunity and extend my heartiest congratulations, as well as those of the Cadillac Motor Car Division, to you and Mrs. Campbell on your coming golden wedding anniversary. I sincerely hope that you continue to enjoy many more and that you have a very pleasant trip to Florida.

        (NOTE: Of all the endings I have seen that pack a human appeal and public-relations wallop, that last one tops them all! It is the last paragraph of a letter written by my friend Art Floethe of the Parts Department at Cadillac. Would you like to see the rest of Art's letter? And Mr. Campbell's letters, too? Fine! You have a real treat in store on the Twelfth Day. See pages 170-172.)

12. *Use any closing that will win friends for you and your company—*

    a. Here's hoping that one of these days real soon we'll be receiving an order from you so we can prove to you that we not only TALK good trailers .... but also MAKE good trailers!

    b. I hope that you will use the enclosed card whenever you are in Washington, and that you will continue to send me your advice on current issues.
       (NOTE: From a former U. S. Senator, no less!)

    c. We join you in hoping that Coulter Motor Company in Phoenix will completely live up to your expectations.

d. We do appreciate your interest in our work and hope that you will compete in future examinations for permanent employment in our Bureau.

e. I hope that we have heard the last of Mr. Adams' 3.36 ratio problem!

f. Believe me, Mr. Russell, we sincerely regret any incon venience you may have been caused. I do hope you'll understand that it was just one of those things that can happen in the best of regulated families, of which FIL-MACK is no exception.

g. It is disappointing to us that we are unable to write you more favorably.

h. I am sorry that you were unable to get up here yesterday, but it was raining like the dickens, so perhaps you can make it another time.

i. We are sorry that we could not send you the exact material you had in mind. Perhaps the next time we can serve you better.

j. Please apologize to Mr. Smith particularly. I believe that shipping the car on November 23 instead of the 29th may help to appease your customer.

Well, there you have them—93 really good letter endings, ones that you can use in or adapt to your own letters with the least amount of effort, and that will leave your reader in a good frame of mind, willing and even eager to do what you want.

If your ending gives you a graceful exit from your letter and if it motivates the action you want, it has done everything that can reasonably be expected of it except, perhaps, to terminate the correspondence. That is another matter worth considering. A safe rule to follow in routine letters or in any other kind is to use any ending that is friendly, confidence-winning, and action-inducing.

Happy endings!

Ninth Day

DON'T FUMBLE IN THE END ZONE!

THIS IS THE SECOND chapter in this book that I wish I didn't have to write. But I know that you should see these weak, ineffective letter endings held up to ridicule so that you won't make the same blunders in your own business letters. It's a job that must be done, so here goes for as painless a treatment as possible.

Wishy-washy, pusillanimous letter endings *must be avoided* as much as a rattlesnake: they are equally poisonous and deadly. They kill your reader's interest when that interest should be at its height. They defeat the very purpose of your ending: to motivate action and to leave your reader in a happy frame of mind.

But let's get at these weak, puny, silly letter endings and drive them out into the open, where we can examine them, diagnose their weaknesses, and prescribe a cure.

RED-LIGHT CLOSINGS

1. *Eliminate that antiquated participial ending—*

    a. Awaiting your further commands, we remain
       (Weak, extremely old-fashioned, and servile. Why not close with:
          May we hear from you again?   *Or,*
          If you need more information, just write me.   *Or,*
          We'll be glad to help you in any way we can.)

114

b. Thanking you, I am

(This writer missed an excellent ending by three little letters—"ing"—and the addition of two words—"I am." But a miss is as good as a mile. Here is the excellent ending he missed:

Thank you. This is as strong and friendly an ending as you can use.)

2. *Avoid incomplete closings and ones that end with "I am," "We are" "We remain" and so forth—*

a. With all good wishes, we are

(Such an ending is just a shortening of the very servile "We beg to remain your most humble and obedient servant" closing, which was so popular years ago. Just drop off the "we are" and you have a good, modern closing:

With all good wishes!   *Or,*
Good luck!   *Or,*
Best wishes to all of you!)

b. Would appreciate any information you can obtain for us.

(This writer not only clipped off his logical subject, "We," but also used "would" when he really meant "shall":

We shall appreciate any information you can obtain for us.)

c. Appreciations for your courtesy.

(Curt and clipped. Not at all friendly. These are much better:

Your courtesy is much appreciated.   *Or,*
We certainly appreciate your courtesy.   *Or,*
Thanks for your courtesy.)

3. *Eliminate trite, hackneyed, stock phraseology—*

a. Enclosed check herewith and attaching order hereto, beg to remain

(How bad can an ending get! These hackneyed words contain good news, but it is nearly smothered by sense less mouthings. Clear and clean it up:

Here is our check—and another order, too.

Or

,

You will be glad to get the enclosed check and order.
Or,
Here's good news for you—a check and another or-
der.)

b. We have appreciated all past favors, and trust you will
keep us in mind when in need of additional merchandise.
(Sounds as if they *did* appreciate the favors, but in the
meantime changed their minds. Also, don't suffer from a
case of "merchandise-itis." It's a vague, baffling disease.
Here's a more friendly rewrite:
Thanks for your nice orders. Keep us in mind whenever you need more parts.)

c. We thank you kindly for calling on us for this quotation,
and trust we will be favored with your order.
(How would you react if someone came up to you and
said this bit of nonsense? Here's how it can be loosened
up and humanized:
Thanks for letting us make this quotation. We really
would like to fill this order for you, Mr. Smith.)

d. Kindly advise by return mail.
(A man of few words, mostly trite ones. How about this
rewrite:
Won't you please reply promptly?   *Or,*
Please reply promptly, won't you?
Exactly the same number of words, but oh, the differ-
ence!)

e. If we can be of any service along the insurance line, please
command me.
(Just try to command the writer of that bit of bombastic
pomposity. Say:
If I can help you with your insurance problems, just
let me know.)

f. We don't anticipate any vacancy in the near future but
will be glad to be acquainted with you in case something
arises in which you might be interested.
(He takes too long to say his piece. It can be shortened
and improved:

Although we don't expect a vacancy soon, we'd like to meet you. You can never tell when something interesting will develop.

Don't overload your sentences. Make little ones out of big ones.)

g. Whenever we may be of assistance to you, kindly do not hesitate to let us know.

(This writer meant well, anyhow. He needs to be brought up to date:

Let us know whenever we can help you.)

4. *Don't have I-trouble or WE-writis—*

a. We trust the literature enclosed herewith will be of assist ance to you in considering the future use of our equip ment.

(Weak and wordy, hackneyed and trite. Use the reader's point of view:

The enclosed literature will give you all the data on our [use trade name here] compressors.

Be specific—take advantage of every opportunity to get free advertising through the use of your trade name in your letters.)

b. We wish to thank you for your very kind interest and trust that we may be privileged to serve you in the very near future.

(Pompous, unnatural, wordy, insincere. Why didn't he use just plain, ordinary talking instead?

Thanks for your interest. Won't you try our service soon? O blessed simplicity!)

c. We thank you for your interest in our company and re main

("Remain" what? where? why? Stiff and incomplete. This is much better:

Thanks for your interest in our company. That's a good, strong, friendly, forceful ending for a letter.)

Don't be stiff, stuffy, or pompous—

    a. We presume that this explanation of our charges and credits will serve your purpose adequately.

        (Take that and like it. It's all you'll get. He could have been nice:

           We are always glad to explain our charges and credits. This rewrite will go a long way toward mollifying the customer.)

    b. We trust same will interest you.

        (Very stiff, pompous, and vague. Have you noticed the preponderance of "WE" openings in these RED-LIGHT closings? That's no coincidence. Whenever you talk overly much about yourself, you tend to become pompous. Instead, think *about* your reader and then talk *to* him.

           You probably will be quite interested in these enclosures. .   *Or,*

           We are sure that these enclosures will interest you. Since I saw the rest of the letter, I knew he was talking about some enclosures. Otherwise, I would have been completely in the dark about the word "same.")

    c. Please rest assured that we will abide by the agreement stated in your letter.

        (This kind of writing should "rest in peace" permanently, it has been dead so long. In fact, it died half a century ago. Here is its modern counterpart: You may be sure that we will abide by the agreement mentioned in your letter of August 30. It is a good idea to mention the date of his letter, particularly for legal purposes.)

    d. Please advise.

        (Short, but NOT sweet. These revisions are   short *and* sweet:

Will you please let us know by [date]?	*Or,*
Please answer immediately.	*Or,*
Your prompt reply will be appreciated.	*Or,*
An early reply will be most welcome.	*Or,*
How do you want this order shipped?	*Or,*

May we hear from you soon?

There are many, many ways of rewriting this stiff, curt sentence in friendly, forceful, clear language—in words that any 10-year-old would understand.)

6. *Don't be repetitious, wordy, or long-winded*—

    a. As I mentioned several times in my letter, I really do appreciate what you have done for us, and I am very grateful.

        (He protests so much that he sounds insincere. Why not be plain and natural:

        Thanks for everything you have done for us, George. There is no finer personal touch than the use of your reader's name once in a short letter, twice in a long one.)

    b. Thank you again for your patronage.

        (Thanking him once is fine—and enough. What is "patronage"? See Appendix, page 255. Here's how I would write it:

        Thanks for your business.   *Or,*

        Thanks for your orders.   *Or,*

        Thanks for your inquiries.   *Or,*

        Your business [orders, inquiries] is [are] much appreciated.   *Or,*

        We certainly appreciate your orders [business, inquiries].)

    c. We thank you for your order and will handle it promptly as soon as we hear from you confirming our assumption that the piece shown on the aforementioned drawing is the piece you actually require.

        (Round he goes, as long as he has some words left. Then —and only then—does he grind to a stop! Say it better and cheaper:

        Thanks for your order, which will be handled promptly. *Or,*

        You may be sure that we'll handle your order promptly.)

    d. Thank you for your cooperation in this little matter, and again thank you for the very valuable business you have given us in the past months.

(Wordy and repetitious. Here are two streamlined versions :

Your cooperation, as well as your business, is much appreciated.   *Or,*
Your cooperation is appreciated as much as is your business.)

e. We shall be very much interested in hearing your reaction to the Film, "The Newest Market," following your showing of it.

(Write from your reader's point of view, not from your own:

After you have seen "The Newest Market," won't you let me know what you think of it?)

f. We wish to thank you for this opportunity of serving you and wish also to extend to you a cordial invitation to visit our establishment, or to write for any further information which you may care to desire.

(Some people are prodigal when it comes to spending their words. Instead, why not write: Thanks for the chance to serve you. Why not visit our plant the next time you are out this way? Also, be sure to write for more information if you need it.

Make little, readable sentences out of big, unwieldy, clumsy ones.)

7. *Don't be curt, gruff, or snippy—*

a. Please acknowledge.

(Obviously, he's the commanding type. When he barks, everyone is supposed to jump, including his reader! Why didn't he unbend and be gracious:

Will you please acknowledge this quotation?   *Or,* I'd appreciate your acknowledging this quotation. Although I usually dislike using the word "please" because it so often is used as if it were pronounced puh-*leeze,* it does have its uses, as in the first rewrite.)

b. Kindly advise manner of shipment.

(Often one mistake is piled upon another so that they are compounded or, in bridge terminology, doubled and redoubled. This doubling of trite, hackneyed wording contributes to the general ineffectiveness of that sentence. Few sentences are all bad; most poorly written sentences have something good to commend them. That is true with the sentence given here. Why didn't this writer say:

How do you want these parts shipped?

Isn't this far more natural and friendly?)

c. Please pay your payment.

(Aside from being a very badly worded sentence, this is an ill-conceived one from the standpoint of tone. How would *you* like to get a letter that ended with this sentence? Soften it up a bit:

Won't you drop in tomorrow and make your pay ment? *Or,*

How about sending us this payment today, please?

These two endings motivate payment, since they request it courteously and considerately, not curtly and crassly.)

d. We believe that this explanation of our service policy will serve your purpose.

(This is all you get, and that's that! Don't you dare ask for more. You won't get it. That's how I feel after reading this sentence. But I would feel much different if I had read:

We are always glad to tell our customers about our service policy. *Or,*

As one of our good customers, you are certainly en titled to know about our service policy. *Or,*

It is a pleasure to tell you about our service policy.)

8. *Eliminate the negative whenever you can—*

a. Regretting our inability to serve you at this time, we are

(Here the writer closes on a great big MINUS sign, whereas he could have closed positively just as easily:

Perhaps the next time we can send you what you need. Add the words, "Try us, won't you?" if you wish to.)

b. It is with great regret that we inform you that at this time we are unable to use your services.

(A short phrase, "at this time/' carries the key to a positive ending. This answer is not an irrevocable, absolute NO! It's a MAYBE, SOMETIME. Capitalize on that possibility:

We should like to keep your application on file. There's no telling when something suitable may develop.

Even if you throw his letter in the circular file, at least you have helped him to keep his chin up, and he'll appreciate that and feel much more kindly toward your company.)

c. Please let me know the number of parts you'll need on this job as soon as you can because this will delay production if the information is not received soon.

(Negative, NEGATIVE, NEGATIVE ALL THE WAY! Say it positively:

Please let me know the number of parts you'll need for this job so that there will be no delay in production.   *Or,*

Just as soon as you let me know the number of parts you'll need on this job, we'll schedule their production immediately.

After all, it's just the way you look at things. Some people view life from the negative side, some from the positive. You can't get better advice on how to write more friendly, forceful business letters than ACCENTUATE THE POSITIVE—ELIMINATE THE NEGATIVE!)

9. *Don't be vague, indefinite, clumsy, or cringing—*

a. The items that you had listed in your letter of May 5 that have not yet been shipped against the above mentioned order numbers have been placed on back order and will be forwarded to you with your next order.

(This fellow is a word spendthrift—and his company has to foot the bill! As long as he has any words left, he keeps on going. Not much thinking behind that type of writing. Writing clearly means thinking clearly beforehand:

Those items listed in your letter of May 5 but not shipped against Order Nos. 149, 169, and 170 have been placed on back order. They will be included in your next shipment.

Anyone can understand this thought with a minimum of effort.)

b. We shall be most happy to play host to the Poultry Hus bandry classes at Cal Poly if you will advise me of the most convenient date, that is, the second or third Thurs day in December.

(This writer is a starter-and-stopper. He could easily have combined these two ideas into one, and he could also have specified the dates involved: We shall be glad to have the Poultry Husbandry classes at Cal Poly visit our plant on either December 9 or 16.)

c. In common with other dies you have made for us in the past, we are also in a rush for this one.

(What could people and dies possibly have in common? This muddled thought could so easily have been un-tangled :

As usual, we are in a rush for this die.   *Or,*

We are in a hurry for this die also. Shorter, clearer, much easier to read and understand.)

d. I hope I will be able to inform you approximately the first of next week of the date on which, in all probability, the construction will commence.

(After a long, fumbling start, he finally blurted out his message. How about:

I'll probably know by next Tuesday just when con-struction will start.)

◆   ◆   ◆   ◆

Thirty-six weak, wordy, wobbly endings that annoy the reader and turn him from your message. You have fumbled the ball in your own end zone. You have lost a golden opportunity to run it out safely.

These 36 spineless endings, together with their forceful revisions, have introduced you to the Dr. Jekyll and Mr. Hyde of business letter-writing. Mr. Hyde is the vicious killer—the weak, old-fashioned, hackneyed ending that fails to get the action you want. Dr. Jekyll is the honored and respected physician, the healer of ills and wounds, the friendly and lovable person—the modern, friendly, forceful ending that keeps your old customers happy and satisfied and wins new friends for yourself and your company.

With just a little effort on your part, you can eliminate Mr. Hyde openings and closings. No magic potion is needed—just some serious thought about *how* your ending will strike your reader, *what* he will think of your parting statement, *how* it will affect him. Just put yourself in your reader's place and then write the kind of ending *you* would like to read. If you will do this, you're bound to write friendly, forceful endings—GREEN-LIGHTS every time!

DON'T PUT YOUR FAITH IN STOCK ENDINGS TO POLISH OFF YOUR LETTERS! Stereotyped endings are dull, drab, depressing. Vary your ending to suit the specific situation at hand. Each ending should be different, unless you are writing identical letters to more than one person, as in a form letter.

When you end your letters, remember two things:

1. HAVE A POINT AND COME TO IT QUICKLY AND CLEARLY.

2. DON'T USE ANY WORD OR GROUP OF WORDS TOO OFTEN, OR ELSE IT WILL BECOME STALE AND HACK NEYED.

Tenth Day

THE SUNSHINE OF YOUR SMILE

MANY YEARS AGO, Dad sang a beautiful song called "The Sunshine of Your Smile." I still play it on the piano once in a while. But what interests me especially right now is that title—THE SUNSHINE OF YOUR SMILE. A most fitting sentiment for those who want to write friendly, successful letters.

With few exceptions, every business letter that you write should radiate the sunshine of *your* smile. You know, a business letter actually takes the place of a personal visit. That's why your business letter should be as friendly and smiling as you would be if you called on your reader in person.

Most of the time when you call on a customer, you smile, don't you? Then why not smile at him in your business letters? If you do, he is much more likely to smile right back at you, because *friendliness is contagious.*

How can a letter smile? Very easily. Just read carefully the following letter and you'll get a mental picture of Mr. Mack smiling at his reader, Mr. Stribling:

Thank you for your inquiry, Mr. Stribling. It's a pleasure to send you the information you requested regarding our trailerettes.

By separate mail we're sending you some samples to give you an idea of what they look like on the screen. When you screen them, you'll notice they are one-frame trailers—10 feet in length and consist of the title of the feature . . . cast of characters ... a still photograph of the stars . . . and a catch-line to arouse interest in the picture.

They're sold outright at 75¢ each if two or more are ordered at one time (in quantities of just one they're $1.00). There's no rental or returns . . . they're yours to keep . . . and we have them available on practically every picture that comes out of Hollywood.

I feel sure that once you get your patrons used to them, they'll do a good selling job for you. In fact, some of the largest circuits right now have used them for years and tell us business hasn't been hurt one bit ... and you can imagine what considerable savings they've been afforded.

It will be a pleasure to serve you with trailerettes, Mr. Stribling. Here's hoping one of these days real soon we'll be receiving a trailerette order from you. I assure you it will be given the immediate personal attention of

Irving Mack

Now remember, I said that letters should *smile*—not laugh out loud, or smirk, or giggle, or snicker, or guffaw. Your smile should be as friendly and sincere as you would be if you met your reader in person. You wouldn't be grinning all the time—nobody likes a Cheshire cat, or a Uriah Heep, either. Sincerity is the foundation of friendly, successful letters.

Mr. Mack starts off without the conventional, old-fashioned salutation, and he eliminates the equally conventional complimentary closing. Instead, tossing aside the insincere "Dear," he gets off to a flying start by thanking Mr. Stribling for his inquiry. Notice that he calls him by name in his very first sentence. And his ending is as natural as it is friendly and sincere. This is the coming style for modern business letters.

Friendliness is contagious. The friendliness and sincerity of Mr. Mack's style of writing have permeated the thoughts and feelings and writing of those who work for him. Here is a letter from his secretary, who likes to sign herself as "Mr. Mack's Gal Friday":

I hope you won't mind, Mr. Riebel, that I'm taking the liberty of answering the cordial letter you wrote to Mr. Mack . . . but the "boss" is in Miami taking a well-deserved rest, and he won't be back until about the 1st of March. I didn't want to hold it up that long.

You said some most flattering things about Mr. Mack's letters ... I know he'll
be very pleased . . . but I agree with you that he's tops in letter writing, and
I really find it a pleasure to work for a firm that has such a friendly style
of writing.

I'm sold on it ... and have spent several enjoyable sessions studying with Cy
Frailey, both at Northwestern University . . . and at his letter-writing
clinics held through Dartnell.

Recently my husband started a little hobby shop, selling artificial flower
material ... the makings for earrings, etc. ... I decided to take a fling at
starting a mail order department, and ran a few ads in Hobby Magazine.

When the inquiries came in, I wrote these fine farm folk as if I were sitting
across from them talking . . . and honestly I'm just thrilled at the results it
has brought. Of course, I can't devote full time to it ... just two nights a
week . . . but it has been fun. To me writing friendly letters is almost a
religion and I wish there were more people to spread the gospel!

That the publication of your fine book is most successful is the sincere hope of
Vi Dane Mr.
Mack's Gal Friday

I have shared Mrs. Dane's letter with you for three good
reasons:

1. So that you can see that the writing of friendly, forceful,
sincere, conversational letters is a religion to some people;

2. So that you can see that this style of writing is infectious—
that you can "catch it" too, if you will only try;

3. So that you can see that the writing of friendly, forceful
letters *does pay big dividends,* not only in winning new friends
for your company, but also in keeping your old and valued cus
tomers satisfied and happy.

Those are the primary thoughts behind every business letter
you write—winning new friends and pleasing old customers.

Here are some more letters that illustrate "the sunshine of your
smile."

On December 18, 1951, the following letter was released by
the Department of Defense through Mr. Robert A. Lovett, then
Secretary of Defense. It is an "open letter" of thanks for the

wholehearted cooperation of the American people for their very generous response to the Armed Forces Blood Donor Drive:

On behalf of the members of the Armed Forces everywhere, I thank every American who is responding so generously to the urgent appeal for blood.

Many servicemen are alive today because of their fellow citizens' contributions. However, the critical need for blood still exists and will continue for some time to come, regardless of what turn events may take in Korea. Battlefield casualties require whole blood or its derivatives in their initial and subsequent treatment; so it is necessary that an adequate supply is on hand at all times.

I feel confident that we here at home will not shirk our duty, but will give generously to those who are giving so much for us.

That's a good letter. The first time I heard it over the radio, I knew it was a good letter. That's right—I *did* hear it over the radio before I read it. When it *sounded* good, I knew it *was* a good letter.

Here is a very easy way to determine whether your letter is well written. This is what you might call the "acid test" of your letter—READ IT ALOUD! If your letter reads smoothly and easily, you can be sure that it is well written. But if you stumble over your words, find yourself tangled in long, complicated sentences, are bewildered and confused—then you can be sure that your letter is badly written. REWORK IT UNTIL IT READS SMOOTHLY!

Whenever you have written a really important business letter, do these two things:

1. SLEEP OVER IT—Sleeping over the letter will give you a fresh, new point of view. You will approach your letter not as your own brainchild, but impersonally and critically, as if someone else had written it. You will then read exactly what you wrote, not what you thought you had written.

2. READ IT ALOUD—Reading your letter aloud will give you an opportunity to catch those

errors that your weary eyes may have missed—wrong words, mistakes in punctuation, bad errors in grammar, awkward wording, confused sentences. Your ear is much keener and sharper at finding mistakes than your eye— probably because you have to use both eye and ear when you read aloud. You have *two* checks instead of just one.

Now let's get back to more letters that radiate the sunshine of their writers' smiles. Here is a fine letter written by a former Cabinet Member, the late Secretary of Defense, Mr. James E. Forrestal. Like former Secretary Lovett's letter, this is also a form letter, which means that the same letter was sent to thousands of persons, not dictated simply for one alone.

This letter was addressed to one of my students, Joe Schrick. When you read the letter, you will find it as personal and friendly as any individually dictated letter could be. After all, it isn't the method of reproduction that makes a letter cold and formal or friendly and personal—it's the feelings in the man that count. Friendliness is something that must come from the heart and soul of the person himself.

Note how this sincere, cordial message literally flowed from the heart of a really great American—a letter written by a man who gave his life for his beloved country just as surely as if he had been a battlefield casualty:

My dear Mr. Schrick:

I have addressed this letter to reach you after all the formalities of your separation from active service are completed. I have done so because, without formality but as clearly as I know how to say it, I want the Navy's pride in you, which it is my privilege to express, to reach into your civil life and to remain with you always.

You have served in the greatest Navy in the world.

It crushed two enemy fleets at once, receiving their surrenders only four months apart.

It brought our land-based airpower within bombing range of the enemy, and set our ground armies on the beachhead of final victory.

It performed the multitude of tasks necessary to support these military operations.

No other Navy at any time has done so much. For your part in these achievements you deserve to be proud as long as you live. The Nation which you served at a time of crisis will remember you with gratitude.

The best wishes of the Navy go with you into civilian life. Good luck!

Sincerely yours,

Notice the emphasis on YOU-words. There are eleven YOU-words and only six I-words. After the introductory paragraph, the letter is entirely from the point of view of Joe Schrick, the reader. Joe did not feel that this letter was any less personal because it was a form letter, identical with those received by thousands of other separated Naval officers. This letter was individually typed and signed.

Please don't despise all form letters. Don't judge all of them by the few that reach your desk every day. I hope that, after reading Secretary Forrestal's letter and some other form letters that I have given throughout this book, you will have a better understanding of this type of letter. Form letters really can have character, can be friendly and personal, can smile and radiate the personality of their writers—even as the skilled artist can appear to be singing to you alone.

Of the nine original letters quoted in the first "Day," five were form letters! The worst letter in the lot—probably the worst in the entire book—was personally dictated. Conversely, some of the finest letters in this book are those so-called form letters. Did you ever stop to think that form letters usually are more nearly perfect than personally dictated ones? Form letters are not the unhallowed inspiration of the moment, but are carefully written, criticized, and rewritten again and again until they say exactly what they are supposed to say. I remember one letter on company policy that I wrote and rewrote about fifteen times over a period of six weeks. That letter *had* to be perfect, because it involved the spending of upwards of a quarter of a million dollars. The approval list of persons who O.K/d the letter included a vice president of General Motors Corporation!

While I am at it, here are some more letters from ex-government men. The first is a friendly, heart-warming letter from Mr. Sheridan Downey, former Senator from California. Although admittedly a form letter, it is friendly, personal, cordial. I want you to share it with me:

Dear Mr. & Mrs. Riebel:

Thank you for your recent letter, which is most helpful to me, concerning the question of the revision of our labor laws. I am happy to have this evidence of the keen interest shown by Californians on a measure which affects each American citizen so deeply. I regret that the heavy volume of mail makes it necessary to give you this form of reply. You may be sure that the labor legislation now being considered by Congress will continue to receive my most active study.

May I refer you to the enclosed card, sent with my compliments and best wishes. I hope you will use it whenever you are in Washington, and that you will continue to send me your advice on current issues.

Sincerely,

IT ISN'T SO MUCH *WHAT* YOU SAY AS *HOW* YOU SAY IT THAT COUNTS!

But to get along . . . Some people have the mistaken notion that if they *say* their letter is friendly, presto, it *is* friendly! Alas, that's not true:

Dear Mr. Blue:

You will agree that to have a letter be successful, it must be both friendly and brief.

Well, this letter is friendly. Please pay your payment.

Yours truly,

If you can find any smile in *that* letter, it's more than I can. Yet it is an actual letter that was sent out. By whom, of course, I won't tell. It was used by a branch office of a parent organization that tries hard to make its letters very friendly and forceful. It may have been effective in collecting overdue payments, but it certainly didn't make friends for the company that sent it out.

Yes, I know what you're going to ask: How can a person feel very kindly toward a company to whom he owes money, toward a company that is trying to collect an overdue account? Ill admit it *does* take a bit of tact and skill on the part of the writer of a collection letter. But if he has a sense of humor and a good knowledge of human psychology, he probably can write as forceful but friendly a letter as this one:

Dear Mr. Cordell:

Will you please send me the name of the best lawyer in your town? You see, sir, I *may* have to sue you!

As I recall it, that was the opening paragraph. The rest of the letter went on to say that unless the overdue account was paid promptly, some form of drastic action would have to be taken.

Perhaps the best example of the humorous type of collection letter that I have ever seen is this one:

Dear Mr. Doe: We want a check of

some kind!

Either a real check, or a pencil check alongside one of the items listed below. We would like to know just where we stand, so just check up on your bankbook today and drop a real check into the mails tomorrow. Or check one of the blocks below and drop this letter into the nearest mailbox tonight—using the enclosed stamped envelope:

☐   I am sending check herewith.

☐   Here is part of your bill to show you that my heart is in the right place.

☐   I'll try to pay each month from now on in the same amount as the enclosed check.

☐   I think I can pay this on the------------------------- so I am enclosing a post-dated check.

☐   Here is all of it—SHUT UP!

Very truly yours,

I have been using that letter in my classes for over fifteen years. I found an old mimeographed copy in the files at General Motors Institute—no name, no company, no author. I wish I knew who wrote that letter, for I'd like to take my hat off to a real letter craftsman—a writer with a beautiful sense of humor and a true O. Henry ability to put snap into his last sentence!

Notice how dead serious the letter is down to the last two

words—and then comes the explosion. Notice the play on the word "check." Notice also how many times the word "check" is used. Notice that each alternative to be checked *includes a check!* Notice that the first and the last alternatives are identical in meaning—but what a difference in tone. Truly, a *very* fine letter.

COURTESY IS CONTAGIOUS

Did you ever stop to think how contagious courtesy really is? Someone you don't especially like is polite to you. What do you do? You are polite to him. He smiles. You, too, smile. Human beings instinctively smile back when someone smiles at them. And smiles, like courtesy, are also contagious. Often smiles are the outward manifestation of courtesy, in letters as in the flesh.

Now let me show you some more letters that radiate the sunshine of their writers' smiles—some letters that, in turn, tend to make their readers smile, too. The first is another form letter, this time one sent out by FORBES Magazine of Business and Money Management in an effort to get a careless subscriber to renew his subscription:

So Long

dear friend,
we'll have to part,
Although it almost breaks my heart!

I wrote to you,
    and wrote,
        and wrote,
But you ignored my every
note.

I really hate to say Good Bye,
So let me make *one final try:*

Four Dollars is not much to pay,
Come on renew—*this very day!*
                              Cordially,

Quite a delightful "poetic" effort on the part of Mr. Norman Bruce of the Subscriber Service Bureau. Who could resist such a clever appeal?

The second form letter was sent out by Mr. Charles Kushins, of Oakland, California. Like all good, friendly, forceful business letters, it best speaks for itself:

Dear Mrs. Nielsen:

Thank you! You have been a charge customer for several years, and we want you to know that your patronage is much appreciated.

Your support has made our steady growth possible. You may be sure that we shall continue in our efforts to merit your good will.

Very sincerely yours,

The third is another form letter that also radiates the sunshine of the writer's smile:

Here is your Commercial Credit Plan

CREDIT COURTESY CARD

Welcome to the Commercial Credit Family. We are glad to add your name to the ever-growing list of our friends.

Your credit record is now established here, and we want you to know that we value your patronage.

You will find the Commercial Credit Plan a simple, dignified way to get a cash loan and an easy way to repay it. If you need additional funds for any purpose, we invite you to call on us.

For prompt service, simply present the enclosed card at our office, or mention your name and card number, if it is more convenient to phone.

Very truly yours,

Too few people realize the opportunity that credit letters give to spread sunshine and good will. Usually only those who owe money get the attention of the credit manager. The prompt-pay customer generally receives little or no recognition, not even a simple "Thank you." Not so with the Commercial Credit Plan Incorporated, affiliated with the Commercial Credit Company, the originators of this friendly, forceful, smiling letter.

And now, in rapid succession, here are three friendly, smiling answers to requests for information, which my friend, Marshall Ganz, gave to me. The first is from The Trane Company, La Crosse, Wisconsin:

Dear Mr. Ganz:

Thank you for your interest in Trane equipment as indicated by your recent letter.

We are pleased to enclose a copy of our Condensed Catalog PB-290. This catalog describes briefly all the products manufactured by The Trane Company.

Also enclosed are descriptive literature and order information for all Trane educational material. If you want to place an order, we will be happy to serve you.

Very truly yours,

The following very short but friendly letter comes from The National Radiator Company:

Dear Mr. Ganz:

Thank you for your recent inquiry.
We are attaching the material you requested. If you need more information, we'll be happy to help you.

Sincerely yours,

I always like to save the best until last. So here is what I think is a friendly, smiling answer to a routine inquiry—a letter that does not lose track of the sales appeal inherent in such an inquiry. This letter is from the Schwitzer-Cummins Company of Indianapolis, Indiana:

Dear Mr. Ganz:

Thank you for your recent inquiry regarding our ventilating fans.

Schwitzer-Cummins Company builds a wide range of sizes and models of FRESH-AIR-MAKER fans that meet practically every need for overall ventilation *IN THE HOME AS WELL AS IN COMMERCIAL AND INDUSTRIAL INSTALLATIONS.* Among these models are:

1. Window fans 10" to 20" diameters.
2. Reversible Window fans 12", 16" and 20" diameters.
3. Combination Window-Portable fans.
4. Portable Floor fans.

    5. Horizontal Attic fans. (Package units)
    6. Belt-Driven Exhaust and Attic fans.
    7. Direct-Driven Exhaust fans.

The enclosed literature describes each model and its many superior features. We are also enclosing a complete price schedule showing cuts of each model together with summary data.

The Schwitzer-Cummins Company, one of the leaders in the fan industry, has specialized in the manufacture of the finest quality ventilating equipment, at attractive prices, for more than thirty years.

We welcome the opportunity of acquainting you with our ventilating line and shall be glad to be of further service to you.

                                                                Cordially yours,

I'm not saying that these letters are perfect. They are not. All of them could be improved. But as run-of-the-mill, routine replies to routine inquiries, I think that they are far ahead of many letters being sent out today by most companies, small or large.

THE TIE THAT BINDS—"THANK YOU"

In closing our study of smiling letters, I want to show you some to illustrate that "the tie that binds" can be those two little words, "Thank you."

My first letter is a friendly thank-you note from that famous radio commentator, Fulton Lewis, Jr.—a letter in which Mr. Lewis thanked me, one of his listeners, for sending him my personal reaction to some of his comments. This was a personally typed and signed letter:

Dear Mr. Riebel:

    Whenever I get somewhat discouraged over the Washington scene, things like your card and the subsequent Senate rejection of the
-------------------- nomination come along to hearten me for the further fight.

    Believe me when I say I am tremendously indebted to you for writing me as you did.

                                                                Cordially yours,

The next is a letter written by Mr. L. I. Kriloff, President of Kriloffice, Inc. Although written without salutation or complimentary close, it is friendly and smiling:

How do you do, Mr. Blank . . .

Naturally, it is the custom of every salesman to say "Thank You" when taking an order in person.

Since this is impossible to do, there remains only one way to convey to you my feelings . . . not only about your last order but all future orders . . . and that is to write and let you know that they are genuinely appreciated.

Our greatest concern is to please you! May

we hear from you more often?

"THE KRILOFFICE HABIT IS WORTH WHILE"

L. I. Kriloff-Pres.

I'd like to close this day's consideration of smiling letters that say "Thank you" by showing you three letters that were written almost twenty years ago—letters that are as modern as any that I have given in this entire book on friendly, forceful, modern business letters:

Dear Asher:

Once again an appreciative trailer maker sends a letter of thanks to a good customer.

I wish that "think-tank" of mine were working a little more smoothly. Then I could think of some really original and more clever way of saying "thank you" so that it wouldn't sound like the last time I said it.

But no matter how I would say it, I don't think it would be any more sincere than just these two small words "Thank you"—for—

It's always nice to hear from you, and here's hoping that the mailman walks in with another nice order from you again soon.

Sincerely yours,

Dear Mr. Banning:

AKHTN OYU!

No, it's not Russian, or even Turkish.

Just my usual "Thank you" with the letters jumbled a bit.

Your trailer orders are always deeply appreciated, and I hope we receive a lot more of them. And you can depend upon it that we will always give you immediate service and courteous personal attention.

Cordially yours,

And, finally, here is probably the best "Thank you" letter I have ever read:

Dear Mr. Shaw:

Appreciation is expressed in a lot of different ways. A dog is apt to wag his tail when he's pleased or happy. A cat will purr, or, arching its back, rub firmly against your shins as a sign of contentment.

A theatre audience will register appreciation by clapping their hands. At a football game the spectators join in collegiate yells for the same purpose.

Now, when I'm delighted over an order, as I am at the one we are shipping you today, all I can do is write you a quiet and modest "thank you," but it means the same as the dog's tail wagging, the cat's purr, the applause of a theatre throng, or the cheers of thousands in a stadium.

My "thank you" comes straight from the heart, and anybody who knows me will tell you that I always mean it. I wish you'd give me cause to say "thank you" more frequently! Sincerely yours,

The first sentence of Mr. Mack's last paragraph contains the hidden secret of success—the art of bathing your reader in the warm, friendly sunshine of your smile, of saying "Thank you" and really meaning it.

Eleventh Day

EVERY LETTER IS A SALES LETTER

You HAVE HEARD ME SAY often throughout this book that *every letter is a sales letter.* Today I'm going to prove it!

Every letter that any businessman writes can be—or perhaps *should* be—a sales letter. Every letter that you write, every letter that goes out over your signature and on your company's letterhead, is trying to "sell" something—a product, a service, company good will, an idea, or a course of action. Yes, *every letter that you write is making some kind of sales appeal to your reader* —an appeal for the kind of action that you want from him.

Fine! Now let's look at some of the different desires or appeals that make a person WANT to act. These are appeals that you can put into your letters to encourage or persuade your reader to act favorably on what you have to offer. These are fundamental human appeals listed under two headings: the general area of the appeal and the specific kind of appeal usable within that area.

Area of Appeal	*Specific Appeals*
PERSONAL	Appearance, artistry, avoidance of trouble, beauty, cleanliness, desire for gain, enjoyment, health, hunger (the satisfaction of), labor-saving, leisure, ornament, painlessness (the avoidance of pain), possession, protection, purity, quality, relaxation, safety, satisfaction, security, self-esteem, self-indul-

gence, sex (romance), success (the avoidance of failure), style, self-preservation, usefulness.

CHARACTER   Acquisitiveness, ambition, caution, courtesy, curiosity, cooperation, desire for gain, desire to get ahead, devotion, fear, friendliness, greed, hope, hospitality, inquisitiveness, loyalty, pride, possessiveness, reliability, self-respect, thrift, vanity, warmth, service.

ECONOMIC   Dependability, durability, economy, efficiency, endurance, handiness, labor-saving, low cost, orderliness, productivity, proficiency, profit, prosperity, timeliness, reliability, good will, security, service, time-saving, timeliness, usefulness, versatility.

FAMILY   Devotion, love of home, paternal and maternal instinct, protection of the home and family, self-perpetuation, self-preservation, pride, hope, fear.

ETHICAL-   Dependability, conscience, devotion, duty,
MORAL   devotion to a cause, fairness, fair play, hope, love, purity, reputation, service, sympathy, worship.

SOCIAL   Acceptance, ambition, approval, avoidance of criticism, distinctiveness, exclusiveness, fear, emulation, imitation, gregariousness, group loyalty, pride, position, praise, popularity, rank, style, success (avoidance of failure), individuality.

Quite a few of them, aren't there? I'm sure I have not listed all of those fundamental human appeals, those motives that make us act like human beings. In fact, this is a never-ending list, but it will give you some idea of the tremendous number and scope of the appeals available to help you make your business letters friendly, successful sales letters, one and all.

Now let's look at some specific types of letters and see why they really must be considered sales letters, since each one appeals to one or more of these basic human motivating forces.

INQUIRIES, REQUESTS FOR INFORMATION, and REPLIES TO INQUIRIES naturally come first, but since I plan to spend all tomorrow proving to you that inquiries should be given first-class treatment, I'll save what I have to say about these types of routine letters and begin with—

1. ORDERS.

Your appeal here is to the company's desire to make you a happy, satisfied customer; to their desire to give you prompt, efficient service; to their desire to make a friend of you; to their desire to build good will for themselves by the careful handling of this order.

It may sound strange to you when I insist that your order should also be a sales letter, but it's true. If you make your reader *want* to reply favorably, if you make your order clear and courteous, it will be filled much more quickly than if you madly dash down a jumble of meaningless words and let your reader guess at just what you want.

In order to motivate a prompt and favorable response, an order should be clear as to the number of items, the size, color, weight, catalog number (if any), price, and any other pertinent information about the article itself. In addition, you should mention the date you want the article shipped, the method of shipment, and the method of payment, as in the following example of a clear, well-written order:

Gentlemen:

Please send me the following items listed in your 1952-53 General Catalog:

1 Hinged extension sides for pickup truck	#87A 7443F	$109.50
1 7-piece micrometer set for mechanics	#84A 5075	39.95
1 Power-Kraft metal lathe, 24" between centers	#84A 2130R	273.95
1 Heavy-duty high-output piston-type paint sprayer, electrically powered	#75A 6435RS	136.95
3 Spray guns @ $10.95	#75A 6402SX	32.85
	Total:	$593.20

Attached is a DO-MRO priority rating under CMP Regulation 5, which is required for purchase of the Power-Kraft metal lathe.

Add these items to my regular account, although I may take advantage of your 2 per cent discount for cash within 10 days. I should like you to send the micrometer set by parcel post immediately. The other items can be shipped by Southern Pacific or California Motor Express, whichever is less expensive.

Sincerely yours,

Note how the order gets off to a flying start, mincing no words; how the various items are tabulated, with the quantity ordered, a clear description, the catalog number (and which catalog was used) and the price of each item; how special attention has been called to the attached priority rating for the metal lathe; how the items are to be paid for; and how they are to be shipped. Such an order will receive prompt, courteous attention.

2. ACKNOWLEDGMENT OF AN ORDER.

You can make your acknowledgment of an order a good sales letter if you will be sincere, courteous, and prompt. Show your customer that you really appreciate his order. Give him what information you can. Sell him your service as well as your product. Make him happy and satisfied that he is getting the most for his money. Your appeal here is primarily economic.

Here is an excellent acknowledgment of an order from a new customer:

Dear Mr. Prone:

It is always a pleasure to meet new friends . . . you feel it in business the same as you do in everyday life.

Your order received just the other day gives us the pleasure of beginning a business friendship which we will try to make permanent through superior quality and unexcelled service.

We feel sure that "Dutch Boy" products will find in your community the same consumer acceptance that has made them so popular throughout the nation.

Our representative, Mr. Blank, will be glad to discuss any item in which you may be interested, and he will appreciate serving you.

Cordially yours,

That is a friendly, forceful acknowledgment from the credit manager of a large company, National Lead. It makes the customer feel welcome. It's like the hearty greeting and handshake of the host when you enter his home: it gives you a warm feeling of satisfaction inside.

Obviously, there can be a strong play for customer good will through letting him know that his order has been received and is receiving prompt, efficient service:

Dear Mr. Holmberg:

Thank you for your nice order which came in this morning's mail. It is always good to hear from old friends again.

Most of the items on this order can be shipped promptly. One, however, we cannot supply now. We haven't had a 10' cornice brake in stock for months. In fact, we haven't been able to get any manufacturer even to accept our order for one, though we have tried a number of times.

If you can give us a little time, we'll look around to see what we can dig up in the way of a good used brake. I know exactly what you want, and I'll do the best I can to get it for you as soon as possible.

Cordially yours,

You can't always fill a customer's order, but you can always fill him with good will and the satisfaction of knowing that you are on his side fighting for him.

3. REFUSAL OF AN ORDER.

When you refuse an order from a customer, you will have to do a good job of selling him on your sincere desire to be of service, even though you are apparently letting him down this time. The author of the previous letter had to do that very thing; so did General Mills in the following letter:

Dear Friend:

Thank you for your order for Medality pattern silverware. However, we regret that this silverware is no longer being manufactured. Therefore, it is not available to fill your order.

When we again packed coupons after the war, we offered a new pattern called Queen Bess. This pattern was chosen as the most popular in a test conducted among housewives throughout the United States.

In fairness to those who had started Medality pattern but were not able to complete their sets before the war, it was decided to make Medality pattern available until January 1, 1949. It was felt that this would allow sufficient time to complete these sets.

A statement that Medality pattern was available for this period was printed on all the coupons packed after the war.

Although we can no longer supply you with the Medality pattern, may we suggest you try our lovely Queen Bess pattern. We are proud to say it is being enthusiastically accepted by the redeemers of our coupons.

If you have coupons which have expired, we will be glad to redeem them for you at this time for Queen Bess pattern silverware. Enclosed is a catalog which pictures this silverware and contains other information about this offer.

We appreciate your use of our products and are very sorry that circumstances make it necessary to return your order.

Sincerely, GENERAL MILLS, INC.

P.S. Enclosed are stamps to reimburse you for the postage you used on the order you sent us.

This letter has been written to appeal to the reader's desire to obtain lovely silverware even if it is of a different pattern from the one originally ordered. The letter is designed to win the confidence of the customer by offering to redeem expired coupons. The company gives not only a "good" but a "real" reason for having to refuse this order: the product is no longer being manufactured !

4. INVITATION.

When you invite someone to do something, you must be sincere and friendly—if you want your reader to react favorably. Your appeal is a personal one. You show him what a favor he will be doing you personally if he will accept; you recognize him as an authority in his field, as one who has something worth while to give. You must be sincere, but you must not be insistent. Don't put your reader in such a position that he cannot gracefully decline. Above all, BE CLEAR AND COMPLETE!

Dear Mr. Paul:

The Mission Belles Chapter of the National Secretaries Association is having its monthly meeting next Friday evening in the home of Miss Irene Horton, 865 Morro Street, at 8 P.M. We should be very happy to have you speak to us on letter-writing problems confronting the modern secretary.

As you probably will recall, Miss Horton talked to you some time ago, and you indicated that you would be glad to speak to us on this subject, which you said was very dear to your heart. You may be sure that all of us will benefit greatly by whatever you care to tell us.

A short business meeting will take place just prior to your talk. If you prefer, come about 8:30. Could you let me know by telephone if you can make this meeting?

Sincerely,

5. ACCEPTING AN INVITATION.

When you accept an invitation, you must be sincere and genuine above all. Graciousness is also high on the list. You emphasize your sincere desire to accommodate, your appreciation of the opportunity, your desire to be of service. It is a good idea to repeat the time, place, and subject as a check.

Dear Mrs. Edwards:

I was happy to receive your letter requesting me to speak to the Anaheim Garden Club on gardening and the use of Terra-Lite.

Of the two open dates that you mentioned, the third Friday in February will be the most satisfactory for me. At what time am I scheduled to speak? I want to be sure to be there on time.

There will be no charge for this service, of course, but it is our usual policy to have a nurseryman in the locality sponsor our presentation. However, we can make an exception in this case if you wish.

It certainly is good to know that you are using Terra-Lite in your own lath house and like it so well.

Sincerely yours,

6. REFUSING AN INVITATION.

When you refuse an invitation, have a good, plausible reason.

Be sincere and at least give the impression of being genuinely regretful that you cannot accept.

Dear Mr. Smith:

Thank you very much for your kind invitation to speak before your business club next Thursday at noon.

There is nothing I should like more than to be able to tell you some of the new techniques I picked up at the American Business Letter Writing convention in Berkeley. Unfortunately, I won't be in town on Thursday. I am leaving for a week's trip into the Valley early Tuesday morning.

How about giving me a rain check on that invitation? As far as I know now, any Thursday in July will be open, if you need a speaker then.

Regretfully,

7. INTRODUCTION.

A letter of introduction is definitely a sales letter. You are selling your reader on receiving favorably the person you are introducing. You are the point of contact, the go-between who hopes to bring together two persons with mutual interests—social, economic, or otherwise. Your letter should be friendly and sincere. It should also indicate the extent to which you know the person you are introducing.

Dear Mr. Otto:

I should like you to meet Mr. and Mrs. George Stout of San Luis Obispo. Mr. Stout tells me that he has purchased a Series 62 Cadillac sedan, and is taking delivery from the factory.

This is the Stouts' first visit to Detroit. Since they plan to arrive several days before their car will be ready, I have assured them that you folks at the factory will do everything possible to make their stay in Detroit a pleasant one.

Any courtesies you can extend to our good San Luis friends will certainly be appreciated by me, also.

Cordially,

8. LETTER OF RECOMMENDATION.

Once in a while you will be called upon to write a letter of recommendation for a friend or employee. To be worth anything, your letter must be clear, sincere, and honest. Don't say anything that you can't prove, if necessary. A fair recommendation is far more valuable than a flattering one. The former is likely to be taken at face value; the latter will certainly be discounted.

Dear Miss Weir:

Miss Henrietta Jones has asked me to write a letter of recommendation in her behalf. This I am very glad to do.

For four years Miss Jones and I have worked together and shared the same office. In this way we came to know each other quite well, for we also taught the same courses. I came to have a very sincere respect for Miss Jones' ability to teach and for her desire to become better acquainted with her subjects. We consulted almost daily about teaching problems and assignments. Miss Jones always contributed her share of worth-while ideas.

Miss Jones is well liked as a teacher. She is cooperative and well informed, genuinely interested in her courses and students, and in helping them get the most out of their college education. She is very well balanced emotionally. In the four years I have known Miss Jones I do not recall ever having heard her say an unkind word about anyone.

It is with mixed pleasure and regret that I write this letter. I am glad to speak for my friend and colleague, Miss Jones. But I am also sorry to know that next year we shall not have the benefit of her calm, helpful, wise suggestions. I know that wherever she goes she will enrich the teaching in that institution.

Sincerely yours,

To be really effective, a letter of recommendation should be sent directly to the person who is to receive it. It should not be given to the person about whom it is written.

9. ACCEPTANCE.

A letter of acceptance—whether it be of a gift, an appointment, an office, or something else—must ring true. It must be genuinely sincere and leave your reader with the impression that he has made no mistake in appointing, selecting, or electing you.

Dear Mr. Brown:

I am delighted to accept an interim appointment as Chairman of the Membership Committee of our Business Men's Group. You know how enthusiastic I am about the work of our Club. You may be sure that I'll do my best to build up our membership to an all-time high while I am in office!

Cordially,

10. RESIGNATION.

Sometimes it is necessary for you to resign from some office or position. This calls for a real sales letter, because you must be sincere, yet firm. Your reasons must be good ones. They may not be the real reasons, but *they must be convincing.* In writing your letter of resignation, don't burn your bridges behind you:

Dear Miss Fischer:

Three months ago when I was elected secretary of the Businesswomen's Club I was very proud and happy, for I have always enjoyed working with our girls. But as you know, I have not been in good health, and my doctor has advised me to take a long rest.

Under the circumstances, it is only fair to all that I ask you as president of our Club to arrange for a special election during our December meeting to elect someone to fill out my unexpired term. Since there are so many capable women in our group, I know you will have no trouble replacing me. Of course, I'll carry on until a new secretary has been installed.

Thanks, Marjorie, for everything you have done to make my association in our Club more enjoyable.

Regretfully,

Obviously, this letter was personally dictated or written, since it is a once-in-a-lifetime letter. Now I'd like you to see a friendly, successful letter of resignation that was sent to many customers. This letter was completely processed with the exception of the inside address and salutation:

Dear Mr. Riebel:

After thirty years as an insurance broker and agent I have decided to withdraw from the active management of my business. Effective October 1, 1952, the business will be operated by Mr. Gerald B. Evans, 1118 Chorro Street, San Luis Obispo. I shall retain an interest in the agency and shall act in the capacity of a solicitor under the license held by Mr. Evans.

This transfer has been approved by the insurance companies which

I represent, and they have appointed Mr. Evans as their agent. All policies will remain in full force and effect, and coverage will in no way be affected by this change.

Statements for all outstanding accounts will be billed from and payable to my office. Premiums on new and renewal business will be payable to Mr. Evans.

I have every confidence in Mr. Evans' ability as an insurance agent, and know that you will receive prompt and efficient service from him. It has been a pleasure to serve you, and I hope that you will favor my successor with the continuance of your business.

Sincerely yours, Maurice

W. Fitzgerald

11. REQUEST FOR AN APPOINTMENT.

Your letter must sell your reader on giving you this appointment or interview. It must be courteous, sincere, clear, specific. It should also be short and stress the reason for the request. You might offer a substitute time in case the original is not acceptable.

Dear Mr. Downing:

When we corresponded several months ago, you suggested that I drop in to see you the next time I came to Riverdale. I find that I will be in that area for three days next week, beginning Tuesday. May I come to see you on one of these days?

I am still very much interested in seeing what you have to offer, as I indicated in my last letter. If you can spare me a few minutes next week, 111 be glad to make my plans accordingly.

Sincerely yours,

12. APOLOGY.

Probably one of the hardest letters to write is an apology. But when it must be done, it must—and it must be done well, or not at all. An apology given with ill grace is worse than no apology at all. In this kind of letter you must sell your sincerity and desire to make amends or to atone for what you did or failed to do.

Dear Warren:

Touché, old man 1 Touché!

I guess there comes a time when the only thing that a fellow can honestly do is to apologize in order to live in peace with himself. And that's what I want to do right now.

I am sincerely sorry for what happened, particularly for my part in this unfortunate affair. I hope that you will accept this apology in the spirit in which it is made, and let bygones be bygones.

Regretfully,

When we come to the Thirteenth Day you will read some other kinds of apologies, for poor service or other business reasons.

13. FOLLOW-UP.

A follow-up letter is an excellent device for getting in some additional sales appeals. Follow-up letters presume that your reader received a previous message from you, that he may have had difficulty in obtaining your products (as in the J. T. Baker letter), or that he needs some additional persuasion to act favorably. The same sales appeals used in your original letter—purity, fineness, skill, reliability, convenience, selectiveness, economy, savings, pride, and so forth—can be repeated to advantage in your follow-up, as in the following two letters:

Dear Customer:

Ease and economy are the keynotes of shopping Wards Catalogs.

As you and your family look through the new Spring and Summer Catalog we sent you a short time ago, you'll discover how easy it is to get most all of your needs from Wards. Whether you want clothing for everyone, carpeting or furnishings for your home, accessories or repair parts for your car, our Catalog offers you over 100,000 selections from which to choose.

This spring you'll also find Wards traditionally low prices are even lower on many lines than they were in our big Catalog last fall. Greatest reductions are in textiles, where you'll save 5% to 26% on sheets, towels, and piece goods; 7% to 23% on nylon hose, lingerie, dress shirts, and work clothing. Note, too, the lower prices on freezers and refrigerators, vacuum cleaners and portable sewing machines.

Everything in Wards Catalogs is guaranteed to satisfy you completely, so just jot down the things you need right now and on through the spring season. Then stop in or call our Catalog Sales Department to plan your order. If you don't want to pay cash, ask about our convenient Monthly Payment Plan.

We appreciate your past purchases and hope you will turn to Wards

Catalogs first whenever you need anything. You'll prove to yourself it's the easy, economical way to shop.

MONTGOMERY WARD

Here is another excellent sales follow-up:

Dear Dr. Boles:

Some of our chemist friends in certain areas have informed us that they are having difficulty in securing Baker's Analyzed C. P. Chemicals from some laboratory supply houses. We are sure that this is not your experience on the West Coast when you send your orders to any one of the three authorized distributors listed below:

Braun Corporation   Braun-Knecht-Heimann Company
2260 East 15th Street   1400 16th Street
Los Angeles, California   San Francisco, California

Scientific Supplies Company 122
Jackson Street Seattle 4,
Washington

For your protection, when you place your order for laboratory chemicals, be sure to specify them by name—BAKER'S ANALYZED C. P. CHEMICALS—and be sure the order is addressed to an authorized Baker distributor.

Over the years we have provided the chemist with the finest Reagent Chemicals that we know how to make. Each Baker label shows an *actual lot analysis*—a record of the degree of purity our chemists have achieved. It is Baker Skill on Parade.

Baker's Analyzed C. P. Chemicals are specified by leading chemists of the nation. If you have trouble securing your requirements, won't you let us know immediately? The enclosed post card is for your convenience.

We and our West Coast distributors want to be sure that you get the laboratory chemicals of your choice promptly.

Sincerely yours, H.
B. Rasmussen

14. GOOD WILL.

Often quite similar in purpose to the FOLLOW-UP is the GOOD WILL letter—a letter written solely to create customer good will. This letter is usually written *after* the customer has made his purchase. You have already seen some fine examples of good will letters, particularly the one written by Mr. W. T. Carpenter for Du Pont.

Here is another fine letter building customer good will. Often after a person has made a purchase, he begins to get "cold feet" and wonders whether he has done the right thing. To keep new policyholders happy and satisfied with their purchase of protection, Mr. R. J. Chrisman, Vice President in Charge of Sales for the Farmers Insurance Exchange, Los Angeles, sends out this excellent good will follow-up:

Dear Mr. Doe:

We are indeed glad to welcome you as a member of our large family of policyholders, and we assure you that it will always be our aim to furnish you the best protection at the lowest cost consistent with safety.

Yours is a "Continuing Policy." This means that after the initial premium is paid, you merely renew by remitting premiums semi-an-nually. Just prior to the end of each six months, a notice of premium due will be sent to you. Payment of this premium before the due date continues your protection for the following semi-annual period.

You keep the same policy right along. If any changes are desired, your policy will be brought up-to-date when we are notified. This method eliminates a considerable resale expense, permitting the savings to be reflected in lower rates.

We are exceptionally proud of our Claims Service. Your local Farmers District Agent is authorized to handle claims as soon as reported. This eliminates red-tape and delay. Policyholders receive immediate service plus prompt payment. Please report all claims to your District Office promptly.

Again we bid you welcome.

Yours very truly,

15. THANKS.

Although this book is filled with letters of thanks, I want to emphasize how important a part of routine correspondence this type of letter is. So with this brief opening, here is a letter that says "Thanks" in the nicest possible way:

An orchid to you, Wilfred, for recommending FILMACK to Mr. Fey Rogers of the Appalachian Broadcasting Corporation in your city.

It certainly makes me feel good to know that there are still people in

this good old world of ours who will do their friends favors without being
   moved by mercenary reasons.

I want you to know that your courtesy is very much appreciated . . . and I hope
   some day I can reciprocate.

When that opportunity does present itself, need I tell you all you have to do is
   just command

Irving Mack
for FILMACK CORPORATION

16. CREDIT.

Any letter dealing with credit is definitely a sales letter. Too
often companies feel that they must write credit letters only when
accepting an account, when refusing it, or when the debtor gets
into trouble credit-wise. Too seldom do any credit managers take
time out to say "Thank you" to those who look upon credit not
only as a privilege, but also as a responsibility.

Credit letters must be tactful, courteous, considerate; they
should have that intangible but very obvious thing called "character." The following credit letters have all of these qualities.

Here is a letter which the Goodyear Tire & Rubber Company
recommends for its dealers to send to customers who have satisfactorily handled their accounts:

Your account is all paid up with us—and we want to thank you for your
regularity in making payments.

Enclosed is your Credit Identification Card, which you are entitled to
because of the excellent way in which you handled your account.

We suggest that you sign the card and place it in your wallet. When you are
ready to reopen your account, simply show the card and you'll get preferred
credit consideration.

If you're not already doing so, we hope you'll make this your headquarters
for everything you need in the way of tires and tire service, batteries, car
accessories. We also carry many other things—radios, electrical appliances,
sporting goods, hardware and other home items.

Come in often—and use your credit to enjoy quality merchandise without
waiting.

An invitation to a potential customer to open a credit account is
surely a sales letter. You must make your offer attractive, convincing, and sincere, for you are trying to persuade your reader

to enjoy the convenience of a credit account. Your letter therefore must be tactful and courteous, like this Seiberling letter sent out by the Kimball Tire Co. of San Luis Obispo:

Dear Sir:

More motorists than ever before are finding that SEIBERLING is not only "A NAME YOU CAN TRUST IN RUBBER," but that a tire has to be better to be a SEIBERLING. We want you to be able to enjoy the smooth-riding, quick stopping, extra long mileage, and genuine peace of mind that comes with the purchase of a new SEIBERLING Special Service Deluxe Tire.

That's why we are taking this opportunity to invite you to open one of our Budget Accounts. Our plan is actually "tailor-made" to suit your individual problems. It is easy, entirely confidential, and takes only a few moments. Just tell us how much you want to pay and when you want your payments and we will do the rest.

For your convenience we are attaching a credit card which automatically opens your account with us. We sincerely hope that you will make use of this card, but in any event, won't you come in and visit our store, tire retreading, and balancing plant?

Please be sure to ask for me when you come in.

> Very truly yours, K.
> W. Robenstine

17. COLLECTION.

Although I'll have much to say about collection letters when I talk about the soft answer that turneth away wrath on the Thirteenth Day, I want to emphasize here that collection letters are very definitely sales letters. Their main purpose is to get the money, admittedly, but a close second is to keep the customer happy and buying. A third and very important appeal in collection letters is that of company good will.

But to get along with today's discussion. Here are two more collection letters, one humorous, one dead serious—both good sales letters:

Dear Subscriber:

In Oklahoma City recently, cafe owners opened a school to teach their waitresses to smile pleasantly.

And before you laugh, you might admit that smiling waitresses have a lot to recommend them.

Here at TIME, we've always felt the same way about "collection" letters.

We just smile pleasantly and say: "Our bill for your current subscription is enclosed."

Wonder if you wouldn't like to substantiate our faith in smiles by sending us your check, please, today?

Cordially,

And now to show you that a collection letter can be friendly, forceful, but still a straight-from-the-shoulder warning that unless the reader pays up promptly, something drastic will happen, I give you this letter:

Dear Mr. Doe:

This is a serious letter about a very serious subject: your long-overdue bill for $185.33, on which you have made no payment for three months.

We have sent you statements, notices, and polite letters in which we have asked you in every nice way that we know for your payment.

We asked you if there was anything wrong with the charge, with the merchandise, or with the service; but we have had no reply from you.

Now we want you to know that we still value your friendship, and we want to retain it, if at all possible. That, of course, depends entirely on you.

For your convenience I am enclosing an itemized statement of your account, together with an addressed, stamped envelope. Use it to send us your check. This envelope will bring your check straight to my desk, unopened.

What do you say, Mr. Doe? Can't we settle this matter in the same spirit of friendship that we had when we opened your account many years ago?

Hopefully yours,

18. SALES LETTERS.

I know you have been wondering whether I would ever show you any real, honest-to-goodness sales letters in this chapter. The answer is: OF COURSE! Here are three very good ones.

This letter uses the appeals to one's natural desire to get a bargain and to fear—two very powerful human appeals:

Dear Mr. Schmitt:

In spite of all the world turmoil, changing credit regulations, etc., I can offer you a tremendous deal on a new DeSoto or Plymouth.

I don't know how long it will be before prices change or production has a drastic cutback because of scarce supplies. If you have been thinking of a new car, come in and see me. For as long as our stock lasts, we are going to make you a deal that you would probably think impossible at this time.

Drop by or call me for an appointment. Just ask for Mack.

Sincerely yours, K.
L. McKinney

Here the appeal is primarily economic:

Dear Mr. Masek:

Bill Jones has just told me that you are interested in some pasture land in the Paso Robles area.

You will be glad to know that I have 780 acres available on the first of January, 1953. This is good permanent pasture just a year and a half old. You can lease it on a ten-year basis, or rent it from season to season. This land is set up so that it can be cross-fenced very easily. Also, three miles of steel fencing goes with the pasture. The boundary fence is stationary. The stock can be watered from five conveniently located wells.

Enclosed are the production report and cost list. From them you can get the exact date and rotation information. Also included are the precipitation dates and rates.

I hope that this information will help you in making your decision as to where you should pasture your calves. If you need further information, write or call me collect.

Sincerely yours,
John T. Smithers

The two previous letters were personally dictated sales messages—written specifically for one person. The next two are form letters, written to the various members of two large groups. Yet each has a warm, personal touch, and each in its way *is* SL good sales letter.

In this letter, the appeal is primarily to the reader's desire to be of greatest service to his organization:

Dear State and Chapter Officers:

Here is your 1953 National Engineers' Week promotional kit.

The material in the kit is designed to *stimulate* ideas, and should be used only after being adapted to *local* conditions. Read the instructions on how to use the kit—you'll find them printed on the back of the cover.

National Engineers' Week can be your Number One public relations activity for the year. It is an affair that has excellent promotional opportunities for the small chapter as well as the large one. Don't fail to do all you can to take part in this nationwide observance.

For your information, the kits are being distributed as follows:

1 copy to each Chapter President
1 copy to each Chapter Secretary
1 copy to each State President
1 copy to each State Secretary
1 copy to each State Engineers' Week Committee Chairman

Please take care of your kit! They are expensive to produce and only a very few additional copies are left. *Make certain that all copies get into the hands of those who are doing the work.*

You will be hearing again from your National Committee as our program progresses. Be on the look-out for more information from Headquarters from time to time. If you need help, your State and National Headquarters stand ready to do all they can for you.

Good luck and don't forget to get an *early* start 1
                              Sincerely,
                              W. W. Perry, Chairman National
                         Engineers' Week Committee

The following letter starts right off by announcing the appeals that will be used: a sound investment and monetary savings. It then proceeds with such strong sales appeals as more pleasant home life, the desire to be in on new ideas, convenience, comfort, entertainment, and relaxation. This sales letter has about as many different sales appeals cleverly interwoven as you could hope to find. Notice also how the second paragraph contains the central selling point, and how smoothly the letter flows from sentence to sentence and paragraph to paragraph:

Dear Friend:

Here's an easy way you can make a sound investment in better family living—and save some money at the same time!

Yes, by entering your Better Homes & Gardens subscription for 24 months for only $5, you'll make home-life more pleasant for you and your family. And you'll be money ahead.

Your home is one of the most important things in your life. But it takes a heap of living to make any house a pleasant, comfortable home. And for the next two years—through winter, spring, summer, and fall —you'll have Better Homes & Gardens at your fingertips with ideas and suggestions to help you and your family squeeze the most possible pleasure out of your everyday living.

Interesting articles and colorful photographs will offer you practical solutions for all your homemaking problems—big and small. You'll receive handy tips for making housework easier and shortcuts for planning meals to please even the most demanding appetites. You'll learn how to stretch your building and decorating dollars and plan a more productive garden—with an eye to the family budget. You'll use the special child training suggestions with comforting confidence.

And you'll like the features on informal home entertainment, indoor and outdoor parties, along with complete outlines for friendly family vacations that will give you more thrills and more relaxation for your vacation dollars.

Month after month more than 1,500,000 people pay 25¢ at the newsstands for Better Homes & Gardens, and copies often disappear in just a few days. But by subscribing now, you'll be sure of having your copy delivered conveniently to your door each month—and at a saving of $1.00 under the single-copy price.

We're looking forward to serving you during the months ahead, and we've made it easy for you to rush your order. Just attach your payment to the enclosed order card, and speed it to us in the handy airmail envelope TODAY!

Sincerely yours,

BETTER HOMES & GARDENS /S/ Ed
Meredith General Manager

To this excellent sales letter there is appended a handwritten postscript:

P.S. Remember—your Better Homes & Gardens subscription will save you
time, work and money.

E.M.

Notice that the ending of this *Better Homes & Gardens* letter fulfills all the requirements of a good, modern sales-letter ending: it makes the action EASY ("speed it to us in the handy airmail envelope"), FINAL ("Just attach your payment"), and IMME-DIATE ("TODAY!").

Well, there is the story—not so full as I should like to make it, but enough, I hope, to prove beyond any doubt that you *can* make any business letter that you write a sales letter—if you will only select the right appeal, put yourself in your reader's place, and then write the kind of letter you would like to receive.

INQUIRIES DESERVE FIRST-CLASS TREATMENT

YESTERDAY WE SAW that every business letter, of no matter what type, must be considered a sales letter of some sort. I purposely omitted any discussion of inquiries, requests for information, and answers to those letters. That's what I want to consider in detail today—routine letters that so often receive little or no consideration in the average office.

Who writes inquiries? POTENTIAL CUSTOMERS, of course —prospective purchasers of whatever you have to sell. Few people write inquiries simply for the sheer fun of fishing to see what kind of reply they will get. Most people who take the time and trouble to write your company are serious in their request. They have some direct or indirect interest in what you have to sell.

For that reason, anyone who requests information should be treated as a first-class prospect. He must not be brushed off with a cursory reply, just to get him out of the way. People who write for information may at times seem like nuisances, but about 95 times out of 100 they aren't.

The very best plan of approach is to put yourself in your reader's place and ask yourself these questions: Why did this fellow write to us? How can I best serve him? What information can I

160

give him that will tell him most about our products and services? How can I make a friend out of him?

How would *you* like to receive this reply to your inquiry?

Dear Sir:

Answering your recent postal, we herewith enclose copy of our latest price list, which should be sufficient for your needs.

Very truly yours,

Now, I'm sure the writer of that letter didn't mean to be cold and unfriendly, but he certainly was. In fact, his letter comes pretty close to being rude, if not downright insulting. It's true, the writer may not have had much to send, but at least he could have sent what he did graciously and courteously. Here is a good rule to follow: what you give, give cheerfully, graciously, courteously ; never give grudgingly or discourteously.

Why didn't that writer say:

Dear Mr. Tuttle:

Thank you for your interest in Blank products. Of course, we are glad to give you one of our latest price lists. I hope it will be of help to you in your work.

Sincerely yours,

There you have a warm, friendly answer that doesn't give him any more than the original letter gave, but how differently! Here is another sales-less reply:

Sir:

Your inquiry received. Have nothing that would interest you.

Very truly yours,

When you turn a customer down, do it gently. Don't drop him like a ton of bricks! This letter is short, but it is too curt, abrupt, unfriendly. It could have been done this way:

Dear Mr. Brown:

Your recent inquiry is much appreciated. I'm sorry we can't send you the information you requested, since it is not available for general distribution.

Very truly yours,

If you want to see how an inquirer can be turned down skilfully and yet without causing any hard feelings, study carefully the following letter:

ABOUT THE GARDEN CATALOG YOU REQUESTED . . .

We regret that we are unable to send you the new Ward Garden Book which you requested.

Our first real effort with a special catalog of this kind in the Nursery field was planned with every intention of sending a Garden Book to all who were interested in buying from it. We felt that the printed quantity of almost a million copies would be adequate.

So many of our customers have requested the Garden Book that the entire supply is now exhausted. If we were to reprint the catalog at this time, the additional books would not be available in time for Spring buying.

We are anxious for you to see Ward's new Garden Book. May we suggest that you contact Ward's local store—a few copies of the Garden Book are on hand there, and they can lend you one to make your selections. In this way you will have the opportunity to buy now or at any time in the future. Thank you for your interest in Ward's new Garden Book.

                                        Yours very truly,

Now I think we are ready to discuss inquiries, requests for information, and answers to these questions from the point of view of potential sales letters.

1. INQUIRIES AND REQUESTS FOR INFORMATION.

When you write an inquiry or a request for information, your appeal is to your reader's fundamental human desire to help someone in need. Indirectly, at least, you can appeal to the potential good will the company will create; to the company as an authority—the final word; and to the company's reputation.

Here is a "before" and "after" example. Years ago a student blithely wrote the following letter to the manufacturer of well-known precision instruments:

Gentlemen:

Please send me all the information you have on precision instrumerits. I'm writing a report on such and will need all the information I can get.

Yours very truly,

That's what he wanted—"ALL THE INFORMATION YOU HAVE ON PRECISION INSTRUMENTS"! Just suppose, for an instant, the company *had* sent him "all the information" they had—their extensive library of highly technical books, their research reports, their files of confidential information, and so forth. Do you think *that* was what this student wanted? Not at all. He wouldn't have known where to start. Actually, what he wanted was some relatively simple information that he could digest easily and put into his report to make it look impressive.

So, after much persuasion, he wrote the following revision:

Gentlemen:

As a student at Blank Technical College I am writing a report on precision instruments. Since your company is well known for the fine tools you manufacture, I wonder if you could help me by answering the following questions, if this information is available for distribution to college students:

1. What types of steel or other metals are used in the manufacture of precision instruments?

2. What special precautions must be used, such as control of humidity, dust removal, and so forth?

3. How are precision instruments calibrated and tested?

I am interested in any type of precision instrument, but am especially anxious to have this information on micrometers and vernier calipers.

My report is due in three weeks. I'll appreciate your sending me whatever material you can by Friday, June 13. If you wish, I'll be glad to send you a copy of the completed report.

Sincerely yours,

When you write a request for information, it is a good idea to indicate:

1. Who you are and why you want this information.

2. What use of it you will make, and what acknowledgments you will give.

3. When you will need this information.

4. That you want only information the company can and will send you.

It's always good not only to motivate a reply, but also to give the writer an out. Sometimes you will ask for information that is confidential and cannot be released. It is quite embarrassing to have people ask for confidential information. I know! In the spring of 1947, word got out that Cadillac was making a radical change in body style and so forth. Many a person wrote in asking for detailed information, which I knew but could not send out. It was quite embarrassing to have to write that such information could not be released until the cars were shown nationally.

2. REPLIES TO INQUIRIES AND REQUESTS FOR IN-FORMATION.

Just as there is a certain amount of sales appeal necessary in writing for information, so are sales appeals necessary in answering these requests. Your appeals are based on your desire to be of help, your desire to create good will for your company, your desire to be friendly, and your desire to substantiate the inquirer's confidence in your company.

Properly handling inquiries and requests for information can build a tremendous amount of customer good will and potential sales for your company. If you don't believe it, read Frank A. South's enlightening article, "Inquirers Deserve First-Class Treatment," in the July 8, 1949, PRINTER'S INK. Now you know where I got the title for this chapter.

Out of 56 inquiries South sent out, only one reply came near being first-class. Eighteen companies failed even to answer his inquiry. That's pretty hard to believe, but it's true.

As we have said before, people don't write inquiries unless they are definitely interested in what you have to offer. That immediately makes them first-class sales possibilities. Here, for example, are several excellent answers to inquiries—letters that do a good job of selling the company to the inquirer:

It is a pleasure to learn through The Saturday Review of Literature of your interest in 16mm sound motion picture films.

As a leading manufacturer of 16mm motion picture equipment, we are happy to assist you in your quest for film and are enclosing a pamphlet entitled "Where To Get Film And Film Information." The film catalogs and directories described therein represent a cross-section of sources for all types of films available on a free loan basis, on a rental basis, as well as for outright purchase.

May we suggest that you contact our distributor in your territory, whose name and address are given below. They will be glad to give you additional information regarding available film and a demonstration of Victor equipment:

Coast Visual Education Company
6058 Sunset Boulevard
Hollywood 28, California

Very truly yours,

M. E. Cain

Here is another answer that has positive sales appeal:

Dear Mr. Ganz:

Thank you for your recent inquiry regarding a Carrier Commercial Weathermaker for your place of business.

I hope the enclosed catalog will answer some of the questions you may have in mind. Others in your business have realized profit advantages and customer attraction with air conditioning. You will find a discussion of these results of interest and value to you.

The dealer whose name and address appear at the bottom of this letter will be glad to give you these facts. I am requesting that he get in touch with you as soon as possible.

Sincerely,
Roy Lansing

Here is a dandy letter from Mr. R. S. Young, Metallurgist for the O.K. Tool Company, Inc., in Milford, New Hampshire. This reply is indeed first-class:

Dear Mr. Wood:

This is a very brief reply to your very interesting letter of October 20 concerning an evaluation of carbide tools.

Your first paragraph indicates that you are primarily interested in lathe tools, and I agree with you that carbide is rapidly becoming dominant in this field. However, its scope is terrifically broad and it would be impractical to give information in detail. The best compilation of data that I know of, comparing high speed steel, cast alloys (such as

Stellite) and carbide lathe tools was made by Gisholt Machine Company, Madison, Wisconsin. They show various operating speeds for a variety of feeds and depths of cut for a great many materials. I suggest that you write them for this material.

Also write to Carboloy Company, Inc., Detroit, Michigan; First Sterling Steel & Carbide Company, McKeesport, Pennsylvania; and The Kennametal Company, Latrobe, Pennsylvania. These companies, especially Carboloy, have much published information concerning your five questions, and I suggest that you ask them in detail.

On many applications, however, carbide has been unable to replace high speed steels, particularly those steels with higher vanadium and carbon contents. It would be impossible to go into this except to say that carbide sometimes has difficulty with large-radius work, and cuts so lightly that it might be termed scraping rather than true cutting.

In an evaluation of carbide tools, it is essential to consider the special requirements of the machine tools used. Planing and milling with carbide are more complicated, and I would be glad to advise you on them, if you desire.

If you have any difficulty in obtaining information from these companies, please let me know.

Yours very truly,

When Mr. Young wrote his answer, he put himself in his reader's place and wrote things that he as a reader wanted to know. Therein lies the great secret to writing a successful answer to an inquiry—in fact, the secret to writing any successful letter, business or personal.

The following form letter could hardly be more friendly, personal, and forceful had it been personally dictated by its author, Mr. John B. Hogan of the Barnes & Jones Company of Boston, Massachusetts:

Thank you for the opportunity you have given us to tell you about Barnes & Jones Quality Heating Equipment.

As an operating engineer you will find a lot of helpful information in the bulletins we have enclosed. Bulletin E45 tells the story of re-evaporation and its effects on the heating system. Bulletin R44 is a maintenance manual covering location and repair of defective traps. Our catalog #76 covers our complete line of steam specialties.

Test a FREE sample of Barnes & Jones Cage Replacement Unit in one of your defective traps, without any obligation on your part. This trial should convince you that Barnes & Jones has the easy, economical answer to trap maintenance. The inside pages show you why.

Just jot down on the enclosed postage-free card the model number of one of your traps and mail the card today.

And now I am pleased to show you some letters that I have used for a number of years as excellent illustrations of how good will can be fostered through the thoughtful handling of inquiries.

The first letter is an inquiry from Mr. W. G. Mitchell, Jr.—an earnest, sincere request for information about parts for an obsolete car, which, as he indicates twice in his letter, he intends to keep running indefinitely. The second letter is an equally honest but frank answer by my friend Roger Browne, Assistant Manager of the Parts Department at Cadillac.

Dear Mr. Otto:

I am writing to you upon the suggestion of Mr. Moutier of your New York Branch. My car is a 1929 LaSalle, Model 328, Engine Number 418709, to which I am very much attached and which I intend to keep running indefinitely. As I am very much worried regarding the parts situation, I would appreciate your kindness in giving me the answer to the following two questions.

First, do you have any parts in stock for this car, and if so, would you be willing to sell me one of each of the vital parts of the motor and transmission? If a small stockpile of vital parts could be accumulated, I should feel more comfortable as to the future. I say one of each, since it is not my wish to hoard or prevent any owner of a similar car from obtaining parts. Of course, I understand that my term "vital parts" is too vague to serve as the basis for an actual order. If you have the parts on hand, I shall determine, with the aid of Mr. Fuller of the Boston Cadillac, precisely which parts I should get.

Second, if you have no parts for a 328 LaSalle on hand, would you be willing to make them for me? I understand that if the dies or molds for these parts have been discarded, the process of manufacture would be expensive, since it would be necessary to reimburse for the cost of the molds as well as the actual parts. But I am prepared for this as necessary to keep my old car running. Furthermore, I doubt that you would be willing to manufacture any parts at the present time, due to the very great pressure for new cars. Therefore, I would be satisfied with your assurance that you would make them for me at a future date.

At present I have in mind spending about $500.00 for parts. In another year I hope to be able to accumulate a larger fund for this purpose.

Incidentally, do you have or could you make any of the Fisher Body parts for my car, which is a five passenger sedan?

I shall be much obliged if you can furnish me with the answers to these questions.

Very truly yours,

Don't say you didn't smile when you read that letter. Yet there is a sincere ring in Mr. Mitchell's words that assures you he isn't fooling, but is dead serious in his request. There is some compelling reason why he is willing to spend his accumulated savings "to keep my old car running," as he puts it.

In his reply to my request for permission to publish this letter, Mr. Mitchell said, in part: "I am really fond of the original La-Salle, as it has been in the family garage since my childhood days. I was only 14 on the day my father brought it home, and I grew up with it and had most of my good times in it."

Roger Browne must have sensed this sentimental attachment when he framed his reply, a masterpiece of tact and diplomacy:

Dear Mr. Mitchell:

Your letter of April 12, addressed to Mr. Otto, was referred to me for a careful analysis on the availability of parts for your car.

I do want you to know that we are anxious to do what we can to keep your car in running order. To say that all parts or even most parts are available would be a misstatement. Our stock is depleted on many items.

In the early days of the War, our Government called upon all manufacturers to make available for the war effort fixtures, dies, molds—in fact, anything that would swell the supply of scrap iron which was so vitally needed to prosecute the War. Call it patriotism, pride, or what you may, we did review our needs at that time on Service Parts, and we did release all such equipment that we felt sure would no longer be needed, particularly on the earlier models.

Owners who normally would purchase new cars had to make their present car carry on, resulting in a demand for some parts far out of proportion to normal service needs.

You and I realize that the combined effort of all our people, together with manufacturing facilities across the nation working day and night, eventually turned the tide of the War in our favor. The War is now over, and we are once again trying to bring our service up to the standard which Cadillac and LaSalle owners have learned to expect.

Some parts are available for your model 328 LaSalle, such as camshaft, crankshaft, connecting rods, almost all motor gaskets, some transmission parts, and a limited number of body hardware items. Our stock of cylinder blocks, cylinder heads, car doors, body springs, etc., is depleted. To make even one or two different major items that are not available would cost more than the price of a new model car.

Realizing the esteem in which you hold your LaSalle, I have a suggestion to offer, although somewhat reluctantly. As you need them, order just the parts necessary to keep your car in running order and we will try to supply them. Perhaps there is another owner in your locality who has a car of the same model, but to which the owner may not attach the same sentiment as you do to yours. It could probably be purchased for a very reasonable sum, and it would assure you of the added protection on the vital parts to which you referred.

Please do not construe this as an evasion, for it is not. I simply want to assist you in any practical way. Your writing us is appreciated, and we will be glad to serve you in any possible way. You will also find Mr. Fuller and his entire organization ready to serve your needs.

Yours very truly,

That is a first-class reply. Did you notice how skillfully Mr. Browne avoided leading Mr. Mitchell to believe that all or even many of the parts are still available? Notice how he tactfully opens with "... a careful analysis on the availability of parts." Notice how the first sentence of paragraph 2 gently breaks the news that there may be some difficulty in getting the needed parts. Notice the appeal to patriotism—excellent preparation for the devastating blow that follows. Notice how he speaks of "earlier models," carefully avoiding the term "old car"—a phrase that Mr. Mitchell could use and get by with, but that he very likely would have resented coming from anyone else. Notice the extremely personalized "You and I know" opening to the fifth paragraph, and the repetition of the call of patriotism.

Then notice how he states positively what parts *are* available, and how he de-emphasizes those that are not. Notice the subtle reference to new cars and the cost of making parts for this 328 LaSalle. Notice how tactfully he "reluctantly" suggests purchasing "a car of the same model, but to which the owner may not attach the same sentiment as you do to yours." This was a stroke of genius. (P.S. That is exactly what Mr. Mitchell did. Now he has an ample supply of spare parts for his original 328 LaSalle.)

You can't read these two letters too often. Every time you go through them, you will learn something more about the tactful handling of inquiries. You must learn to take seriously any inquiry or request for information. Had Roger Browne taken lightly Mr. Mitchell's request, either through the tone of his letter or by what he said, his answer would have created much ill will toward the company. Instead, he has made a lifelong friend and booster.

Another series of letters consists of two from the customer and one from the company. Too often, as in the Mitchell-Browne exchange of letters, the correspondence terminates with the company's answer to the request. The company never gets to know how the customer reacted to its reply.

That is not true of this series. But let's get along with the letters themselves.

Gentlemen:

Last April I placed an order for a rear right fender for my 41/61 Cadillac with the Forest Cadillac Olds Co. from where I bought the car. The fender had been twisted by a fruit truck turning into my rear at Vero Beach, Fla. The fender is not fit for repair and I am anxious to have a new one sent to the above concern at 4100 Laclede, St. Louis, because there are other repairs to be made and I would like to have the new fender put on and the other damages cured.

The Forest Cadillac Olds Co. has been quite sympathetic to my urgent requests and has kept me posted as to your inability to supply the fender. Mr. Reddon of that concern showed me today a memo dated 10/11/46 hoping to ship the fender within 60 days.

Mrs. Campbell and I have been married 50 years in the near future, and we are planning to go to St. Petersburg, Fla., November 29, and we would be so happy to get that fender and the Cadillac repaired before that date. I am retired, having leased my paper to faithful employees, and I wish you would send me some definite word to my St. Louis address.

Yours respectfully,

Now, there isn't anything unusual about that request ... or *is* there? Is it exactly like the hundreds of other requests the company received almost daily about fenders, bumpers, and other parts for earlier model cars?

Let's see what Art Floethe of the Cadillac Parts Department thought about it, and how he answered it. Let's see whether he saw in it anything to lift this letter above the level of the ordinary routine request:

Dear Mr. Campbell:

We are sorry to learn from your letter of October 21 of the damage to the right rear fender on your series 41-61 Cadillac.

Our supply of these fenders became exhausted during the war years, and because of certain government restrictions, additional quantities could not be manufactured.

Of course, it was our earnest desire to again make these fenders available to Cadillac customers, and it has only been within the past few weeks that we have been obtaining a very small number of them, inasmuch as manufacturing facilities have not yet reached the point where we can receive them in any sizeable quantities. At present, we do not have a 1097346 right rear fender on hand, but we expect to have one within the next ten days. You may be assured it will be shipped at that time to our St. Louis distributor, Forest Cadillac Olds Company, on back order B52872-2A tagged for you.

We suggest you keep in touch with our distributor, and we are sending them a copy of this letter so they will be familiar with this transaction.

Thus far, there is nothing out of the ordinary in this reply. It is like many other good letters that I have given you in this book. But Art Floethe saw in Mr. Campbell's letter a golden opportunity. Reread, if you will, Mr. Campbell's last paragraph in which he mentions his coming golden wedding anniversary. That was the inspiration for Art Floethe's last paragraph:

The average individual very seldom has an opportunity to congratulate a couple on their 50th wedding anniversary. Inasmuch as I have not yet had this privilege, I wish to take advantage of this opportunity and extend my heartiest congratulations, as well as those of the Cadillac Motor Car Company, to you and Mrs. Campbell on your coming anniversary. I sincerely hope that you continue to enjoy many more, and that you have a very pleasant trip to Florida.
                                                          Yours very truly,

This last paragraph literally lifts a routine answer far, far above the average. It adds the dignity of *character* without one bit of sentimentality. True, that paragraph wasn't really necessary in a strictly business transaction, but Art saw in Mr. Campbell's last paragraph an opportunity to build an extra bit of good will that might remove some of the sting of having had to wait so long to have his damaged fender replaced.

Or it might have been the natural reaction of one friendly human being to another who has made a notable achievement— having lived long enough to celebrate fifty years of happy married life, an achievement shared by so few couples that it becomes truly a mark of distinction.

A letter, like an individual, *can* have character—that quality which elevates a person or thing above the ordinary. Many of the letters you have read in this book have character in the true meaning of that word. And if you wish, every letter that you write *can have character.* It's entirely up to you, for you alone select those words that can and will give distinction to your letters.

I promised you *three* letters in this series. Here is the third letter, a reply from Mr. Campbell. Without it, this series would not be complete. In this third one we learn how Art Floethe's last paragraph affected Mr. Campbell. In this letter we realize what a tremendous impression Art's unnecessary last paragraph made on his reader:

Dear Mr. Floethe:

Your letter of October 25 last, concerning a right rear fender for my Cadillac, was greatly appreciated. Mr. Smoky, assistant service manager for the Forest Cadillac Olds Co. accorded me a high rating on account of your letter. He said it was unusual, and his concern joined in the business of putting the new fender on and making other repairs with alacrity, unusual in these days of delays and confusion.

It was three days less than a month from the date of your letter until the fender was replaced, and I shall not forget the attention a great company accorded me in a matter seemingly more vital to Mrs. Campbell and me than a mere fender. It was our intended departure for Florida and our expected golden wedding which made the arrival of that fender a most happy event, and we thank you again and also for your thoughtful and friendly felicitations.

Yours very truly,

If that isn't living proof that friendliness and courtesy beget friendliness and courtesy, I don't know human beings!

*   *   *   *

Although this Campbell-Floethe series would be an excellent one on which to close today's study, I have one more letter that I know you will enjoy. There is a definite moral behind this delightful bit of nonsense: WHEN YOU WANT TO KNOW SOMETHING, COME OUT AND ASK FOR IT IN UNMISTAKABLE LANGUAGE—DON'T JUST HINT AROUND AT WHAT YOU WANT!

The way I heard it, a young couple about to be married went house-hunting in the country. On their way home the young woman fell into a deep meditation, which caused the young man to ask why she was so silent. She replied that she liked the last house they had inspected, but didn't remember having seen any W.C., by which she meant the water closet. Recalling that he too hadn't seen any such outfit, he wrote to the landlord asking where the W.C. was located. The landlord, who didn't know what W.C. meant, concluded that his prospective tenant was referring to the Wesleyan Church. Accordingly, he replied as follows:

Dear Sir:

I regret very much the delay in answering your letter, but I have the pleasure to inform you that the W.C. is located nine miles from the house on a good paved road, and is capable of seating 240 people. This is unfortunate for you if you are in the habit of going regularly, but you will be glad to know that a number of people take their lunch and make a day of it. Others who can't spare the time go by auto, but generally they are in such a hurry that they cannot wait. The last time my wife and I went was six years ago, and we had to stand all the time. It may interest you to know that a Bazaar is to be given soon to raise funds to furnish plush seats, as many of the members feel that this is a long felt want. I may mention that it pains me greatly not to be able to go more often.

Respectfully yours,

What a delightful bit of nonsense, which probably was actually sent. For fifteen years I have been trying to run down the source of that letter, but to no avail. Recently, Mr. Joseph Garretson of the Cincinnati *Enquirer,* published the entire story as I have given it to you, with a request that anyone knowing anything about this uproariously funny letter get in touch with me. Unfortunately, no one has replied as yet.

Now I want to give you 10 simple rules that you can follow in order to make your inquiry or request for information more forceful and friendly:

1. *Be clear*—If your reader doesn't understand what you want, he can't possibly send it to you; he is like the puzzled land lord in the W.C. letter.

2. *Be complete*—This is a close corollary of being clear. Err on the side of giving too much information, rather than too little.

3. *Be courteous*—It's so easy to be nice to someone who has been nice to you. Abe Lincoln said that a pint of molasses catches more flies than a barrel of vinegar—and he was right.

4. *Be specific*—The more specific you are as to what you want, the more likely you are to get what you ask for.

5. *Be considerate*—You are writing to another human being. Don't ask for the impossible and expect to get it.

6. *Be helpful*—Tabulate or list the things you want or the points you want information on. If possible, frame your requests in question form. Questions are easier to answer.

7. *Be reasonable*—Don't ask for "all information." Give your reader an out in case he can't give you the information you want.

8. *Be honest*—Tell him who you are and why you want this information. Companies like to know this information before they start giving out material.

9. *Be modest*—Don't pose as a "big shot" in order to high-pressure information that you are afraid you couldn't get otherwise. Your scheme might backfire and embarrass you con siderably.

10. *Be fair*—Express willingness to give credit for information sent you and used. Often that is the only way you can repay the company for their trouble—and it is the least you can do and still be fair.

And here are 10 pointers that will help you write more friendly, forceful replies to inquiries and requests for information:

1. *Be prompt*—A prompt reply will cover a multitude of sins.

Your reader may have waited until the last minute to write you, but he won't appreciate your keeping him waiting. A prompt reply helps build good will.

2. *Be clear*—If you aren't clear, your reader will merely write you again to try to get the information you didn't give him the first time. People are persistent.

3. *Be complete*—Give all the information you can in your first letter. Your reader will like that. If you can't send every thing at once, send what you can and indicate that the rest will come later.

4. *Be courteous*—You may be seething inside when you write your letter, but don't let your reader know it. This time it will pay to be two-faced. Let only the friendly, smiling one show.

5. *Be specific*—Be as definite and specific as you can. This will help not only to build good will, but also to terminate the correspondence.

6. *Be considerate*—Remember, your reader had a reason for writing, probably a very good one. He will appreciate any con sideration you care to show him.

7. *Be helpful*—Your reader wrote to you for help. Give it to him. Even if he wrote a jumbled-up letter, organize your ma terial. If he should know more than he asked for, tell that to him also.

8. *Be patient*—Your reader doesn't know as much about the material as you do, or else he wouldn't be writing you. Don't in sinuate that he's dumb because he may not be able to grasp a highly technical point explained to him in highly technical lan guage. Talk to him on his own level, in simple, nickel-and-dime words. He'll like that.

9. *Be fair*—Praise your own product, of course, but not at the expense of your competitors. Every product has its own merits. Select yours and hammer away at them.

10. *Be a good salesman for your company*—Recently I bought a pair of binoculars from the Westlake Camera Stores, Inc., in Los Angeles because of the fine way in which Mr. Charles E. Arensten of their Special Order Desk handled my inquiry. He was a good salesman for his company. And you can be, too, if you will make a practice of writing friendly, forceful answers to every inquiry or request for information that comes to your desk.

I want you to see Mr. Arensten's letter, not only because it is a good letter and a good sales letter, to boot, but because Mr. Arensten was not born in this country and has spoken English for only seven years! Here is his excellent letter:

Dear. Mr. Riebel:

Thank you for your letter of June 27 regarding 8 x 30 binoculars which we recently advertised for $17.95.

The total price for these binoculars is $28.23. This includes $5.00 for the case, $4.59 federal excise tax, and 69¢ state sales tax. Upon receipt of your remittance, we shall be happy to make shipment to you.

With reference to your inquiry in connection with the Practiflex 35mm camera, this camera can be focused as closely as two feet, and therefore can be focused closely enough for a sheet of letterhead paper to fill one frame.

If there is any additional information you desire, please contact us.

Very truly yours,

A SOFT ANSWER TURNETH AWAY WRATH

THERE'S AN OLD SAYING to the effect that a barking dog never bites. I wouldn't like to bank on that. Here is one thing I would certainly agree to—I'D NEVER LET A "BARKING DOG" WRITE LETTERS FOR MY COMPANY!

A barking dog may not bite, but he certainly scares away a lot of people. So with a barking dictator or letter writer. He may never bite customers, figuratively or literally, but he will scare a lot of them away. And that isn't the way to win friends for your company and to influence customers favorably.

How would *you* like to get a letter that said, in part:

Either you are of a mind to do business, or you aren't. Now I don't give a damn which it is. All I want to know is which.

or:

You know that we cannot permit you to take this unearned discount. Surely you must have *some* sense of fair play left in you.

or:

I have done business with crooks and shysters before, but never ones like those at your Blankville agency. They take the cake! Those thieves would steal the gold fillings out of my teeth if I dared to open my mouth!

177

Fortunately, there are relatively few letters today that go to such lengths to insult a customer—to drive him to buying from a competitor. Still, there are far too many people writing letters with that proverbial chip on their shoulders.

Voltaire once said: "We cannot always oblige, but we can always speak obligingly." There is the secret of speaking softly and turning away the potential wrath of a customer. Therein lies the secret of writing successful complaints, and acceptable answers to complaints; of refusing an individual's application for credit; of asking a customer to pay his overdue bill; of writing any kind of letter that is likely to arouse anger or hurt feelings.

A letter is such a permanent thing. A business letter is usually filed and preserved for years and years. If it is a good, friendly letter, it will bless not only the receiver but also the writer and his company. If it is nasty, sarcastic, cutting, it will hurt not only the reader but also the writer and his company. It will kill all desire to do business with them.

Today, I don't want to show you ill-conceived letters, ones spewed out in anger and filled with vitriol. Instead, I'd like to show you how you can speak softly and turn to friendship the potential wrath of your reader. That will make your reader feel that you are, after all, a pretty fine fellow.

DON'T BE AFRAID TO SAY "I'M SORRY"

That's right—don't be afraid to say that you're sorry. But when you say it, mean it! Don't say: "I'm sorry BUT . . ." That immediately qualifies your sorrow and makes your reader feel that you really aren't as sorry as you appear to be.

Some people have the queer notion that it is unethical or unmanly for someone to say he is sorry for something that happened or that he cannot do. I once worked with a man who *never* said that he or his company was sorry for any mistake or incident that happened. His excuse was that a company couldn't feel anything anyway, and therefore it couldn't feel sorrow.

That is a foolish, short-sighted view. Of course, a company—an impersonal entity—cannot actually feel sorrow as you and I do. Likewise, a company cannot actually *do* anything, except as things are done by individuals within that company.

Therein lies the secret. Some companies are made up of abstractions, including the people who work for them. Those individuals are not really people; they are automatons. Once they pass through the doors of that company, they lose their own individuality; they become just badge numbers or "positions," not human beings of flesh and blood. Ice water—or is it vinegar?—runs in their veins. Some of these letter-writers remind me of a sign that I have seen in quite a number of places:

WHY BE DIFFICULT

when, with a little more effort,

YOU CAN BE IMPOSSIBLE?

No company or organization can rise above the level of the individuals who compose it. Every person, at some time in his life, has done something which he regrets, for which he feels constrained to say, "I'm sorry." Since a business is made up of human beings, it is only natural that occasional mistakes are made. And it is equally natural that someone should apologize for these mistakes.

Here is a letter in which the writer is not ashamed to say, at the very outset, "I was certainly sorry . . ."

I was certainly sorry to learn, Mr. Russell, that you were disappointed in the MAIN ATTRACTION trailer we made for you recently.

There's one thing we at FILMACK strive for—that's a customer who is satisfied 100%, whether he spends $2.50, $25.00, or $250.00 for a trailer.

If we in any way slip up on our workmanship or service, we want to be the first ones to know about it, because our work is unconditionally guaranteed.

Would you be a good scout and return the defective trailer to us so that we can screen it and hold a post mortem over it to find out just where we went wrong?

When we see what happened, we'll be happy to remake it and furnish you with a trailer for which neither of us will have to apologize.

Believe me, Mr. Russell, we sincerely regret any inconvenience you may have been caused. I do hope you'll understand it was one of those things that can happen in the best of regulated families, of which FILMACK is no exception.

Sincerely,

There is an excellent example of a soft answer turning away the wrath of an irate customer. Who could stay angry with a man who took such a cooperative attitude toward a common human error?

Here is a letter that makes no bones about saying, "I'm sorry that we did not serve you to the best of our ability." This letter helps to restore amicable relations between customer and company:

Dear Dr. Maurer:

We have your letter of the 8th and are naturally sorry that you came across a can of our peanuts that were not "The Best You Ever Tasted."

You did exactly the right thing in writing us. In fact, we are most appreciative of your kindness in letting us know of your experience.

It so happens that occasionally a can will not hold the vacuum and will permit the air to enter, thereby causing rancidity. These instances are rare, but they can and do happen. We pack and ship about 400,000 cans each month. We have the most modern testing equipment, but at that, a small pin hole which might not show up at the time of packing and testing can later allow air to enter and spoil the contents.

Our representatives have instructed all stores to make immediate replacement when such incidents occur. Sometimes, however, stores are reluctant to handle such replacements on account of the details involved. The quickest way, of course, is to write, as you did in this instance.

We are sending you a fresh can in perfect condition. We guarantee our merchandise to be of the finest quality. If at any time you buy a can of CIRCUS that is imperfect, please let us know.

We do hope that this will be the last can of CIRCUS you ever obtain in that condition.

                                        Sincerely yours,

When Mr. N. Unini, Assistant Secretary of Circus Foods Inc., wrote that letter, you know that he meant every word he said. His sincerity is unmistakable, and he is trying hard to "appease" an irate customer. The letter is not absolutely perfect, however, for it is a bit too long and repetitious. It could easily be shortened without damage. Also, it seems to protest too much. But the man's heart was in the right place when he wrote and told

Dr. Maurer that he was sorry that a can of CIRCUS peanuts was not up to par.

Here is another letter in which the writer turned the wrath of the customer by the softness and reasonableness of her answer. As did Mr. Unini, Mrs. Charlotte S. De Armond, Advertising Manager of the Dinnerware Division at Gladding, McBean, explained why certain actions were taken. She gave the "reason why" explanation, and thus showed the irate customer that profit would accrue from the company's action, even though the customer would lose a small commission on the china sold directly to the college:

Dear Mrs. Hart:

The copy of your letter to Mr. Robert Saving has just reached my desk. We are sincerely sorry that there has been any misunderstanding regarding the shipment of Franciscan Fine China direct to the Home Economics Department of State College. Gladding, McBean & Co. is very much aware that your firm is our exclusive china representative in Boyd. However, home economics department orders are not sales in the usual sense, but are rather another instance of the advertising and sales promotion program which has been designed to help build customers for Franciscan Dinnerware.

It is standard practice for manufacturers of china, silver, crystal, and appliances, to attempt to place their products in the best outlets to promote future sales for the retailers who sell their various lines. By placing Franciscan Fine China in the home management houses and demonstration dining rooms of State College, we are insuring that every girl who studies home economics is completely familiar with our products. By using the china and arranging tables with it, she gains first-hand knowledge of the beauty and quality of the product and the attractiveness of the design. When these same girls are ready to furnish homes of their own, the knowledge they have gained about our china will make them think first of Franciscan when buying for their own homes.

As our exclusive representative in Boyd, your store will enjoy the benefits of these future customers. Since sales such as the one you mentioned to State College are entirely an Advertising Department promotion and are made possible from funds allocated to advertising, they in no way conflict with the regular operation of the Sales Department. Results have shown that this program is one of the most successful yet developed to promote future sales of Franciscan Dinner-ware. Many retail accounts find it most advantageous to cooperate with the home economics departments of the various colleges and universities by arranging special table-setting promotions in cooperation with the schools.

You might like to consider a special promotion with the Home Economics Department at State College, at which time you might offer to lecture to the girls, or invite them to participate in a table-setting contest in order to make them familiar with your store and your operation. You certainly would want to make sure that every home economics student at Boyd knows that she can buy at your store the same Franciscan Fine China that she has been used to in college work.

We sincerely hope that this explanation will clear up the matter to your complete satisfaction.

Cordially,

Again the letter is a bit too long, but there is the matter of sales policy that must be explained to the complete satisfaction of the customer. In such letters, it is better to write more than is necessary than to be too brief. Above all, you must not be curt or abrupt. The customer's feathers are already ruffled, and anything untoward that you say will be taken up promptly—to your disadvantage.

This brings up the second thing I want to say about using soft answers to turn away the wrath of your customer—

WHATEVER YOU GIVE, GIVE
GRACIOUSLY—NEVER
GRUDGINGLY

Many companies have learned the great secret of successfully handling complaints and adjustments: *what you give, give graciously and cheerfully—never give anything grudgingly.* Often it is better to refuse courteously but firmly a request than to give grudgingly and with obvious ill will.

You might as well try to make a friend of your dissatisfied customer as to make an enemy of him, especially if you are going to allow some kind of adjustment anyway.

When Mr. Unini gave Dr. Maurer a replacement can of CIRCUS peanuts, he did it with the best of grace. Dr. Maurer said that he felt he was doing Mr. Unini a favor by accepting the replacement can; that's how good a job of selling his customer Mr. Unini did.

Here is an exchange of correspondence about an unsatisfactory-purchase. The young man wrote the company a courteous letter, and the company promptly replied in kind, thus making an enthusiastic booster and satisfied customer out of Earl Weinstein:

Gentlemen:

Recently I purchased a V-5A Vacuum Tube Voltmeter kit and last week assembled it. The instrument works fine electrically, but on any range when the needle moves past the 24-30 volt markings, it sticks. It doesn't appear that the pointer end of the needle is rubbing on the front scale of the meter, but rather that the movement which is attached to the needle is rubbing in the housing at this deflection.

Upon your advice, then, I shall either send the meter removed from the VTM or the entire VTM to you for repair or replacement.

I like my Heathkit VTM and am anxious to put it to use. Since the end of the college year is June 7, and after that date I'll be living at my home address in Los Angeles, I'm enclosing an addressed airmail envelope so that your answer may reach me while I'm still at college.

Sincerely yours,

This is a good letter of complaint, or request for adjustment. Note the calm, quiet tone, the feeling of assurance that the company will stand behind its product, the complete description of the trouble, the choice given the company, and the motivation for a prompt reply. If more people would write letters like this one by Earl Weinstein, they would get better and prompter replies.

Here is Mr. G. Krepp's reply to Earl's request:

Dear Mr. Weinstein:

We are very sorry to learn that you have been inconvenienced by a defective meter movement with your model V-5A VTM. You may be sure that the Heath Company will provide you with the necessary replacement.

You will soon receive a replacement meter movement, and we should appreciate the return of the unused meter at your convenience. Of course, there will be no charge for this service, and we sincerely hope that no further difficulty will develop.

If there is any question at all concerning your Heathkit VTM, you are invited to write to the Heath Company at any time.

Very truly yours,

A friendly, courteous, satisfying reply. Notice how soon after expressing regret at the incident Mr. Krepp assures Earl that the company will give him the necessary replacement. This is indeed a successful sales letter, one that will win the confidence of an unhappy customer.

POLITENESS WILL GET YOU MORE THAN WILL RUDENESS

Once I saw a sign that read: Courtesy is not rationed! That was during the war, of course—World War II. What a pity so many letter-writers have never seen that little sign, for politeness will certainly get a person much, much more than grouchiness or rudeness. Here is a series of letters that illustrates this very point. Gruffness or discourtesy on the part of either writer could have resulted in something far different from the happy outcome:

The first letter is from Miss Grace Branson, City Librarian at Paso Robles, California:

Dear Mr. Matzinger:

According to our records, the following books are charged to your library card:

Durant—Story of Philosophy

Berne—Mind in Action

Pearl—Rate of Living These

books were due Dec. 1.

Several requests have been received for these books. We shall appreciate your cooperation in helping keep them available to the public.

This is your third notice. Please see me about the books, won't you?

Very truly yours,

To this restrained request, Guy Matzinger replied, with equal restraint and courtesy:

Dear Miss Branson:

Your letter of January 4 arrived today, and I was both startled and shocked to learn that there are three delinquent books charged to my card.

As I recall, the last time I used the card was in May of last year. On August 15, my wife and I moved to San Luis Obispo so that I could enroll for the Fall Quarter at California State Polytechnic College here.

We haven't been in Paso Robles since August 15, so I am quite sure we don't have the books you mentioned. As a double check, however, I have gone through all of our belongings, but the three volumes are not among them.

Please hold my card on the inactive list or destroy it so that no further charge will be made on it. Let me know if there is any way I can help in solving this problem.

Cordially yours,

A friendly reply to what could easily have degenerated into a name-calling contest, each side sure that it was right. But Guy's soft answer had its reward:

My dear Mr. Matzinger:

Thank you for answering my letter so promptly. On checking the files, I found a mistake had been made in reading the number of the book cards. Your number is 6548 and the books were charged to 6648.

Because of your kind cooperation, the mistake made by a member of the library staff has been corrected, and the proper notice sent to the person whose number is 6648.

I regret having cause you inconvenience and am sorry the mistake was made.

Sincerely yours,

As Alexander Pope once said, "To err is human; to forgive, divine." As long as human beings continue to transact business, mistakes will occur. The only sensible thing to do is to face them squarely, admit the mistakes, and then try to correct or eliminate them as best we can.

YOU CAN'T WIN AN ARGUMENT WITH A CUSTOMER

It seldom pays to get in an argument with a customer, because you just can't win. If you win your argument, you probably will lose your customer. And if you lose your argument, it'll so rankle you inside that you may do or say something that will annoy your customer. So it's best not to argue with him.

Once I corresponded with a man who complained because his new car wouldn't go more than 100 miles an hour! I couldn't tell him that no one in his right mind should be driving a car 100 miles an hour. So I asked him to take his car to the Miami dealer for a checkup. After carefully going over the car, the dealer reported the car standard and normal in every respect.

Still the customer was dissatisfied. So I asked the Jacksonville distributor to send down a service engineer to check the car. The results were the same. Still the customer was unhappy. So I had our district service manager *fly* from Atlanta to Miami to see the car and consult with the service representatives from both the dealership and the distributorship. After three days of testing, the results were the same—the car was standard and normal in every respect.

But the customer still was unhappy—after the company had spent several hundred dollars checking and rechecking his car. There was simply nothing to do but close the complaint as "still dissatisfied." After my fifth or sixth letter, I heard nothing more from this disgruntled customer. But you may be sure that he was treated with the greatest of courtesy, and no attempt was made to argue with him. He was told simply and directly that his car was standard and normal according to all our standards, and that was that. After a final letter, he quit writing.

You can't expect to please every customer, or to settle satisfactorily every complaint. Don't hope for that, or you'll be bitterly disappointed. But, above all, avoid whenever you can any reference to "company policy." Customers buy service and products, not company policy. Too often company policy is something to hide behind when you don't have a really good reason for refusing a request.

Some years ago, I wrote to a number of large companies to see whether they would be interested in having me put on some kind of better-letter program for their correspondents during the summer vacation. Here is the brush-off that I got from an officer in one of these companies:

Dear Sir:

This office recognizes the need everywhere for the type of service you have to offer in your clinic for letter writing.

However, as far as we are personally concerned, our office manager has developed a planned approach for the improvement of letter writing in our company.

To the best of my knowledge and belief this plan calls for no outside assistance and for this reason I do not feel it would be possible to employ you in this capacity during your summer vacation.

Very truly yours,

Well, what do you think of it? ... So did I! Of course, he was perfectly within his rights in not encouraging me, but couldn't he have done it a little more gently, a little less brusquely? I think so.

Dear Mr. Riebel:

We are glad to know that others are also interested in improving the quality of business letters. However, our office manager has developed for us what we think is a very carefully planned approach.

Since this plan does not call for outside assistance, we cannot offer you any encouragement for the coming summer. But I do very much appreciate your thinking of our company.

Sincerely,

Yes, I know what you're saying: why should he bother with the feelings of an outsider, a total stranger? Why should he be concerned with treading lightly on my toes, after I was brash enough to ask him for a summer job? Maybe he shouldn't, but I still think it would have created far more good will toward his company had he been a little more diplomatic in turning me down. What do *you* think?

In other words, I think he could have accentuated the positive tone of his letter and eliminated the unpleasant negative, which has lingered with me these many, many years.

I just can't resist showing you another letter, which I received not too long ago from Mr. F. G. Vaughan, Vice President of the Grolier Society in charge of the Book of Knowledge Division. In a sense, this is a turn-down letter because he could not get me what I wanted. This one will show you not only how considerately he did this distasteful job, but also how much trouble companies often go to in trying to fill a customer's order:

Dear Mr. Riebel:

As much as I hate to admit it, I must confess defeat in my effort to acquire for you a Volume 2 of the 1938 printing of The Book of Knowledge.

Inquiries made to every one of our branch offices have brought the information that such a volume is not obtainable.

I sincerely regret this, as I know how much you must dislike having the usefulness of your set impaired in this manner.

Sincerely yours,

CREDIT AND COLLECTION LETTERS

Two kinds of letters that need special attention and care are credit and collection letters, especially when you are turning down a request for credit. Some wit once said that the tenderest part of a person's anatomy is his left rear pocket—or was it his left hip? Anyway, what he meant was that you are treading on precarious ground when you ask for money or refuse to let a customer have credit.

For example, here is a heartless way of turning an applicant down:

Dear Mr. Jones:

We find it impossible to grant your application for credit at this time.

Yours very truly,

Just like a razor cutting through a piece of quick flesh, sharp and stinging. No reason why, no explanation of any sort, yet there is in this letter some ray of hope—the words "at this time." Why didn't the writer say:

Dear Mr. Jones:

Thank you for your application for credit at the Vogue. We are always glad to know that new customers want to open accounts with us.

After a careful investigation, Mr. Jones, we believe that it would be unwise for both of us to open this account just now. You do have some heavy obligations outstanding. However, as soon as you clear some of them up, send in your application again.

Credit, you know, is a convenience and not a necessity. It is also a tremendous responsibility, and we don't want to add to your burdens at this time. How about letting us hear from you in three months?

Very sincerely yours,

You don't give him anything but HOPE. But maybe, in his case, that's the best thing you can give him—encouragement to get busy and clear up some of his outstanding bills. You don't do the customer a favor when you let him overextend himself credit-wise. The revised reply has taken the time and trouble to explain to Mr. Jones *why* you can't grant him credit "at this time." The rest is strictly up to him. You have turned him down gently, but firmly—not finally.

Throughout this book I have showed you a number of credit as well as collection letters. Here is a paraphrase of a collection letter about as bad—for a "first appeal" letter, at least—as any I have seen.

Dear Sir:

I'm afraid that you have made a very, very bad start on your account.

You have made only a down payment, which you sent along with your order. Your first payment is overdue and you apparently have chosen to ignore the notices which we sent you. Surely you know that no company can afford to do business in that way, don't you?

The only reason that we extended credit to you was because you promised to pay regularly each month. We accepted your promise in perfectly good faith and you may be sure we expect *you* to keep *your* promise. We do appreciate your business and would like to keep your account, but we have to have some tangible evidence on your part that you intend to keep your part of the bargain.

We are giving you just five days in which to live up to your word and keep your promise. Unless you make up your past due payment and give us your assurance that you will make your payments regularly in the future, we certainly will have to take steps necessary to protect our interests in this contract.

Yours very truly,

That is without doubt the strongest "first appeal" letter I have ever read. If I received such a letter from any company, I'd never do business with them again. The letter is entirely from the company point of view except when the reader is jerked upon the carpet and singled out with scornful YOU-words. Also, if the company's only reason for granting credit was the debtor's promise to pay, the company deserved to lose. The deadest dead-beat will make the sweetest sounding promises, but only a fool will believe him!

Here's how he could have written this "first appeal" letter to persuade the debtor in a friendly, convincing way that it's good business to pay his obligations when they come due:

Dear Mr. Doe:

Not so long ago we had the pleasure of opening an account in your name. In fact, we considered it a real privilege on [insert date] to open this account for [insert amount].

And we felt sure that you also considered it a privilege as well as a responsibility to be able to purchase [company name] merchandise in such a convenient way. That's why we are puzzled at not receiving your first monthly payment, as you promised, on [insert date].

Now I know that you don't like to get off on the wrong foot. Credit, as you know, is one of the most valuable assets a businessman can have. "Credit" means that the person selling you merchandise has faith in your word—that he believes in you enough to let you take his goods simply on your promise to pay as you agreed.

So why not get back on the right foot immediately? Send us your overdue monthly payment immediately, and keep sending your payments on time, as you agreed. Then we'll know that we weren't mistaken when we trusted you, as we did on [insert date of opening account].

What do you say, Mr. Doe?

Hopefully yours,

Here is a straightforward, personal, friendly appeal, positive rather than negative, helpful rather than threatening, friendly rather than fierce. Remember: YOU CAN ALWAYS GET ANGRY AND SAY NASTY THINGS, BUT YOU CAN'T UNSAY WHAT YOU HAVE SAID! Wise old Omar Khayyam said, many centuries ago in his exquisite *Rubáiyát:*

The Moving Finger writes; and, having writ,
Moves on: nor all your Piety nor Wit
   Shall lure it back to cancel half a Line, Nor
all your tears wash out a Word of it.

That doesn't mean you can't use straight-from-the-shoulder talking to your customer, if that kind of talk is called for. Here is an excellent letter written by another of my Gladding-McBean friends, H. F. Smith. Although it is certainly straight talking, Mr. Smith never had occasion to want to cancel even "half a line":

Dear Mr. Blank:

Thanks so much for your order for the #ll-B Folker cutting machine.

I am sorry I was unable to ship this machine yesterday because I ran into a financial snag. It seems that before you went to Mexico, we made a c.o.d. shipment to you in care of the SP depot in Salinas. But you had already left town, and we had to assume the freight charges both directions.

Therefore, if you don't mind, we should appreciate receiving from you a check for the full amount of the cutting machine, itemized as follows:

#ll-B Folker	$186.87	(½ h.p.)
	10.40	hose attachment
	9.60	protractor
	206.87	
	6.18	tax
	$213.05	total

Just as soon as we receive your check, this machine will be forwarded to you.

Cordially yours,

This customer not only sent his check promptly, but became one of the company's best customers—all because of a delicate credit situation tactfully handled. And what better advice can I give you at the close of today's important study than to TURN ME DOWN GENTLY, BROTHER!

Fourteenth Day

PUNCTUATION-GESTURES IN WRITING

Do YOU PAY MUCH ATTENTION to those little curlicues called "marks of punctuation" often scattered promiscuously throughout business letters? Or do you let your secretary worry about them? No matter what your answer, come along with me today for a brief excursion into the art of using punctuation.

Years ago I read an article entitled "Punctuation—Gestures in Writing." That's where I got the idea for the title to this chapter. After all, that's exactly what punctuation is—GESTURES IN WRITING.

When you speak, you move your arms and body—you gesticulate—you raise and lower your voice. That's called inflection. You emphasize one word or a series of words. You soft pedal others. You put *life* into your spoken words.

When you write, you can put life into your written words, too, by using appropriate marks of punctuation. Look at the following letter from TIME magazine. It's a long letter, but an extremely effective one. Certainly this letter has plenty of life and zip. Notice how various marks of punctuation have been used throughout to give life and animation to the plain black words on white paper:

Dear Reader:

   *You don't have to know Tito's real name (Josip Broz)

192

*or the formula behind the atom bomb ($E=MC^2$).

*You don't have to memorize the footnotes to be well-informed these days.

But you should know what Stalin is doing about his rebellious onetime satellite. And how the U. S. and Canada are moving to defend the West against atomic attack.

And you should be table to talk confidently and intelligently about the future of television and Russia's next move in Asia and what Congress is likely to do about the federal deficit.

For the truly well-informed people you know are not those who can give you countless details about one facet of the news; they are those who can talk well on a great many significant and interesting subjects —about what is being discovered, written, painted, preached; about what is happening in Business and Medicine, Music and Theatre, Education and Sport.

This changing world is so interesting they want to get the picture whole—to read and know its many-sided story complete.

And reading TIME, they know. Recently, for example, they had the satisfaction and the fun of knowing . . .

... what signs point to a boom in 1950 (TIME, Jan. 9, p. 75) ...

how it feels to fly faster than sound (TIME, Dec. 19, p. 28)

... who's the biggest thing on Broadway since Ethel Merman (TIME, Jan. 9, p. 50)

... what kind of parents teachers like (TIME, Jan. 16, p. 47) ... if American Business needs psychiatry (TIME, Jan. 16, p. 41)

... how many A-bombs it takes to equal one "H"-bomb (TIME, Jan. 16, p. 19)

... the good news for coffee-drinkers (TIME, Jan. 16, p. 32)

... how safe are the "cold cures" (TIME, Dec. 5, p. 69)

◆   ◆   ◆

Added all together, the answers to hundreds of questions like these give more than 1,500,000 TIME-reading families a quick, clear, vivid grasp of each week's essential news—the important news they <u>can't afford to miss</u> and the entertaining news it's so fascinating to follow.

That is the job TIME was invented (more than a quarter of a century ago) to do. Invented—for TIME in 1923 was an entirely new way to gather, organize and write the news. (And no magazine since then has ever quite been able to duplicate TIME's way of bringing you the news you want to know.)

To do this job, TIME gathers the news from many sources: from the Associated Press, from hundreds of newspapers in a dozen languages, from TIME's own News Bureaus in 26 cities at home and overseas, from TIME's own correspondents in every other news-capital.

The editors of TIME examine every bit of this news, discuss what is vital, what is trivial—often argue, sometimes even fight over it. Then they write the meaningful news so you can enjoy, understand and remember it—tersely because TIME will not waste your time, dramatically because TIME will not dull an exciting story with faded words.

They arrange this news into one coherent story of the world's week, divided into 21 logical chapters:

National Affairs	Science	Medicine
International	Theatre	Business and Finance
Foreign News	Religion	Motion Pictures
The Hemisphere	Art	Books
People	Radio and TV	Milestones
Sport	Press	Miscellany
Music	Education	Letters

And because many of these subjects are the kind that matter intensely to many people, every word you read in TIME is checked for accuracy by trained researchers whose watchfulness is as unflagging as is humanly possible. (That is why you will always find TIME as reliable as it is readable.)

But only by reading TIME regularly can you understand why so many of the most successful people in the U. S. turn to TIME every week and vote it their favorite of all the magazines they read—both for the information it gives them and the fun they have getting that information.

They include businessmen (more than half of all the officers and directors in Poor's Register)—government officials (half of all the key people in Washington)—doctors (more than 40% of all the members of the American Medical Assn.)—lawyers, churchmen, college presidents, newspaper editors—and more than 1,500,000 busy, intelligent families like yours from coast to coast.

So won't you join that group and share its understanding—just by picking up your pen and signing the enclosed card?

This card entitles you to a Special Introductory Rate that will bring you TIME for the next 44 weeks for only $3.57— saving you $5.23 under the single-copy price, $1.51 under the $5.08 these copies could cost you at the regular sub-scription price.

No need to send any money now. But this special introductory offer is available for a limited time only. So please mail the card right back to us at our expense today.

And welcome to TIME's Circle of the Well-informed!

Cordially,

Commas, semicolons, colons, periods, dots, dashes, question marks, exclamation points, quotation marks, parentheses, aster-isks—all of them were used, including even capitals, underlining, and specially penned-in large parentheses (in the third-from-the-last paragraph). This letter illustrates the skilful use of almost every common mark of punctuation that the average letter-writer needs to know how to use.

But, you say, this is a form letter, in which the writers had plenty of time to plan ahead and make use of all these different marks of punctuation; such opportunities don't come in everyday dictation. My answer is the following personally dictated letter, which includes almost all the different marks used in the TIME letter:

Dear Miss DeVore:

Yes indeed we'll give you a place on our program at the American Business Writing Association's Western Region convention in Los Angeles on May 5! Just when that time will come—morning or afternoon —I can't say for certain. But you may be very sure that we teachers of business writing want to know about your novel plan for auditing letters.

As it stacks up at the moment, the most likely spot will be in the morning ... for here is our "tentative" program—

MORNING: Opening (at 9:30 or 10:00)—Keynote address, "There IS Money in Your Mail," by Waldo J. Marra, Director of Banking Relations, Walston, Hoffman & Goodwin, San Francisco.

Mrs. Holdridge's Businessmen's Panel:
Ray Kibler—Goodrich Tire and Rubber Company
Kenneth J. Forshee—National Lead Company Robert
Hemming—Burroughs Company Marion
Tompkins—United States Air Forces Eleanora
Nail—Naval Ordnance Test Station, Pasadena

TOPIC: "Can YOUR Students and Employees Write
Money-Making Letters?"

Cora Day DeVore—General Insurance Companies of
America

LUNCHEON: Dr. Robert R. Aurner, guest speaker—Topic to be announced.

AFTERNOON: W. W. Baldwin, University of California at Los Angeles,
Subject: "Student Projects"

Mary Louise Lynott, Long Beach City College,
Subject: "Company Letterheads"

Dr. E. Dana Gibson, San Diego State College, Subject:
"The Business Letter"—a filmstrip

Dr. Jesse Graham, Los Angeles City Board of Education
and A.B.W.V. Vice President, West—Summation of
the Conference

Your program for auditing letters by mail sounds so good to me that I
suggest you write it up and send it in to some business publication. I for one
will be eager to read about it. Whatever illustrative material you care to use
will be welcomed.

I owe you a very sincere apology. Last April I promised to send you some
material that I use in my classes. When I returned from San Jose, I found I had
misplaced your address—and wasn't even too sure about your name! I blush to
admit it, but it's the truth; so to make amends, here is a complete set of
everything I use. I hope you find it interesting.

Am I forgiven?

Cordially,

Punctuating is like acting or singing or swimming—anyone can
learn to do it well, BUT IT MUST BE LEARNED. As with most
actions, there are certain generally accepted rules that help keep
people on the right track.

Years ago there was a very popular song entitled "Every Little
Movement Has a Meaning All Its Own." So also *every little*

mark of punctuation has a meaning all its own. That's a good thing to remember, for even though some marks do overlap in their usage, such as ...

> commas for semicolons—and vice versa
> semicolons for periods—and vice versa
> commas for dashes—and vice versa
> commas for parentheses—and vice versa
> sets of three or four dots for dashes—and vice versa

... each mark has its own distinctive use—that little "meaning all its own."

*   ♦   *   *

In this chapter, I want to tell you briefly but clearly—and with examples—how to add life and feeling and movement to your letters through your skilful use of punctuation, GESTURES IN WRITING.

Let's take a brief look at each mark of punctuation, find out what it can do, and then see it in action.

1. COMMA. *The comma is what the radio announcer calls "a brief pause."* Yes, I know that the dictionary defines "pause" as something brief, but I like that wording. It helps me distinguish between the comma (a brief pause) and the semicolon (a longer pause, but still not a full stop like the period, the question mark, the exclamation point).

Here are three sure-fire uses for the comma:

a. *To separate an introductory word or group of words.* This not only prevents misreading, but gives each word-group the emphasis it deserves.

> To do this job, TIME gathers the news from many sources.
> Naturally, there is nothing we would rather do than ship your order complete.
> Because you have not responded to our urgent appeals, there is nothing left for us to do but sue.

b. *To separate a series of words or groups of words.* This is often known as the A, B, and C series.

Please complete, sign, and airmail the enclosed card *today*. You'll have several short, fast-reading articles on every aspect of current business imaginable. To do this job, TIME gathers the news from many-sources: from the Associated Press, from hundreds of newspapers in a dozen languages, from TIME's own News Bureaus in 26 cities at home and overseas, from TIME'S own correspondents in every other news-capital.

    c. *To enclose a word or group of words within a sentence.*
And those are some of the reasons why, with recent issues, *Esquire* has hit the greatest circulation in its history.
Recently, for example, they had the satisfaction and fun of knowing that their predictions proved correct. Mr. Jones, our vice president in charge of production, will be glad to see you at 10, Friday morning.

    2. SEMICOLON. *If a comma is "a brief pause," a semicolon is a "pause"*—and it is generally used to separate parts of sentences that contain commas. It stands about midway between the comma and the full stop at the end of a sentence. SEMICOLONS ARE NOT USED FREQUENTLY IN MODERN BUSINESS LETTERS. Today, writers prefer to make two sentences instead of linking them with a semicolon. But that does not mean that the semicolon is never used. Here are some sentences in which semicolons have been used successfully:

If you can have the examples mimeographed, fine; if not, send them to me for processing.
Mr. Hemming will handle the sales letter; Mr. Kibler, application letters; Mrs. Tompkins, Air Force communications; Mrs. Nail, Navy communications; and Mr. For-shee, credit letters. Don't take our word for it; see for yourself!

    The semicolon is frequently misused. Here are a few sentences showing how it has been misused:

The maximum life of the diesel engine is about 200,000 miles; much greater than that of the average automobile engine being manufactured today. [Use comma or dash here.]

Four different types of measuring tools are used on different lathe operations; the scale, calipers, snap gauges, and micrometers. [Use a colon.]

3. COLON. *The colon is a mark of expectation or anticipa tion:* whenever you see a colon, you know that there is more to follow. It's like the mathematical equal sign. Note the use of the colon in each of the letters given in this chapter. In the TIME letter, the colon introduces a long series of topics that were dis cussed in recent issues of TIME; in the dictated letter, the colon introduces the program and also the various sections of the pro gram. Here are some additional examples of the use of the colon:

Let me tell you how this comes about: [Then follow five points.]

We are pleased to enclose your copies of the following:
Catalog BX-4
Bulletin 194
Report AJ-16

Whatever problem you choose to write on, be sure that these ideas are included: (1) a clear statement of what your problem is and why it is a problem to you; (2) how you went about getting facts or information that would help you solve your problem; (3) the final decision that you reached; and (4) whether or not your solution was a good one as far as you are concerned. [This shows excellent use of the semicolon also.]

4. DASH. *A dash indicates a break in thought, a change, or an afterthought.* It offers the writer an effect not obtainable with any other mark of punctuation. As you probably have noticed, I have used dashes quite liberally throughout this book. Dashes give sales letters a friendly and informal tone quite unlike the stately formality of the colon, or the coldness of the semicolon, or the bookishness of parentheses. A WORD OF WARNING: DON'T OVERWORK THE DASH! Here are some uses of the popular dash, taken chiefly from sales letters:

Since we probably won't arrive in Los Angeles before late in the afternoon or early in the evening—about 7, I hope —we want you to be sure to hold these rooms for us. In the last year the retail value of the books which the Club gave its members—not sold, mind you!—was OVER TWO AND A HALF MILLION DOLLARS WORTH. You'll know immediately why SUNSET is first choice in more than 450,000 Western homes, when you see how practical it is—filled with "how-to" information on every aspect of Western homemaking.

Foamglas—a cellular glass insulation—is unique as an insulating material that is waterproof, fireproof, and verminproof.

We are sending you today, under separate cover, a sample of ULTRALITE, and the literature that you requested. *Look for this "jump" sample!* It will illustrate to you the fine texture of ULTRALITE—its *toughness*—resiliency —ease of handling—dimensional stability. Walk on it— try to burn it—pour water on it—jump on it—fold it tightly in your hands—do anything to it that you think of that we haven't—and you will see for yourself how easily and quickly ULTRALITE will return to its *original thickness.* Does ULTRALITE answer your problem?

[This is an excellent illustration of how a number of short, sharp ideas can be jammed into a sentence— much like a boxer raining short, sharp blows on his opponent before he has time to recover and defend himself. In other words, the dash creates a very definite atmosphere that no other mark of punctuation can achieve in such a situation.]

5. DOTS. During the past decade a new use has developed for the dot. *A group of three or four consecutive dots indicates a break in thought or an omission in some quoted material.* In indicating a break in thought, the periods and the dash overlap somewhat. In modern business writing, a series of dots . . . sometimes two, sometimes three, sometimes even four ... is used primarily to give added emphasis ... to give the reader a

chance to pause between ideas or thoughts, as in the following illustrations . . .

> We promise you a full measure of "old time" service . . . the kind that keeps your car vigorous and young. [A dash could have been used.]
>
> Eight months ago, I had an idea .... as revolutionary as Edison's electric light. [A dash is also O.K.] In the coming year the AMERICAN HOME will be more valuable than ever to you. New ideas for your garden . . . space-saving gadgets . . . the new technique of flower arrangement . . . the increasing trend toward the modern . . . coming styles in wall paper . . . and a host of other fascinating articles.
>
> So ... we'll be expecting you about 5 Thursday afternoon, Bob. Please don't disappoint us this time.

6. QUESTION MARKS. *Every direct question should be followed by a question mark.* That rule still holds good today. As you learned in our Sixth Day's study, a question opening is very strong; people just can't ignore questions. That's why I prefer using a question mark after such a sentence as—

> Will you please send me these papers immediately? Some authorities consider this a request or command and use only a period. I think that the addition of a question mark gives added incentive to answer the request. You needn't agree, however. Here are some good examples of the use of question marks in business letters:
>
> How are those Hampshires doing for you? Did you have good luck with the litters? They are a mighty valuable investment, you know!
>
> It's no wonder we're confused. Each day brings another "significant development." Significant to whom? Why? What's it mean? . . Whom does it affect? . . What's it all about?

7. EXCLAMATION POINTS. *Exclamation points indicate strong emotion or feeling*—and if the trend toward using them continues, typewriter manufacturers will have to add another

key to their machines. Today, forceful business writers use occasional exclamation points in order to give added force and emphasis to their writing—to give a gesture not possible with any other mark of punctuation. Don't go overboard in your use of exclamation points—USE THEM JUDICIOUSLY, for they are the strongest marks of punctuation that have yet been invented.

> Start NOW! Put your spare time to profitable use! Turn your talent into PROFESSIONAL INCOME! Yes, PERCOFLASH is different! Higher in efficiency— a patented product—with tremendous layman appeal, based upon an understanding of the Percolating Principle !
> You asked how I find time to keep all of you posted—I don't! I just take it!
>> [NOTE: In personally dictated letters, the exclamation point is not used frequently. In certain situations, however, it can be tremendously effective in giving that added bit of "oomph" needed to get across your point. Use this mark when necessary, but use it sparingly.]

   8. PARENTHESES. *Parentheses are always used in pairs to enclose a word or group of words.* Although used infrequently, parentheses have very definite meanings to convey, I think the best way to explain the use of parentheses is to say that you should put in parentheses what you would put in a postscript. In other words, parentheses enclose what is a part of the letter as a whole but apart from the body itself—that is, unnecessary to the meaning of that particular sentence, as indicated in these illustrations :

> Remember, the Weather-Flo (list price $72.00) can be used on any hot water or warm air heating installation. It will draw a straight-line temperature curve on all jobs including radiant (floor or ceiling panel) installations. By actual test, at 95 degrees temperature and 60 per cent relative humidity, the Airmaster removed 46 pounds (22 quarts) of water from the air in 24 hours. And because I believe you are one of the men for whom FORTUNE is written, this letter is to tell you about that

issue, and to invite you to begin reading FORTUNE with it (at an introductory rate that is exceptionally attractive) .

9. CAPITALS. *In letters, capitals are used to give emphasis.* In the TIME letter and in certain examples, certain words were written in all capitals. That not only makes those words more emphatic, but also may indicate the title of the publication, generally a book or magazine. For example, here are the capitalized titles of magazines used in the illustrations given in this chapter: TIME, FORTUNE, SUNSET, AMERICAN HOME. Here are some words that have been capitalized merely for emphasis: OVER TWO AND A HALF MILLION DOLLARS WORTH, ULTRALITE, PROFESSIONAL INCOME, PERCOFLASH. Here are some additional illustrations of titles of publications in capitals and capitals for emphasis:

> The one dependable blueprint for obtaining maximum benefit through entertainment deductions is available to you now through the special study, HANDLING TRAVEL AND ENTERTAINMENT EXPENSES.
>
> [This one uses both capitals and underlining.] We hope you will be persuaded that THE TIMES (London) LITERARY SUPPLEMENT—of which a second copy is sent to you—provides the answer.

One thing must be taken into consideration: TOO MUCH EMPHASIS ANNOYS YOUR READER AND DULLS HIS SENSES. If you use too much emphasis, your reader will tend to discount everything you have to say. Not everything is equally emphatic or important.

Here is a letter that loses effectiveness through overcapitalization. Each set of capitals was *printed* in boldface type, thereby making it seem to jump out of the page at you. To me, that creates an undesirable impression. You need not agree with me. Here is the letter:

Dear Friend:

Would you pay $5. per acre FULL PRICE for good, level ranch land suitable for cattle raising or for growing a variety of field crops???

Can you afford payments of $5. per month (after a down payment of $5.) on a fine San Joaquin Valley Rancho??? Don't you agree that $12.50 per acre is an extremely low price for a fine tract of timber and ranch land with an all year 'round trout stream crossing the property???

Well, **HERE IS YOUR OPPORTUNITY** to buy **LAND BAR-GAINS** like those described above **DIRECTLY** through "The Coast Land Club."

"COAST LAND CLUB" members receive twice monthly bulletins filled with descriptions of **GOOD** ranch, timber, and grazing lands priced as low as $5. to $15. per acre. They are sold to **MEMBERS ONLY** for cash or on **VERY EASY TERMS.**

If you would like to buy a small or large tract of **GOOD LAND** at a price you can afford, here is **YOUR OPPORTUNITY** to join **"THE COAST LAND CLUB."** The yearly membership fee is $5. This $5. fee covers **ALL** COSTS . . . there are no monthly or weekly dues or extra charges of any kind. While you are a member you are free to buy the parcel of your choice in the location you select **DIRECTLY THROUGH THE CLUB** at the low quoted price for cash **or on VERY EASY TERMS.**

HOW IS THIS ALL POSSIBLE??? The answer is simple. Part of the membership fees received from our thousands of members is used to hire expert land buyers. These thoroughly experienced men travel through California, Oregon and Washington buying small and large tracts of farm, grazing, timber and ranch lands which are then re-sold to **COAST LAND CLUB MEMBERS ONLY** at prices 'way below the regular Real Estate Market.

$5. will get you $25. YES SIR! you can really increase your money five fold! **HERE IS THE DEAL!** . . . Enclosed with this letter you will find a $25 **LAND CERTIFICATE.** When you send in your membership application and fee of $5., return this certificate to our office. It will be signed, sealed and dated by our Secretary and returned **to** you for **IMMEDIATE** USE! You can apply this $25. towards the down payment, monthly payments or cash price of any parcel of land listed in **"THE COAST LAND REPORTER,"** the official paper **of** the **CLUB** which is mailed to all members twice each month.

$5. will get you $25. if you **ACT TODAY!** This is a limited offer, subject to withdrawal notice. So send in your membership application **TODAY** and $5. will get you $25.

                                                  Sincerely yours,

10. UNDERLINING AND ITALICS. Underlining **a** word in **writing or** typing is usually **a** signal to set that word in italic

type—type slanted to the right. It is done to achieve emphasis. Form letters are much more likely to use underlining than personally dictated letters. Throughout this book you have seen many letters that contained underlining. Here I want to show you just one example—a forceful *Coronet* letter. Notice how the fourth paragraph stands out because it is not only short but also underlined:

Dear CORONET Reader:

If all you had to do was push a button . . .

   . . . Ill bet your CORONET renewal would be in our subscription department right this minute.

But we haven't reached the "push-button age" (and frankly, I'm glad we haven't because then I wouldn't have this chance to write to you) ... so it takes a little more than just a slight pressure from your finger to keep CORONET coming to your door each month without interruption.

<u>But not much more.</u>

All you have to do is check the enclosed order card . . . slip it in the enclosed reply envelope . . . and drop it in the mail box the next time you go out.

I'll be glad to pay AIRMAIL postage to make sure that your renewal gets back in time so that your subscription will continue without interruption.

                                  Cordially yours,

Here are two rules that will help you do a better job of punctuating your business letters—to help you make more effective gestures in your business writing:

1. DON'T PUNCTUATE UNLESS YOU HAVE A GOOD REASON—Be sure you are right; then punctuate.

2. DON'T OVERPUNCTUATE—Whenever possible, eliminate needless punctuation rather than adding it.

Fifteenth Day

THE PAUSE THAT REFRESHES

COCA COLA REALLY HAS SOMETHING in that slogan, "The Pause That Refreshes" That's exactly what sentences and paragraphs do for the reader of your letters. To a lesser extent, of course, any mark of punctuation is a pause that gives your reader a chance to catch his breath, dwell briefly on what you have said, and then proceed.

Equally true is the fact that the paragraph is the strongest mark of punctuation. Years ago, sentences were written without **a** break of paragraphing. Then along came someone with a symbol that looks like a reversed P (¶) and marked the larger divisions of thought. But I'm not going into that today. What I'm concerned with is teaching you how to do a better job of using sentences and paragraphs in the writing of more successful business letters.

SENTENCES

Don't worry, this is not going to be a dull discussion of sentences and what makes them tick. Instead, I want to show you how some letter-writers have been able to divide their thoughts into short ideas that were easy for their readers to digest mentally and that could be understood with the least effort.

So let's begin by looking at some letters that are composed of comparatively short, easily understood thoughts:

Dear Mr. Carry:

Your constant promptness in meeting your obligations has earned you something invaluable ... an enviable 24 words credit record . . . one of which you may well be proud.

16 words It is true that in many credit departments accounts like yours are unnoticed and seemingly unappreciated. Those

13 words who are slow in paying their bills get most of the atten-

5 words tion. This should not be so.

Please consider this letter an expression of our sincere 21 words "thanks" for the splendid way you have handled your "Dutch Boy" account.

9 words We look forward to further opportunities to serve you.

Cordially yours,

See how the sentence lengths vary—from a low of 5 words to a high of 24. Each sentence is clear, easily understood. Here is another good illustration:

Dear Fellow Mustang:

16 words You may have noticed some new bulletin boards along the basement corridor of the Administration Building. They were built and installed to improve

14 words student participation in worthwhile organized student activities.

Please spend a few minutes with your fellow officers 21 words to decide how to make the most of your "private" bulletin board.

4 words Here are some suggestions—

5 words (1) Minutes of your last meeting
3 words (2) Constitution and by-laws
5 words (3) List of purposes and objectives
7 words (4) List of activities planned during the year
6 words (5) Dates, time, and place of meetings
6 words (6) List of members and/or officers
3 words (7) Photographs, clippings, etc.
3 words (8) Qualifications for membership

11 words A board has been designated for the use of your group. 10 words We hope that you will make good use of it.

Sincerely yours,

Now, I know what you're going to say: "Your second-to-last paragraph is really only one long sentence. Those 'suggestions' are merely a part of the introductory thought. They are not really separate sentences."

You are quite right—technically (that is, grammatically). But I'm not considering sentences from the grammatical point of view. I'm looking upon each of these "suggestions" as a separate idea—just the way Danny Lawson, Cal Poly Activities Officer, set this letter up. That's what he intended to convey—separate ideas, just as if they were in separate sentences.

In this illustration the sentences varied from 3 to 21 words, but each one is perfectly understandable. That brings me to the point I want to hammer home early in today's discussion: IT DOESN'T MATTER HOW MANY WORDS YOUR SENTENCES CONTAIN—WHAT REALLY COUNTS IS HOW EASY YOUR SENTENCES ARE TO UNDERSTAND AT THE FIRST READING.

Here is what Mr. Carl F. Braun has to say about sentence length in letters:

AVERAGE LENGTH For the sake of avoiding monotony, we want sentences of varying lengths—some short, some long, some medium. But let's not have any of them too long. Long sentences are hard to construct. They are apt to make difficult reading. If a reader spots one or two long sentences in a letter, he is apt to pass the whole letter up. But let's not go overboard. Too many short sentences sound choppy and juvenile. Ten words, on an average, is plenty—especially for an untrained writer. Twenty words is a good upper limit. But remember that a dash at the right spot in a sentence may provide a break that is just as effective as a period.[1]

◆   ◆   ◆   ◆

Now let's see whether we can list some suggestions about sentences—something that will help you dictate and write more easily understood thoughts.

1. *Avoid writing excessively short, choppy sentences.*

Although short sentences are to be preferred to long ones, your sentences should not be choppy, jerky, and childish, like these:

[1] Braun, Carl F., *Letter-Writing in Action,* pp. 98-99. Alhambra, California: C. F. Braun & Co., 1947.

Dear Sir:

I have your letter of the 10th. Thanks for your interest. We are glad to send you some catalogs. They describe all of our products. We hope they will help you. Call on us if you need more information. Thanks for writing.

Yours very truly,

There you have a seven-sentence letter that gives the impression of seventh-grade thinking. Why? Simply because the sentences are short and jerky. They insult the reader's intelligence. They sound as if they had been written for a child, not an adult.

Notice the number of words in each sentence: 7, 4, 8, 6, 6, 8, 3 respectively. Don't mistake me. I'm not against short sentences, but I certainly don't like this letter. Do you?

Although the writer used only 42 words in his 7 sentences, his letter is still too long. He could have written:

Dear Mr. Bryce:

Thanks for your letter of July 10. We are glad to send you catalogs describing all our products. We hope they will help you very much. Call on us if you need more information.

Sincerely yours,

There you have the same thoughts expressed in 4 sentences of 7, 11, 8, and 8 words respectively—a grand total of only 34 words. A better letter with 8 fewer words.

Here is another series of choppy sentences:

When the extinguisher is to be used, it is merely inverted. The acid is thereby mixed with the soda water solution. The acid mixing with the soda reacts chemically. Large amounts of carbon dioxide are formed. The formation of this carbon dioxide forces the water out of the container. The water thus forced out extinguishes the fire.

These sentences are not only short and choppy, but repetitious —6 sentences of 56 words, whereas 3 sentences of 43 words would have been more forceful:

When the extinguisher is to be used, it is merely inverted. This mixes the acid with the soda-water solution and causes a chemical reaction. The large amount of carbon dioxide formed forces water out of the container and puts out the fire.

2. *Avoid undue repetition in your sentences.*

The example given just before the last contains sentences that begin by repeating the last few words of the previous sentence. This is childish writing. Here is another example of repetitious writing, in which the writer says the same thing over and over without much progress:

In compliance with your request of March 10th, we are very much pleased and happy to enclose herewith considerable quantities of descriptive literature on various types of equipment and parts which we have manufactured in the past, as well as those parts and items which we are now currently manufacturing at the present time.

These 54 words merely repeat over and over what he has said. Here's how it could have been said in 3 sentences and 32 words:

Thanks for your request of March 10. We are glad to send you literature on our products. These bulletins describe equipment which we now manufacture, as well as our former products.

3. *Avoid stringy, long-winded sentences.*

Another kind of sentence to avoid is the long, stringy kind that we have already met in that impossible paragraph on page 23. For a moment, turn back and take a look at the original; then read the revision and determine which is easier to understand. Here is another of the same type:

With reference to your recent request, we are pleased to enclose herewith a quantity of literature relative to the products now being manufactured by this firm, which literature contains engineering data, prices and other various and sundry related information, which we trust you will find of value to you in your studies in college.

Around and around he goes! The writer of that 54-word monstrosity hated to let go of the ball, once he received it. Here's how this elephantine sentence could have been broken into more easily understandable bits:

Thanks for your recent request. We are glad to send you information about our products. This literature contains engineering data, prices, and other material which we are sure will be helpful in your studies.

There in 3 sentences and 34 words you have even more than the author crammed into his 54-word sentence.

4. *Avoid vague, muddled sentences.*

John Dryden, an Englishman who died in 1700, said that the first duty of the writer is to be understood. What a pity so few writers of business letters failed to hear about Dryden when they went to school! If your message isn't crystal clear, no matter how forceful, how friendly, how beautifully written, your reader won't understand you. Here is a mellifluous sentence that was written as a joke:

The voluminousness of the multiplicity of operations involved in the manufacture of the connecting rod renders such a description prohibitive.

Sounds like Federal gobbledegook—what someone has called "Federalese"—the kind of language that so many Federal directives, income-tax forms, and other documents are couched in. Well, that sentence sounds great, but what does it mean? Boiled down to 4- and 6-cylinder words, it means:

There are too many operations in the manufacture of connecting rods to describe all of them.

Here is another puzzler:

Our records indicate that you withdrew on January 15, 1949, on which date you were training as a student under Public Law 346, and have been automatically interrupted.

Who or what has been "automatically interrupted"? Maybe he meant:

Your training as a student under Public Law 346 was interrupted when you withdrew on January 15, 1949.

And still another:

I hope our services will bring you to our office still, and that it will not inconvenience you in any way.

I'm still wondering what he meant by "still," and whether "it" refers to "still."

Here is an amusing apocryphal story that came out of World War II: It seems that a foreman was having considerable trouble with a woman riveter. She wasn't doing her job right; so he decided to give her some personal instructions. After carefully going through the proper procedure several times, he gave her the hammer and said: "When I nod my head, you hit it with that hammer, understand?" She said she did. He nodded his head, and woke up in the hospital three days later!

Now for three more short examples of vagueness of pronouns:

From tests IT was found that IT took 400 pounds pressure to move the locator when IT was under ITS maximum load.

When the holes are drilled, they have burrs on the inside, and they must be taken off on a machine. [What, the holes?]

To move the locator, the operator must use a lead hammer and pound it in place. [The hammer?]

   5. *Avoid awkward sentences.*

Awkwardness is usually the result of haste or carelessness. One of the easiest ways of detecting awkwardness is reading your letters aloud. You can't always do that; so the next best thing is to read them carefully to yourself *before you sign them.* When you find an awkward or incorrect sentence, rewrite it on the page and then have your secretary retype it. Here are some examples of inexcusable awkwardness:

Awkward: Beauty is what all modern cars are trending to.

Improved: All modern cars are becoming more beautiful.

Awkward: It should be stated, that the Blue Print Room should in its files, contain every print which any use is made of in the plant.

Improved: The Blue Print Room should have in its files a copy of every print used in the plant.

Often awkwardness is the result of getting the order of words mixed up. Don't get the idea that there is only one correct order for the words in a sentence. Here is a sentence that can be written in four different ways—all equally good, all saying exactly the same thing:

(1)   (2)   The Receiving Department is   one of the most impor-
   (3)   tant units   in an assembly plant.

(2)   (3)   One of the most important units   in an assembly plant
   (1)   is   the Receiving Department.

(3)   (1)   In an assembly plant the Receiving Department is
   (2)   one of the most important units.

(3)   (2)   In an assembly plant   one of the most important units
   (1)   is   the Receiving Department.

Never let anyone tell you that there is only one right way to say something. Usually there are a number of correct ways, although one may be the best.

6. *Be sure that your words are in their proper places.*

Nothing can be quite so humorous—or so tragic—as getting your word order mixed up, as in this sentence:

The two lines show the difference in visibility, head room, foot room, and any other increase or decrease in dimension at a glance.

What the writer meant to say was:

The two lines show at a glance the difference in visibility, head room, foot room, and any other increase or decrease in dimension.

Here is another:

You will be entitled to a course of "Comprehensive Instructions" on the use of equipment purchased without further charge.

I'm sure he didn't mean what he said! He probably meant:

You will be entitled (without further charge) to a course of Comprehensive Instructions on the use of equipment purchased.

Quite different, isn't it? Now I'm going to play a trick on you, if I can. Here are five sentences identical in the number of words, identical in the words themselves, but different in the order in which those words have been set down, There is no punctuation, of course, except a period at the end of each one. Yet *every one of these five identically worded sentences is different!* You don't believe me? Then look for yourself:

1. *Only* I offered to buy the horse. (No one else offered.)
2. I *only* offered to buy the horse. (I didn't buy it—I merely offered.)
3. I offered *only* to buy the horse. (I didn't offer to feed or care for it.)
4. I offered to buy *only* the horse. (I didn't offer to buy the colt, the harness, the buggy, or anything except the horse.)
5. I offered to buy the *only* horse. (There was only one horse for sale and I offered to buy it.)

It's almost unbelievable that in a short sentence of only seven words there can be five different meanings—all because the little word "only" belongs to (or modifies) a different word! But it's true.

   7. *Avoid sentences that don't read smoothly or easily.*

Euphony is a 16-cylinder word, but it is very important in modern business letter-writing. Too many modern letters seem to have been literally hacked out of the writer's mind—they don't flow smoothly and easily. Behold:

In high school my attention centered in my intention of attending college after graduation.

Just try to read that sentence aloud. Then try this one:

While in high school, I became interested in attending college after I graduated.

   Here is another jaw-breaker:

This report gives a description of a few tests given gears produced on the gear-generating machines.

This revision is easier to read:

This report describes a few tests made on gears produced on gear-cutting machines.

   8. *Watch your punctuation.*

Yesterday we learned that the function of punctuation is to prevent misreading, and to provide minor pauses that refresh your reader. Today I want to talk about only one common error: jamming two complete thoughts into one, either with or without the use of a comma. This is a very serious mistake, **for it is very** confusing to the reader.

WRONG: Your representative was quite friendly and made me **feel** right at home, I guess he could see that I was very nervous.

RIGHT: Your representative was quite friendly and made me feel right at home. I guess he could see that I was very nervous.

WRONG: I have been accustomed for some time to deal with your sporting goods department up until the present I had always received courteous and satisfactory service.

BETTER: For some time I have bought things from your Sporting Goods Department. Until now I have always received courteous, satisfactory service.

9. *Avoid monotonous sentence patterns.*

Nothing is more boring than reading sentence after sentence beginning with the same word. Look back at those letters that had many sentences beginning with I—pages 11, 27, and **216;** and those beginning with WE—pages 12, 30, 33, and 34. They make pretty monotonous reading. And so does the following selection:

Cemented carbide is a metal which is made from the carbides of tungsten, titanium, molybdenum, and others. These carbides possess extraordinary hardness, high compressive strength, and less heat conductivity. Because of the brittleness of these carbides, they cannot be used as a tool bit in the same manner as high speed steel. These carbides must be brazed onto a bar of steel. Cemented carbides are able to withstand cutting speeds and temperatures many times that of high speed steel. [And so it goes on and on, each sentence opening with almost the same words.]

Here's how it could have been said less monotonously:

Cemented carbide, made from the carbides of tungsten, titanium, molybdenum, and other metals, has extraordinary hardness, high compressive strength, and less heat conductivity. Because of their brittle-ness, cemented carbides cannot be used as a tool bit, as high speed steel can. They must be brazed onto a bar of steel. However, they are able to withstand cutting speeds and temperatures much greater than high speed steel can withstand.

I don't want to close this discussion of sentences on a negative note. Here is a good letter that shows not only excellent sentence structure, but also careful paragraphing:

Dear Mr. Blank:

When you purchased your car, you undoubtedly made a careful examination of the motor, the body, and the interior. But how much attention did you give to the *tires?*

Perhaps your tires are in good shape both inside and out. It's also possible that a little attention given to them now will save you trouble and expense later.

Let us make a FREE inspection of your tires. We'll carefully examine them inch by inch. If we find anything that seems to require repair, we'll put it up to you for decision. When we've finished, you'll KNOW the condition of your tires and you'll have that knowledge completely FREE.

What's our angle? It's quite simple. We're betting that if we give you this free service now when you need it, you'll come back to us when you need new tires.

Give us a ring today and tell us when to expect you. Or just drive in.

Sincerely,

That's an excellent sales letter put out by the Goodyear Tire & Rubber Company. It's also an appropriate transition into the next part of today's discussion—

PARAGRAPHING

How would you like to have to plow through the following letter?

Dear Sir:

I am glad to send you, as you asked in your letter of November 10, my version of the accident which occurred at North Broad and Foothill Boulevard last Thursday evening at 6:45. Shortly after the traffic light had turned green for north- and south-bound cars—I presume eight or nine cars had crossed the intersection—an old woman started to cross Broad Street from the northwest corner. As nearly as I could see, she walked into the side of a south-bound car a little ahead of me and just to my right, and was knocked down. I stopped my car and went to her. When I reached her, she was unconscious, but regained consciousness by the time I lifted her into my car. With Officer James, No. 636, who was handling traffic at the corner, I drove her to the emergency ward of the Mountain View Hospital. When she got there, she was conscious, though somewhat dazed, and was bleeding slightly from a cut in her head. Shortly after we reached the hospital, the man whose car was directly involved in the accident arrived and gave his name and address to Officer James. I hope that these details will give you the information you want. At all events, it is as complete a version of the accident as I can give.

Very truly yours,

That's hard reading. Not because it isn't a good letter. It is. The sentences are short and clear. They have a definite "flow" from beginning to end. BUT THEY ARE TOO MUCH FOR ANYONE TO READ AND GRASP IN ONE MENTAL CHUNK. In other words, the writer simply failed to give his reader time to pause and refresh himself with suitable paragraph stops. Now let's see what magic thoughtful paragraphing can work:

Dear Sir:

I am glad to send you, as you asked in your letter of November 10, my version of the accident which occurred at North Broad and Foothill Boulevard last Thursday evening at 6:45.

Shortly after the traffic light had turned green for north- and southbound cars—I presume eight or nine cars had crossed the intersection— an old woman started to cross Broad Street from the northwest corner. As nearly as I could see, she walked into the side of a south-bound car a little ahead of me and just to my right, and was knocked down.

I stopped my car and went to her. When I reached her, she was unconscious, but regained consciousness by the time I lifted her into my car.

With Officer James, No. 636, who was handling traffic at the corner, I drove her to the emergency ward at the Mountain View Hospital. When she got there, she was conscious, though somewhat dazed, and was bleeding slightly from a cut in her head. Shortly after we reached the hospital, the man whose car was directly involved in the accident arrived and gave his name and address to Officer James,

I hope that these details will give you the information you want. At all events, it is as complete a version of the accident as I can give.

Very truly yours,

This is infinitely easier to read and digest. Few writers realize that there actually is such a thing as mental indigestion. Long, complicated sentences and paragraphs certainly can give your reader a bad case of it.

Here is another illustration of an overloaded paragraph:

The Audio-Visual Department plans to include in its 1953-54 budget a request for equipment and materials for instructors' use in preparing visual aids. Several departments have requested various materials for this purpose from time to time. We want to be able to supply these requests, as we realize that some of the best teaching aids are often those made by the teacher himself for his specific purpose. We have no way of knowing just what you would like to have available unless you tell us. We are thinking of materials and equipment for making such aids as large charts, graphs, posters, mounted pictures, prepared specimens, models, exhibit boards, etc.

This long paragraph can be made much easier to read and digest if it is broken up into shorter ones:

The Audio-Visual Department plans to include in its 1953-54 budget a request for equipment and materials for instructors' use in preparing visual aids.

From time to time, several departments have requested various materials for this purpose. We want to be able to supply these requests, for we realize that some of the best teaching aids are often those made by the teacher himself for his specific purpose.

We have no way of knowing just what you would like to have available unless you tell us. We are thinking of materials and equipment for making such aids as large charts, graphs, posters, mounted pictures, prepared specimens, models, exhibit boards, etc.

Why paragraph? Under what circumstances should you start a new paragraph?

1. *Paragraph for every new thought.*

2. *Paragraph for a change in the direction of your thought.*

3. *Paragraph for emphasis*—this is especially true in letters.

In your desire to make your letters readable, don't go to the other extreme and chop up your letters into too many short paragraphs:

Dear Dr. Mays:

Under separate cover we are sending you catalogs covering our complete line of equipment.

This will give you information concerning the construction of the units and specifications.

Also included is a Manual covering service and installations on vaporizing type of oil burners and gun type burners.

We believe you will find the above both useful and instructive. If we can be of further assistance to you, please let us know.

Yours truly,

Five sentences—five paragraphs! That's carrying paragraphing too far!

Dear Dr. Mays:

We are glad to send you catalogs of our complete line of equipment. They will give you information on the construction of each unit, as well as detailed specifications.

Also included is a manual on the servicing and installation of vaporizing types of oil burners and gun-type burners.

We believe that you will find this material useful and instructive. If we can help you any more, let us know.

At first I started merely to paragraph this letter, but it needed revision so badly that I did a complete face-lifting job on it. I don't want you to think that I am going back on one thing that I said earlier in this book.

Now, don't get the idea that all letters composed of one-sentence paragraphs are ineffective. That's not true. Here is an excellent letter by Mr. Paul R. Andrews, Vice-President of Prentice-Hall, Inc. Note that each paragraph is only one sentence long. But each paragraph contains either a different thought or a change in the direction of the thought. Note also the use of paragraphing for emphasis:

Dear Professor:

We are pleased to send you the enclosed booklet describing this widely-adopted text . . .

PRENTICE-HALL HANDBOOK FOR WRITERS

by Leggett, Mead, and Charvat

In outstandingly attractive format, the text presents the essentials of composition, mechanics, and grammatical usage in a concise, readable, and constructive way.

As their comments indicate, professors agree that this handbook is the practical teaching tool they need for their classes.

The accompanying booklet describes a number of the features your colleagues have found most useful . . . and illustrates many of these points with facsimile pages from the text itself.

You, of course, will find many more features of value to you and your students when you examine this text.

See for yourself. Mail the enclosed postage-free reply card today, and your copy will be sent promptly.

Sincerely yours,

Paragraphing in modern business writing bears a close resemblance to paragraphing in advertising copy—both are short and to the point, with never more than one idea to a paragraph.

PARAGRAPHS GIVE YOUR LETTERS EYE-APPEAL. The only reason why the letter on pages 216-217 is hard to read is that IT DOESN'T HAVE EYE-APPEAL! The reader's eye just can't take it in at a glance. His mind is repelled by the number of words that he has to plow through before he gets to the end of the thought.

The rewrite, however, does have pleasant eye-appeal. The paragraphs are comparatively short. In this version, the reader can take five stops to grasp the thought that he had to get in only one in the original.

Although the sentence is the unit of writing, the paragraph is our unit of thinking.

PARAGRAPH FORMS

Most people have the idea that there are just a few paragraph forms, That's not true. There are many different forms. The following are perhaps the most frequently used. All of them will give eye-appeal to *your* letters:

1. *Indented*—The oldest form, still in good repute today.

Dear Mr. Loring:

Here is the HORIZONTAL CAPACITY CHART that you requested. We hope it will prove useful in your studies.

If we can be of further service by sending you catalogs or bulletins of Armstrong products, just check and mail the enclosed business reply card.

Very truly yours,

2. *Block*—The most commonly used form today.

Dear Mr. Riebel:

Thank you very much for your recent letter. We are always happy to hear from another satisfied Times reader.

I am sure the enclosed clipping is the ad you referred to. It appears every week on page 1 of the Sunday section.

Sincerely,

3. *NOMA Simplified Form*—Suggested by the National Office Manager's Association, this form has many advantages, but as yet has not had the acceptance it really deserves:

July 27, 1952

Mr. John P. Riebel

1933 San Luis Drive

San Luis Obispo, California

AUTOMOBILE ACCIDENTS CAN BE REDUCED

I guess we all realize the terrific toll that highway accidents are taking. There are actually more casualties from highway accidents than from all our wars.

Anything that *can* be done to reduce these accidents *should* be done.

Goodyear *has* done something about it! What this is and how it works is being shown in a demonstration we have here at our store. I would like to have *you* drop in and see this demonstration. It takes only about five minutes, but . . .

. . . this little five-minute stop might save *your* life and the lives of others, as well!

And it can also save *you* money! So won't you drop in and look me up? Let me show you this unusual demonstration. There's no charge or obligation, of course.

Why not come in TODAY?

GOODYEAR TIRE STORE

4. *The Half-Page Form*—This novel device is especially good in collection and credit letters, and in getting replies to inquiries:

Dear Friend:

WILL YOU MEET US ....HALF-WAY?

                    Here's Our Half

You haven't been in for service for a
long, long time . . . and we don't know
the reason for your absence.

Perhaps you'll tell us. We realize there
are always two sides to every story, so
we've left the opposite half of this
letter for *your* side—the side we'd
very much like to get.

You see, we've missed you and we're
really concerned, for losing an old
customer is like losing an old
friend—we couldn't let either drift
away without finding the real reason.

Please meet us half-way, then, by
using the other half of this letter to tell
us just what is wrong. We'll consider
it a personal favor, for we really want
to straighten things out with you.

Thanks a lot.

            Sincerely,
            GLENDALE MOTOR CAR CO.

This is YOUR Half

5. *Overhanging*—Often used by Irving Mack, this form can be very effective, especially when the opening words have partic-

ular significance, as in this letter written by a former student of mine, D. Q. Miller:

Dear Member:

ACTION must spring from you, or the United Railroad Operating Crafts will fail in San Luis Obispo! Don't say: "I'm too busy to attend the meetings." Come this Sunday (May 20) at 10 A.M. to the meeting in the Carpenters' Union Hall at the corner of Chorro and Palm Streets.

RESULTS will spring from your action! Tell the fellow working with you, or the man in the locker room, to attend this Sunday's meeting. Only through an active membership will we have an active organization *that can get results!*

SUCCESS comes only after you and I and the next fellow place our full weight behind the UROC. Offioers to lead the organization must be elected, but first we will have to nominate candidates. Nominations will be made at the Sunday meeting for the following officers: President, General Secretary-Treasurer, and Vice Presidents.

BE SURE TO COME!

Sincerely yours,

D. Q. Miller, Secretary

6. *Varying Margins*—One of the best way of achieving emphasis (and eye-appeal, too) is by varying your paragraph margins:

Dear Friend of QUICK:

*If you are busy—busier perhaps than you have ever been before .
. .. . .* then I know you will welcome this invitation to become acquainted with QUICK—the pocket-sized news weekly that thousands of people are calling one of the greatest time and energy savers ever invented in the field of news reporting.

You will find QUICK *different from anything you have seen.* For it takes the vast mass of the week's news—cuts out the dull, unimportant detail . . . translates into plain English the double-talk of politicians, the gobbledegook of diplomats ...

. . . and in a few short, well-chosen words, tells you exactly what is happening in the world *this week.*

Then, after uncovering the basic facts . . . after carefully analyzing background material and relating it to events and developments in today's news, QUICK GOES OUT ON A LIMB . . .

> . . . and dares to predict what you and I may expect to happen in days and weeks to come!

Add to this . . . THE WEEK'S OUTSTANDING NEWS PHOTOS ... the best quips and quotes of the week in "WHAT THEY'RE SAYING" . . . facts and figures on the BUSINESS outlook, the TAX outlook, the BASKETBALL outlook . . . what's new in HEALTH and MEDICINE, in FOOD and FASHION, in EDUCATION and ENTERTAINMENT ... in literally every phase of human activity that you and I and the man down the street are interested in ...

. . . and then realize that you can cover all this ground in just a few minutes each week—in a magazine that makes it fun to keep informed !

That's why we are so anxious to put QUICK *in your hands* on a trial basis for a few weeks—so that you can see for yourself how much QUICK can do for you—how much of *your* time it can and will save.

Because QUICK'S up-to-the-latest-minute news content is printed simultaneously at Eastern, Midwestern, and Southern plants every week . . .

> . . . your own personal copy comes off the press just a few miles from your own home . . . and reaches your mailbox so promptly that QUICK'S crisp news summaries seem to stem directly from *today's* headlines 1

We are so convinced that you will become a QUICK fan immediately after receiving your first issue that we are enclosing a special $2.00 Discount Certificate, made out in your name, exclusively for your use. Endorsed and mailed to QUICK'S Des Moines, Iowa, Subscription Office, along with a $2.00 additional remittance of your own, this Certificate will bring you—

A FULL 40 WEEKS (MORE THAN NINE MONTHS) OF QUICK

. . . at the rate of just a nickel a copy! The newsstand price of 40 issues would be $4.00, but your certificate covers half of this—so you receive QUICK for the better part of a year *for just $2.00 of your own.*

And you take no risk. For, if after seeing and reading QUICK, you do not agree that it is all I say it is, you may cancel your subscription at any time and receive a full refund for the unused portion.

Publishing costs have risen tremendously—and they're still rising—so this offer is subject to withdrawal without notice. So please accept our invitation now *while the $2.00 price is still in effect.*

Cordially,

7. *Numbered paragraphs*—This is a very effective way of pin pointing essential information that you want to call to your reader's attention.

Dear Friends—

Now for the first time the people of the San Luis Obispo area have the opportunity of seeing not *one* but *TWO* really great foreign films on the same program!

That's right—not one but TWO great pictures:

1. *The Walls of Malapaga*—The Academy Award Winner as the
   best foreign film of 1951! and

2. *Adam and Evalyn*—A sprightly comedy, romance, and drama
   all in one delightful picture!

The Walls of Malapaga is a fine dramatic effort utilizing the joint talents of Italian and French players, writers, and director—but with an American cameraman! This is one picture in which language is no barrier to an appreciation of fine motion-picture artistry. Although the dialogue is bi-lingual (French and Italian) there are English subscripts. American audiences have no difficulty in following the tense exposition.

Adam and Evalyn is a perfect counterpart to *The Walls of Malapaga.* It relates the adventures of a young girl in an orphan asylum and the delightful situations which she gets into through corresponding with her father. But he used the name of a friend, Adam Black, and even sent her Adam's picture as his own! The father is ...

But I'm not going to tell you the rest of this sprightly comedy. I want you to get the full enjoyment by seeing for yourself just what comes next!

So ... just make a date *now* to come to the Elmo Theatre in San Luis Obispo on Wednesday or Thursday—January 23 or 24—for a most delightful evening's entertainment.

How about passing on this information to some friend you think will enjoy seeing these two outstanding pictures?

Cordially yours,

8. *Unusual*—The different paragraph forms are limited only

by limits to the writer's imagination. I could go on and on, with example after example. Instead, 111 show you two of the most striking I have ever seen. Neither uses salutation:

PERSONAL: TO THE COLLECTOR
WHO IS LOOKING TO MAKE A $

DON'T BE MIS-INFORMED WHEN YOU
BUY U.S. STAMPS FOR INVESTMENT!

GET YOURSELF A GOOD INVESTMENT
GUIDE—FOLLOW IT AND PROFIT!

GET THE MOST IMPORTANT, MOST
PRACTICAL GUIDE AVAILABLE-GET
"PRICE PREDICTIONS ON U.S. STAMPS"
(2 vols.) BY GRANVILLE

SEE THE ENCLOSED CIRCULAR FOR
COMPLETED DETAILS AND ORDER FORM

Sincerely yours, H. L.
LINDQUIST
Publications

P. S. We're serious. If this isn't the best guide to the best buys in the U.S. field you ever saw, send it back within 5 days for full and immediate refund.

H.L.L.

This unusual letter is self-explanatory. I'm sure you'll enjoy reading it, and maybe it will give you some good ideas for writing terse, concise sales letters:

This is a sample of the "new thought group idea" of letter writing. Why not try it and see if it is easier to read than ordinary writing?

You	products	like	best electric
want	that	Toastmaster	water
more	sell easy	for instance	heater
Won't lime	in	people	Toastmaster
or	hardest	want	is highest
scale	water	quality	quality
Price	people	sell	use
is	won't	10%	ABC
secondary	resist	down	Budget Plan

see	FOR TOASTMASTERS
or	AND
call us	ABC BUDGET PLAN

N. O. NELSON CO.

P.S. What do you think of it? Fun? You'll have more fun selling Toastmasters—they're easy to sell if you talk up the features and you'll see that price is actually secondary.

♦   ♦   ♦   ♦

My last example is a letter with such unusual paragraphing that I must show it to you. This letter was written by Mr. Doug Scott, of the Doug Scott Advertising Services, 3 Frederick Place, Ottawa, Canada. When I wrote to Mr. Scott asking permission to use this unique letter, here is what he replied, in part:

These letters were written for an engineering supply outfit here who pride themselves on giving extra fast service to their clients, and they have built a nice business on that angle. If a client wants a certain machine part, they will phone or wire to any part of the country for it and bring it in by Air Express where necessary. Hence the copy slant in the letter, to remind their clients of the kind of service they offer. The letters were individually typed on automatic typewriters, and the baseball players were run on from a Multilith plate. I have a battery of Robotypers as part of my operation, and as you can imagine, it was some fun setting up the master record to type in this form.

This just goes to show you what the possibilities are if you use a little ingenuity in setting up your form letters. More power to you—only be careful about throwing your customer too many curves. The Scott letter is reproduced on page 228.

In closing today's discussion of the pauses that refresh your readers, I want to leave some suggestions for improving your sentences and giving your paragraphs eye-appeal.

Sentences:
1. Make your sentences short and easy to read, but not choppy.
2. Make your thoughts complete.
3. Make every sentence have a point and a purpose.
4. Vary your sentence structure so as not to bore or tire your reader.

TEN BAYSWATER AVENUE

April 30

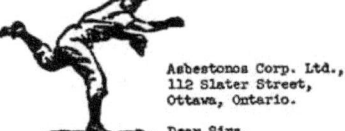

Asbestonos Corp. Ltd.,
112 Slater Street,
Ottawa, Ontario.

Dear Sirs,

                        Baseball
                 time's here again..and
               we like to think of our re-
             lationship with you and your firm
           in terms of the way a good ball team
          works. You're the pitcher, let us say,
         and we're on first. When you toss us
        an order or enquiry, we try always to be in
       a position to handle it. Maybe it is a real-
      ly snappy throw, when you're in a spot and
     speed means everything. Or maybe it's a case
    of a double or triple play, where we not only
    have to make a fast catch of your throw, but
    have to get it to the next man in a hurry, in
     order to complete the play. We're proud to
      be on the same team with you and we take a
       lot of pleasure in our past record of be-
        ing able to handle anything you can
          throw at us, no matter how fast you
           toss them. So just keep your or-
             ders coming our way - and we
               will   do our best to
                    merit them.

                        Yours sincerely,

                        LEGERE ENGINEERING SUPPLIES LTD.

                        A.W. Legere, President.

5. Test your sentences by asking yourselves three questions:
   A. Does it read smoothly?
   B. Can I understand it on the first reading?
   C. Will my reader be able to understand it on the first read ing?

Paragraphs:

1. Make your paragraphs as short as possible, but not choppy.

2. Paragraph not only for a change of thought, but also for a change in the direction of the flow of thought.
3. Have some definite order in your presentation of your facts.
4. Paragraph for eye-appeal.
5. Develop your ideas presented by using one or more of the following methods:

   A. Definition and/or explanation, analysis
   B. Description, details, classification
   C. Reasons or proof, sales appeals, reasons why
   D. Facts, examples, illustrations
   E. Question and answer; a series of questions
   F. A plea for action, or an explanation of what you are doing for the reader
   G. An explanation of how to do something
   H. A quotation from an acknowledged authority, a testimonial
   I. Repetition—statement and restatement of your point J. Cause to effect; effect to cause; purpose to result; result to purpose
K. History, time sequence, narrative, story, anecdote L. Comparison and contrast; similarity, difference M. Any other method that will help your reader better understand your ideas and points.

6. Link your thoughts within your paragraphs, as well as each paragraph with the others in the letter.
7. Have flow from one thought to the next. This can be achieved best by the careful use of—

   A. *Connectives*—conjunctions (and, but, since, because, after, when, etc.)
           prepositions (in, on, by, without, for, etc.) linking words or phrases (first, then, next, thereafter, finally, of course, for instance, etc.)

   B. *Repetition* —Either repeating the same word or using a synonym.

   C. *Pronouns* —Among the best connecting words we have

are our many pronouns—words that
take the place of nouns: personal (I, my,
you, your, yours, they,

his, she, etc.) demonstrative (this, that,
these, those,

etc.) relative (who, whose, whom,
which, that,

what, whatever, etc.) indefinite (some,
any, all, no, each, every,

one, etc.) compound (whatever,
whosoever, anyone,

something, etc.)

8. Use any mechanical aids to give your paragraphs punch and
   pull.
9. Don't be afraid to experiment with your paragraph form
   until you get the exact effect you want. THERE IS
   NOTHING SACRED ABOUT THE PARAGRAPH OR
   PARAGRAPH FORM, as you probably realize now.

NOW THE DAYS ARE OVER

Our daily studies have drawn to a close and you are about to step out boldly on your own, to face your daily quota of letters, to talk to your unseen friends through your letters, to let your own personality shine through the typed or mimeographed page in broad, friendly smiles.

Here are a few brief points that I should like to leave with you —a summary of my own philosophy of life and of letter writing. These are what I consider the twelve cardinal points of successful business letter writing:

1. *Think of your reader first—of yourself last.*
2. *Dictate with a big YOU.*
3. *Make marginal notes on every letter you read, as you read it.*
4. *Plan each letter carefully, thoughtfully.*
5. *Tabulate and/or number your points for clarity.*
6. *Your opening and your closing sentences are two especially important parts of your letter.*
7. *Know what you want to say—then be sure you have said it.*
8. *Keep a chronological file of carbon copies of your own letters for study and ready reference.*
9. *Start your own collection of business letters for criticism and for ideas.*
10. *Read your letters carefully before you sign and mail them,*
11. *Join the American Business Writing Association, Urbana, Illinois, and read everything you can about modern business letters.*
12. *Remember: Letter writing is your best and cheapest form of public-customer relations.*

231

In closing, I want to share with you a masterpiece by Stanley Marcus of that great store, Nieman-Marcus in Dallas, Texas. This letter practices what I have so religiously preached throughout this book:

Dear Mrs. Sewell:

It is with genuine pleasure that we have opened a charge account for you, and we want you to know that this means considerably more to us than a mere formality. Having a charge account has come to rep-' resent good will, and that to us is a point of great importance.

Good will in this sense means simply a natural inclination on your part to deal with those who have pleased you. We shall endeavor in each transaction to show you that we deserve such an indication of your confidence.

You have every right to expect that all of us at Nieman-Marcus will do everything that we can to make you satisfied both with our merchandise and with the way in which it is supplied. It is a tradition of Nieman-Marcus to prefer to conduct our business in the manner of friends, and we are rather particular in choosing for our staff people who like to be pleasant.

If any one of us should ever fall short of your expectations, as humans sometimes do, we would consider it a favor of you to let us know.

Sincerely yours,
Stanley Marcus

NEVER UNDERESTIMATE THE POWER OF A LETTER!

MODERNIZING HACKNEYED EXPRESSIONS

Too OFTEN THE POSTSCRIPT to a letter is merely an afterthought —something that should have been added to the body of thought, but somehow was left out. Not so with this postscript, or Appendix. I didn't forget it when I was writing this book.

Instead, I have purposely put this alphabetical list of trite business-letter expressions in this Appendix because I think they make better reference material than straight reading. In some respects, this portion may contain some of the most useful information in this entire book. Here's why:

Whenever you are wondering about one of your own pet expressions, check it against this list. If it appears here, it is threadbare and should be eliminated; if it does not appear here, it probably is fresh and forceful, usable in modern, successful business letters.

Like anything that is overworked, any spoken or written expression can lose its brightness and punch. That is why these expressions have become hackneyed and stale. So without further ado, let's turn to the most extensive list of lifeless words and phrases that I have met anywhere—and then see how easily they can be modernized, humanized, and vitalized.

1. *above, the above*—vague, old-fashioned, and
hackneyed. I am interested in *the above*. May I have
the above information?

Instead, say exactly what you mean (parts, items, service, catalogs, etc.), or use "it," "them."

> I am interested in your service program. *Or,* I am interested in it. May I have this information? *Or,* May I have them?

2. *above-mentioned, above-listed*—trite and ungrammatical; stilted and stiff.

> Your #2 brick can be sent in the same car as your order for the *above-mentioned* items.
> When can you ship the *above-listed* parts?

If you *must* use "above," then place it after the word "mentioned" or "listed."

> Your #2 brick can be sent in the same car as your order for cement and Spanish tile.
> When can you ship these parts? *Or,* When can you ship the parts mentioned above?

3. *accordance, in accordance with*—wordy and stilted.

> *In accordance with* your request, we are sending you herewith two price lists.
> *In accordance with* this request, we are pleased to forward to your attention under separate cover copy of our latest catalog.

Rather, say "according to," "in," "as," or omit entirely.

> As you requested, here are two of our latest price lists. *Or,* Here are the latest price lists, which you requested. We are glad to send you a copy of our latest catalog.

4. *acknowledge*—a cold and lifeless word when used as follows:

> This will *acknowledge* receipt of your post card requesting literature describing our products.
> I am pleased to *acknowledge* your letter of March 31st. We *acknowledge* with thanks your letter dated October 28, 19—, in which you advise us that you are writing a thesis on ....

Be friendly and natural—it doesn't cost any more.

> Thanks for your request for literature about our .... (Use your trade name—that is good, free advertising!)
> Thank you for your letter of March 31. (The "st," "nd," "rd" aren't necessary after the date.)
> Thanks for your letter of October 28. We are glad to know

MODERNIZING HACKNEYED EXPRESSIONS   235

that you are writing a thesis on .... (Certainly "19—" is not necessary this late in the year.)

5. *advise*—one of the most sadly overworked words in modern business correspondence. Eliminate this word.

> Please *advise* which design you want. Please be *advised* that your order has been shipped. Yesterday I was *advised* that the Black Construction Company is the general contractor on this job.
>
> We regret to *advise* that we will not ship the order for five dozen style #645 which we received by mail today.

Use "advise" *only* when you actually give advice. Otherwise say "told," "said," "written," "notified," "indicated," etc.

> Please indicate which design you want. You will be glad to know that your order has been shipped. Yesterday I heard ("learned," "found out," etc.) that the Black Construction Company is the general contractor on this job.
>
> We will not ship your order for five dozen style #645, which we received today. (This is stronger and more direct. It also does not put the writer in the ridiculous position of regretting something that he voluntarily refuses to do.)

6. *aforementioned*—very stiff, old-fashioned, and legalistic.

> We do not feel that, under the *aforementioned* circumstances, we are qualified to impart to you the information requested.

This word could well be eliminated from business correspondence. You never use it in your conversation, do you? Then don't use it in your business letters.

> Under these circumstances, we do not feel qualified to give you this information. *Or,*
>
> Under these circumstances, we are not qualified to answer your questions.

7. *agreeable*—Of course, it's perfectly O.K. to be agreeable, but please don't use the word in this way:

> *Agreeable* to your request, we are pleased to send you under separate cover a wiring diagram of our heavy-duty press, X-5378.

Instead, say it naturally by writing:

> As you requested, we are glad to send you a wiring diagram of our heavy-duty press, X-5378.

8. *amount*—a perfectly respectable word except in the phrase "in the amount of."

> Your check *in the amount of* $165.73 has been received. (This is a silly thing to say, isn't it? It's also wordy.)

Why not use the simple Anglo-Saxon preposition "for"?

> Thanks for your $165.73 check. *Or,* Thanks for your check for $165.73. (Either of these revisions says something worth hearing. They are shorter, too.)

9. *anticipate*—as a word meaning "to expect." It really means "to look forward to." Although sometimes used separately, it is used most frequently with another hackneyed, silly expression, "in a position to."

> We *anticipate* with pleasure having you with us, and assure you we will do our utmost to make your stay most pleasant and enjoyable. (Too effusive.)

> We *anticipate* we will be able to ship your order Monday. We *anticipate* that we will be *in a position to* ship your order within the very near future. (Words! Words! Words!)

Wherever possible, use simple rather than scholarly, pedantic words. The simpler the word, the more likely is it that your reader will understand it, and the less likely is it that you will get tangled up in your expression.

> It will be a pleasure to have you with us. You may be sure that we'll do our best to make your visit enjoyable (or "memorable").

> We expect to ship your order Monday. *Or,* We'll ship your order Monday.

> We can ship your order soon. (Look how much shorter and better that sentence is. It comes to the point quickly and surely.)

10. *appreciate*—It's only natural to appreciate things, such as good service, prompt delivery, etc. But don't be awkward about it, as in the "appreciate it if you would" combination.

> We would *appreciate it if you would* furnish Mr. Jones one of our handbooks.

> I'll *appreciate it if you will* have these names checked before mailing the books.

> I should *appreciate it very much if you would* get in touch with me immediately.

It's so easy to avoid awkward, wordy constructions. Our trouble is usually habit—we get in the habit of using awkward expressions, and we hate to give them up, or to have to think of some bright, new substitute.

>We should appreciate your sending Mr. Jones one of our handbooks.
>
>Won't you please have these names checked before mailing the books?
>
>Get in touch with me immediately, won't you?

11. as *per*—Besides being a mongrel hybrid of Anglo-Saxon "as" and Latin "per," this combination is very old-fashioned and trite.

>*As per* your letter of the 15th to hand, beg to state that we are giving your proposition due consideration. (Not only hackneyed, but also confusing.)

Resolve right now never, NEVER to use this expression; write "in," "according to," or something else simple and natural.

>We are glad to consider the offer given in your letter of May 15. (Is this what he meant to say? I don't know. Your guess is as good as mine. Trite expressions are often confusing.)

12. *at all times*—wordy for "always."

>We are *at all times* glad to be of assistance to you.

Instead, write "always."

>We are always glad to be of assistance to you.

13. *at an early date*—also wordy.

>We will contact you *at an early date.* Why

not use the simple word "soon"? We shall

write you soon.

14. *attached hereto, attached herewith*—the height of silliness! How could you attach it in any other way?

Attached herewith is our check in the amount of $5.67. Our

latest revised price list is *attached hereto.* Omit "hereto" or

"herewith." They are unnecessary.

>Attached is our check for $5.67. *Or,* Our check for $5.67 is attached.
>
>Here is our latest price list. *Or,* Attached is our latest price list.

15. *attention*—It's perfectly proper to pay attention, but don't send something to someone's "attention."

>Please address your letter to my personal *attention.*

Instead, send it to him, and he'll probably give it his personal attention.

Please address your letter to me personally.

16. *at this time, at the present writing*—wordy and trite.

> *At this time* we are prepared to make you a very attractive offer.

> Mr. Smith is, *at the present writing,* on vacation. Use

"now," "today," or omit entirely.

> We can now make you a very attractive (or "good") offer. Mr. Smith is now on vacation. *Or,* Mr. Smith is on vacation.

17. *avail*—"avail" means "to have force or efficiency," "to be of use; serve," etc. "Avail yourself of" is illogical, wordy, and moss-covered.

> *Avail yourself of* this opportunity to purchase these sport coats at half price!

Say something simple, and say it simply! Why not say "take advantage of"?

> Take advantage of this opportunity to buy handsome, quick-selling, all-wool sport coats, beautifully tailored in the latest styles—at only half their usual price! (Remember, every letter *is* a sales letter, as you learned on the Eleventh Day.)

18. *balance*—incorrectly used for "rest" or "remainder" except when referring to a bank balance.

> The *balance* of your order will be shipped February 1.

Instead, use "rest" or "remainder."

> The rest (or "remainder") of your order will be shipped February 1.

19. *beg*—*DON'T!* In modern business correspondence, you don't have to beg. This word is sadly overworked.

> We *beg* to acknowledge receipt of your order of recent date. For your information, *beg* to call to your attention that the transaction which we had with you last season did not turn out satisfactory. (Wordy and ungrammatical.)

Omit this word entirely. Don't be a beggar in your letter-writing.

> Thanks for your letter of.............. (Be specific—give the exact date.)

> As you will remember, we were not pleased with the way you paid your bill last season.

20. *be good enough to*—a very annoying phrase, chiefly because of its implication: "If you don't do what is requested, you are a bad, bad boy."

> Would you *be good enough to* send me a list of dealers who make a specialty of this kind of service?

Although I don't like the word "please," as you will see when we come to that word, it certainly is preferable to "be good enough to."

> Would you please send (or "mind sending") me the names of dealers who specialize in this kind of service?

21. *claim*—This is almost a fighting word in business correspondence.

Although the claim letter is a definite type, forceful letter-writers avoid using this word because it is irritating.

> The letter about breakage which you *claim* was caused by our driver's negligence has been received. (A stupid, cold, insulting sentence that will annoy your reader and immediately put him on the defensive.)

> He *claimed* the reason he hadn't answered sooner was that he didn't know any names to suggest. (You really doubt his word, don't you?)

The word "claim" can be eliminated completely from business correspondence if you will only say what you have to say in courteous, considerate language. There is no need to irritate further a customer who already is annoyed.

> Thank you for your letter about the breakage that you believe was caused by our driver's negligence. *Or,* We certainly appreciate your calling to our attention the breakage that, in your opinion, was caused by our driver's negligence. He said that he did not answer sooner because he had no names to suggest. (This at least gives him the benefit of any doubt that might exist. In this case, you can afford to be generous, since it doesn't cost you one penny.)

22. *client*—generally reserved for the customers of professional people, especially lawyers.

> From all the information I can gather, I don't think Mr. Jones in Mudville will make a very satisfactory *client*. We have taken the liberty of expressing a sample of each of the above, so that you may submit same to your *client*. (This one's a dilly, isn't it?)

Don't be afraid to call a customer a customer. He'll like that. Call him a client and hell be afraid that you plan to give him the works,

From all that I hear, I don't think that Mr. Jones in Mud-ville will make us a very satisfactory customer. He doesn't pay his bills.

You can show your customer the sample hangers sent you by prepaid express.

23. *command me*—This expression was O.K. a couple of hundred years ago, when men were ruled by kings with iron hands and had little or no freedom of their own.

If I can be of any service along the insurance line, kindly *command me*. (And be sure you do it gently.)

Today, most of you reading these words live in a democracy, where you are relatively free of commands. People react better to suggestions.

If I can help you with your insurance problems, just write me.

24. *complaint, your complaint*—more fighting words! Avoid if at all possible.

We have received *your complaint* about our last shipment of parts.

It will be necessary to investigate the *complaint* before coming to a conclusion.

Instead of saying "complaint," why not use "suggestion," "request," "comments," etc.?

We are glad to have your comments about our last shipment of parts.

You may be sure that we shall investigate this matter and let you know our decision.

25. *compliance, comply with*—old-fashioned use of these words.

After due consideration, we have decided *to comply with* your terms. (Nice of them, wasn't it?)

In compliance with your recent request, we are pleased to enclose herewith copy of our latest catalog.

Say it naturally, in nickel and dime words that any reader can understand.

We agree to your terms. *Or,* Your terms are quite satisfactory.

We are glad to send you our latest catalog, which you requested.

26. *confined*—sounds too much as if someone or something is in jail or in a hospital.

Our production at the present time is *confined* to that of producing domestic ice refrigerators. (Sounds like some kind of double talk.)

Why not use "limited" or "restricted"?

Our production is now limited to domestic ice refrigerators. *Or,* We are now making only domestic ice refrigerators.

27. *consensus of opinion*—redundant; "consensus" includes "opinion."

The *consensus of opinion* around here is that Joe is soon to be replaced.

Use "consensus" by itself—drop off the words "of opinion" and you'll be 100 per cent right.

The consensus here is ... *Or,* Around here, we think that Joe will soon be replaced.

28. *contact*—a sadly overworked word.

Contact us at any time.

Will you *contact* Bill and give him this information? Be specific and say "write," "call," or "telephone." / Write us at any time. Will you give Bill this information?

29. *contemplating*—This means "to observe thoughtfully." Remember that.

We are *contemplating* installing a public address system in our Taft plant. (They are meditating or cogitating on the problem.)

Say what you have to say simply, naturally, and interestingly. Don't go high-hat on us.

We are thinking about installing a public address system in our Taft plant. (That's more like plain talking.)

30. *contents noted*—These words are insulting! The least I expect from a company is to read my business letter without bragging that they have read it.

Your letter of the 26th to hand and *contents noted.*

Just use plain common sense when you write. Put yourself in your reader's place and ask yourself how you would like to receive what you have written.

Thanks for your letter of June 26.

31. *costs the sum of*—wordy, repetitious.

This part *costs the sum of* $6.00 wholesale. It retails *for the sum of* $9.50. Simply use the word "costs."

This part costs $6 wholesale and retails for $9.50.

32. *cover*—another loosely used word. Always reminds me of a blanket.

The check enclosed herewith *covers* your expenses to and from Santa Monica.
We are enclosing our line folders *covering* our sealed condensing units.

Generally speaking, the prepositions "for," "on," or "about" are good substitutes. Or use an appropriate verb.

Here is a check for your expenses to and from Santa Monica.
Enclosed are folders describing our sealed condensing units.

33. *data*—This is the plural form of the Latin word *datum,* which is singular. It is therefore incorrect to say:

This *data* is incorrect and incomplete.

Avoid using this overworked word. In its place, use "information," "facts," etc.

This information is (or "These facts are") incomplete and incorrect.

34. *date, at an early date, to date, recent date, under date of*—trite and hackneyed language.

Under date of January 5, we have your cancellation of Order #4562. Is this right?
We can hold a committee meeting *at an early date.*
To date no word has been received concerning the status of your application.
Your letter of *recent date* received and contents noted.

Be specific. Give the exact date, or say "recently," "as yet," "soon," etc.

Are we correct in cancelling your order #4562 as requested in your letter of January 5?
We can hold a committee meeting soon (or "tomorrow afternoon").
As yet we do not know whether your application has been accepted.
Thanks for your recent letter. *Or,* Thanks for your letter of December 31.

35. *depleted*—trite and overworked.

> Our stock of part #25397 is completely *depleted.* Say

what you have to say simply and naturally:

> We have completely sold out of part #25397. *Or,* We have no more part #25397 in stock.

36. *due to*—It is not good practice to start a sentence with "due to."

> *Due to* a previous engagement, I cannot meet you tomorrow, as we planned.

> My secretary is ill, *due to* pneumonia. (This is very bad.)

Instead of starting your sentences or main clauses with "due to," use "because of."

> Because of a previous engagement, I cannot meet you tomorrow, as we planned. My secretary has pneumonia.

37. *due to the fact that*—wordy.

> *Due to the fact that* our production is running far behind schedule, we will have to change the delivery date on your Order No. 756.

> This type of breakage and loss has been rather common in the past *due to the fact that* the paper sacks are on rough railroad car floors, which chew the bags open during transit.

Just use "since" or "because."

> Because our production is running far behind schedule, we shall have to change the delivery date on your order No. 756. This type of breakage or loss has been rather common in the past, since the paper sacks of cement are stacked on rough railroad cars, which chew the bags open during transit.

38. *in due course of time*—stiff, stuffy, snobbish. It means: "Keep your shirt on. Don't rush me. I'll get around to you when I feel like it."

> We received your order and it will be processed *in due course of time.*

Be positive. At least, it won't hurt to say "as soon as we can."

> Thanks for your order. We'll ship it just as soon as we can. (This rewrite really says something worth hearing, and in a friendly, courteous way.)

39. *duly*—another pompous, officious, supercilious word that should seldom be used.

We hope the books will be *duly* received in good shape.

Please forget this word, and you'll write far more successful letters.

We hope that the books will arrive in good condition.

40. *each and every*—a form of doubling that, illogically, has become very popular among certain letter-writers, who consider it forceful.

Each and every one of us wishes you a very pleasant trip home.

Use one word or the other—not both. We Americans tend to use doublings: "first and foremost," "the sum total of," etc.

Each of us wishes you a very pleasant trip. *Or,* All of us wish you a very pleasant trip.

41. *earliest convenience*—My "earliest convenience" is when I'm ready, not before.

Please send me your bid at your *earliest convenience.*

Will you do this job at your *earliest convenience?*

Instead, say "immediately," "soon," "promptly." Or better still, be specific and give the exact time; then there can be no room for doubt or misunderstanding.

Please send us your bid by noon Friday, December 21.

Will you do this immediately?

42. *to the effect that*—wordy for plain, simple "reported that."

Jones reported *to the effect that* our production rate had dropped 33 per cent last month.

Don't pad your letters just for effect. Streamline them as much as possible.

Jones reported that our production rate had dropped 33 per cent last month.

43. *esteemed*—This means "highly regarded," a qualification unlikely to be applicable to a business letter. It's pompous, servile, and antiquated.

Your *esteemed* order has been duly received and will be duly processed. (Now, how silly can a writer get?)

Be yourself! Be natural and contemporary. "Esteemed" was indeed much used fifty or a hundred years ago.

Thanks for your order, which will be handled with our usual promptness. (This is something your reader will be delighted to hear.)

44. *even date*—Does this mean today? Yesterday?

> Your letter of *even date* to hand and contents noted.

Be specific. Give the date of the letter you are answering. Then there can be no doubt.

> Thanks very much, Mr. Neill, for your letter of December 31.

45. *in the event that*—wordy.

> *In the event that* you want samples, kindly advise. Just use "if" and your letter will be much more forceful. If you want samples, just let me know.

46. *favor*—Call a letter a letter, not a favor or an esteemed com munication. Is a complaint or a cancellation a "favor"?

> Your esteemed *favor* of the 12th inst. has been received. (Shades of Major Hoople!)

Call a spade a spade, and a letter a letter. A rose by any other name would smell as sweet. Shakespeare said that. But he also said: "Name me no names!"

> I was delighted to read your encouraging letter of July 27.

47. *feel*—Too many correspondents do too much "feeling" in their letters.

> We *feel* our experience in this line of work is considerable. (Sounds silly to me. What do *you* think?)
> We feel you will understand. (Keep your hands to yourself, please!)

Don't go around "feeling" this or that or the other. Instead of this weak word, use a stronger one: "think," "believe," "know," etc.

> We have had considerable experience in this type of work. *Or,* Our experience in this type of work has been extensive. We are sure you will understand. (You see, it can be said without "feeling" anything.)

48. *feel free to*—Every time I hear or read this expression, I feel like screaming. I don't need anyone to tell me I can "feel free." Do *you?*

> Please *feel free* to advise the writer. (Just try it and see what happens.)
> *Feel free* to contact the writer for any further information desired. (Very pompous.)
> Please *feel free* to contact us at any time.
> You are perfectly *free* to rewrite this or edit it in any man-

ner you think would improve its presentation. (I appreciated the permission, but not the language.)

It's dandy when a letter-writer is magnanimous, but when he swells up with his own importance and graciously allows me to "feel free" ...?!? Say "please" or "just" or "Why not ... ?"

> Won't you please give me your suggestion? *Or,* Send me your suggestion, if you will.

> If you want any more information, just let me know. (That's the way you would *say* it to him in person. Why write language you wouldn't speak?)

> Please write to us at any time. *Or,* Please call us at any time.

> Just rewrite or edit this material in any way that you think will improve it. (Simpler and more natural, forceful.)

49. *field*—Here is another bit of jargon at which Sir Arthur Quiller-Couch took such a delightful crack in his essay "On Jargon." If only more of our so-called modern business letter-writers would read this essay.

> The accompanying report, entitled *The Functions of the Layout Department,* has been written as the result of my past month's experience in this *field.*

> I should like a job in the Works Engineering *field,* if they have a job open.

> The *field* of refrigeration is one that is growing rapidly. The *field* of welding has found innumerable applications in which it excels. (Let's go over that one again. Who did what to whom and why?)

> The cost of lamps per lamp life is much less in the fluorescent *field.*

> The plastic *field* has grown to be a very outstanding industry.

> This subject covers a very large *field.*

Quiller-Couch did not limit his invectives to "field" alone, but took healthy pokes at the other stocks-in-trade of the professional jargoneer: "case," "nature," "character," "instance," "condition," "degree," and others. Read "On Jargon" sometime.

> The accompanying report, *The Functions of the Layout Department,* has been written as the result of my last month's experience in this department.

> I should like to be in the Works Engineering Department, if there is a job open. Refrigeration is becoming increasingly important.

In many types of construction, welding is superior to riveting, bolting, or any other method of joining two metals. (Be as specific as you can.)

Fluorescent lamps are cheaper to maintain than any other type.

The plastic industry has become quite important economically. This subject is very extensive.

50. *find*—another perfectly good, simple word sadly overworked by many letter-writers.

Enclosed you will *find* suggested specifications for heating and ventilating ducts. (Why make your reader hunt?) Also *find,* with our compliments, our handy pressure temperature chart ruler which you will *find* a useful addition to your tool kit. (He likes doubling—makes his reader hunt twice in the same sentence.) You will *find* this information enclosed.

Omit this word, and your letter will certainly be more forceful and natural.

Enclosed are some suggested specifications for heating and ventilating ducts. (Here you don't have to hunt for either the specifications or the ducts.)

We are glad to send you one of our handy pressure-temperature chart rulers. This will be a useful addition to your tool kit. (Whenever your sentences begin to get too long, look for places where you can cut them into two.) This information is enclosed. *Or,* Enclosed is this information. (Some people just can't write simply. They have to mix up their words for good measure.)

51. *first and foremost*—another example of doubling.

First and foremost, let me say that we are very *pleased and happy* to receive your letter communication. (This writer doesn't know when to stop doubling.)

If you omit "and foremost," you probably will have a very acceptable sentence.

First, we are pleased to have your letter of ... (date). (See how simple and easy it is? Just like talking to him. Simple words are more forceful.)

52. *first of all*—wordy for "first."

First of all, your letter was delayed a week due to the Christmas rush, I presume. (Stiff and unfriendly.)

Omit "of all," or omit the entire expression, if you wish.

> Your letter was delayed because of the Christmas rush, I am sure.

53. *hand, to hand, at hand*—too many "hands" also spoil the letter.

> We *hand* you our latest quotation, enclosed herein. (Then why send it through the mail? You're inconsistent.) Your letter of the 26th *to hand* and contents noted. (Wow!!!!!)

I have *in my hand* your letter of recent date which I am now answering. (Now you have heard everything.) Your letter of the 15th is *at hand.* Be natural, simple, conversational.

> Enclosed is our latest quotation. *Or,* Our latest quotation is enclosed.
>
> I am glad to have your letter of February 29.
>
> It is a pleasure to answer your letter of ... (date). *Or,*
> I am delighted to answer your recent letter. (If you don't know the date, use the second revision.)
>
> Thanks for your letter of January 15.

54. *have before me*—What do you care where he has your letter, as long as he answers it?

> I *have before me* your letter of April 1st, which I am now answering.

Be as simple and natural as you can, and your letters will be far more successful.

> I am glad to answer your letter of April 1.

55. *herein, hereto, herewith*—Here are three timeworn words, which no self-respecting modern business letter-writer would think of using. But I see them every day.

> The quotation *herein* given is our latest and is up to date in every respect. (This is an antiquated form of doubling.)
> Attached *hereto* please find latest stock quotation. We enclose *herewith* the information you recently requested us to send to you. (That fellow hates to let loose of a sentence once he has it going.)
> We are returning *herewith* and attached *hereto* copies of the subject invitation to bid. (More doubling.)

Avoid these three words as you would rattlesnakes. They are unnecessary and add nothing. They merely get in the way of the flow of thought.

This quotation is our latest. (It's just as simple as that. But so many letter-writers are suspicious of plain talk and simple writing. Why?)

Attached is our latest stock quotation. *Or,* Here is our latest stock quotation.

We are glad to send you the information you requested. *Or,* Here is the information you requested. *Or,* Enclosed is the information you requested recently.

Here are our copies of the invitation to bid on the new dormitories at California State Polytechnic College in San Luis Obispo. (No one can misunderstand that.)

56. *hesitate*—He who hesitates is lost. That's doubly true in letter-writing.

Please do not *hesitate* to call on us for additional information that we can send you. (How do you know that you "can send" the information he may ask for?) I *hesitate* to tell you this, but . . . (Do you, really?)

Don't hesitate. Be confident and sure of yourself; then go ahead and say what you know should or must be said.

Just call on us if you need more information, and we'll try to send it to you. *Or,* . . . and we'll send it to you if we have it. (Much better.)

57. */ beg to remain, I remain, I am* and their plural variants, *We beg to remain, We remain, We are*—servile, hackneyed, meaningless letter endings completely out of harmony with our modern idea of forceful, friendly closings. When you close your letter, don't beg—leave nothing but a lot of good will for you and your company. (See Sixth Day.)

With all good wishes for the coming Christmas season, *I beg to remain,*

Hoping to hear from you in the near future, *I remain,* (See also "Trusting.")

Thanking you for your kind consideration, *I am,*

Make your letter endings simple, natural, friendly. See Eighth and Ninth Days—good and bad, forceful and weak letter endings. The easiest way to correct this old-fashioned jargon is to end your letter with whatever immediately preceded "I beg to remain," etc., except without participles.

All good wishes for the coming Christmas season!

Let me hear from you soon.   *Or,*   I hope to hear from you soon.

Thanks for your consideration. *Or,* Your consideration is much appreciated.

58. / *wish to state that, May I say that,* etc.—florid and ill suited to our friendly, forceful idea of modern business letter-writing practice.

> *I wish to state that* your order was shipped yesterday. (Go ahead and say it. Why ask permission? This is a long-winded windup before letting go of the ball.)
>
> *May I state that* we are delighted to have you visit and inspect our plant next Monday at 9. (A stuffed shirt wrote this.)

Go ahead and say it. You'll do it anyway. Why fiddle around wasting time by asking permission? Start with whatever follows "that" and you'll probably have a strong ending.

> We are delighted to have you inspect our plant next week. (This is bright, cheerful, human.)
>
> Your order was shipped yesterday. *Or,* You will be glad to know that your order was shipped yesterday. (This adds something.)

59. *inasmuch as*—a 16-cylinder word for "since" or "because."

> *Inasmuch as* I have had so many requests for our catalogs, our supply is completely depleted. (Naturally! How could it be only partially "depleted"?)

Use "since" or "because" and you will be writing on the mental level of 95 per cent of your readers—and they'll love you for doing it. It cuts down their mental strain.

> We have had so many requests for our catalog that we are completely out of them. (Why not follow this bit of negative information with: "As soon as we get another shipment, we'll send you one promptly"?)

60. *inform*—This simple word has jumped into the trite category.

> Please be *informed* that your order was shipped today. (Brrr! It's cold outside.)
>
> We are glad to *inform* you that we shall ship your order within the next few days.
>
> We are sorry to *inform* you of this turn of events.
>
> As you probably have been *informed* by this time, we are contemplating making several changes in our personnel.
>
> We have been *informed* by our Los Angeles office that the blanks can be delivered during the latter part of June.

Be simple and natural, not ornate and stiff. Use a colloquial synonym, such as "say," "tell," etc. Or just eliminate the offending expression entirely.

> Your order was shipped today. Your order will be shipped in a few days. We are sorry about what has happened. By now you probably know that we are thinking about making some changes in our staff.

> According to our Los Angeles office, the blanks can be delivered late in June.

61. *instant, inst.*—Although not used very often today, this old relic of yesteryear still crops up once in a while. It is a very poor substitute for the name of the current month. (See also "prox.")

> Your request of the 24th *inst.* has been received.

Today we don't believe in mincing words. We call a spade a spade, a letter a letter, and the months of the year by their proper names, not by such subterfuges as "instant," "proximo," or "ultimo."

> Thanks for your request of November 24.

62. *kind, kindly*—This word is very much overworked. Business letters should be kind without having to advertise that fact.

> Would you please be *kind* enough to refer this order to our Denver office? (Sounds as if you are trying to shame your reader into being as kind as you are.)

> *Kindly* place your order through our Customer Shopping Service. (That one appeared in the first letter given in this book.)

> Will you *kindly* handle the reply for us.

> If we can be of further service, *kindly* advise. (Inflated, trite, ridiculous.)

> We wish to thank you *kindly* for your recent request. (You wouldn't thank him gruffly, would you?)

> *Kindly* let us hear from you by return mail.

It is better to omit this word entirely than to use, misuse, and abuse it as in the examples given. Note how friendly these rewrites are. Compare them with the originals.

> Would you mind referring this order to our Denver office?

> Won't you (or "Just") place your order through our Customer Shopping Service.

> Please reply for us. *Or,* Won't you please reply for us? (You wouldn't handle it roughly or gruffly, would you? Say "please," if you wish.)

If we can help you any more, just (or "please") let us know. (This is the way one person would talk to another.) Thanks very much for your recent request. *Or,* Your recent request is very much appreciated.

Let us hear from you immediately, won't you? (You could have said "soon/" "promptly," or by some specific time, such as "by Monday sure.")

63. *kind order*—poppycock! How can an order be kind or unkind?

Thank you very kindly for your *kind order* of the lOst inst. (It really happened! I have written proof!)

Words like "kind" and "esteemed" qualify persons, not letters.

Thanks for your generous order of the tenth. *Or,* Your generous order of January 10 is much appreciated. (This is the way you would say it in person.)

64. *let me say, may I say, I wish to say*—Some people have to fight for every word they get in.

Let me say here and now that we are irrevocably opposed to any such measures. (Trite, wordy, and repetitious. More doubling.)

May I say that you are most welcome to visit us at any time. *I wish to say* that I have enjoyed reading your snide comments about old Jonsey.

Don't be a pompous eager beaver.

We are irrevocably opposed to any such measures. (Even with the word "irrevocably" omitted, this revision would be strong, forceful, straight-from-the-shoulder talking.) You are welcome to visit us anytime. *Or,* We are delighted to have you anytime. I enjoyed reading your snide remarks about old Jonsey.

65. *liberty*—We all cherish our liberty, but we don't like to have it bandied about by bombastic letter-writers.

We have *taken the liberty of* expressing a sample of each of the above, so as to permit you to submit same to your client at your earliest convenience.

I have *taken the liberty of* referring your inquiry to our Mr. Bill Jones, our local dealer in your community.

I *took the liberty of* wiring you this morning.

There is a vast difference between "taking the liberty of" and "taking liberties." Don't take too many liberties with the American language. It's pretty good as it is. Just learn how to use it more forcefully.

So that you can show them to your customer on Friday, we have sent you by express a sample of each color now in stock. Your inquiry has been referred to our local dealer, Bill Jones. I'm sure you will hear from him promptly. I telegraphed you this morning. *Or,* I sent you a telegram this morning.

66. *line, along this line, see our line*—Here is another jargoneers' favorite.

We feel our experience in this *line* is considerable. (Not one, but *two* hackneyed words. Some sentences contain three, four, or more.)

I feel that with the academic and practical training that I have had *along these lines,* I could be of use to your department, if you think my application worth considering. (What a brave, confident chap he is! Scared of his own shadow— and just about as vaguely outlined, too.) Our product is something new in the polishing *line.* (The line forms to the right.)

John knows that he will have to start at some simple job and work up, because of the fact that his high school education and short experience *along industrial lines* will not permit him to do otherwise.

We hope that you will let our salesman show you our *line.* (Some "lines" are so transparent that they are very easily seen through.)

If you *must* use "line," then say "line of merchandise." "Line" reminds me of a string of clothes flapping in the wind—like some words flapping in hot air.)

We have had valuable experience doing this kind of work. (Direct, specific.)

With the academic and practical training I have had, I know I could be very useful to your department. When may I come for an interview? (This fellow is really confident, sure of himself.)

Here is a really *new* polish for your new automobile.

John knows that he will have to start with simple jobs and work his way up because of his high school education and limited industrial experience.

We hope you will let our salesman, Mr. A. J. Nichols, show you our complete line of beautiful imported bone china.

67. *meet with your approval*—This phrase is rapidly becoming threadbare.

We trust our actions will *meet with your approval.*

Say it simply and naturally.

We hope you will approve of our action.

68. *merchandise*—Don't have "merchandise-itis." Are you afraid to speak out plainly and name what you have to sell?

It is a pleasure to send you this *merchandise* with our compliments.

Use every legitimate opportunity to mention your products by trade name. This is free advertising; it distinguishes your product from those of your competitors.

It is a pleasure to give you a set of our lovely Coalport bone china cups and saucer[1]"

69. *near future*—shopworn.

Would you please contact Mr. Miller in the very *near future* and explain to him our sales policy?

We trust we may serve you in the *near future.* (Stiff and ostentatious.)

In the very *near future* we will be publishing an entirely new service manual.

Instead, say "soon," "promptly," "immediately," etc.

Call on (or "Telephone") Mr. Miller immediately and explain our sales policy, will you?

Why not send us a trial order today?   *Or,*   How about giving us a chance to *prove* that we give the best service west of the Rockies? Our new service manual will be out very soon.

70. *note*—Under certain conditions, such as those given, this word is supercilious, snippy, snobbish. I feel like crawling when I read examples like these:

I *note* that all your other questions have been answered. I *note* that you plan to visit us shortly, and I am very happy. (He certainly forced that smile.)

Be yourself! Write as you talk! Try these revisions:

I am glad that all your other questions have been answered. I am delighted that you plan to visit us shortly. (This expresses genuine, wholesome welcome, not a "Quick, Watson! The cyanide bottle! Joe Blokes is visiting us.")

71. *oblige*—a wicked hangover from the ante-bellum era. It still occurs once in every 500 letters written, even today.

> I trust you will send this merchandise in the very near future, and *oblige.*

Today, people try to be obliging without bragging about it, or without demanding it from others.

> I'll appreciate your sending these gaskets promptly. I have three cars tied up, and I need these parts badly.

72. *our*—Some companies are too possessive—they brag about own
ing their employees.

> *Our* Miss Jones will send you a credit memorandum. *Our*
> Mr. Smith, our treasurer, will see you at noon.

Just relax and be natural. I know that the possessive personal pronouns are important, but soft pedal those in the first person: *I, my, mine, me; we, our, ours, us.*

> Miss Jones will make out your credit memorandum.
> Mr. Smith, our treasurer, will see you at noon.

73. *party*—When is a person a party? Only in legal documents. You know the lingo: "The party of the first part assigns to the party of the second part, etc."

> A certain *party* is interested in our product. His name is
> Marshall Hinks.
> Thanks for the information on the *party* from San Luis
> Obispo.

In business letters, don't call a person a party—unless you are referring to a group. Even then it is better to use the word "group."

> A certain person (or "dealer") in your territory, Marshall
> Hinks of Huston, is very much interested in our products.
> Thanks for the information about a prospective customer in
> San Luis Obispo.

74. *patronage*—Years ago, writers, artists, and the like had patrons, who supplied them money, food, and shelter while they practiced their art. But that doesn't hold true today. We now have cus
tomers, whom we serve—not patrons.

> Many thanks for your *patronage.*
> Thanks again for your *patronage.*

Let's be sensible and call business business, not patronage.

> Many thanks for your order.   *Or,*   Many thanks for your fine
> order.
> Thanks for your business, Mr. White.   *Or,*   We certainly
> appreciate your business, Mr. White.

75. *per*—This trite bit of jargon is a half-brother to "as per." It is equally bad and should also be avoided.

> *Per* your request of March 23rd, are forwarding under separate cover two photographs for your files. We are herewith enclosing one of our catalogs, *per* your postal card request.

When a cat purrs, he's supposed to be happy and contented; when a letter writer "per"s in his letters, he's simply antiquated.

> As you requested on March 23, we are sending you two photographs.
> We are glad to send you one of our catalogs, as you requested.

76. *period, for a period of*—another perfectly good word when it isn't in bad company, as it is in this sentence:

> Your subscription is *for a period of* two years. *For a period of* two months we shall not be hiring.

Wordy. Just strip off the words "a period of" or "the period of" and leave "for."

> Your subscription is for two years.
> For two months we shall not hire any new employees.

77. *permit me to say*—This is a full-brother to *let me say, may I say,* and / *wish to say.* All of them are stilted, florid, creaking at the joints. Avoid them.

> I hope that you will *permit me to say* that I am delighted to send you this information.

Can't you see Senator Snort swelling up like a balloon while spouting: "Permit me to say, my worthy constituents . . . ." Turn off all the hot air, PLEASE.

> I am delighted to send you this information. *Or,* It is a pleasure to send you this information.

78. *peruse, perusal*—I thought that these old chestnuts were buried with prohibition, but they still creep up every once in a while. I don't know why.

> We are herewith sending you under separate cover a copy of our catalog for your *perusal.*
> *Peruse* this contract carefully; then sign both copies and return the original to me, if you please.

Instead, say "study," "read carefully," or "check over." These are good, modern words.

> We are glad to send you a copy of our catalog to study.

Check over this contract carefully; then sign both copies and return the original to me, please.

79. *please*—If there is one word in the English language that has al most lost its pleasant connotation, it is this sadly overworked word "please." Every time I see it, I am reminded of those nu merous signs: "PLEASE Keep off the Grass" or just "PLEASE." I always want to pronounce it *"puh-leeze!"*

> *Please* be assured we shall abide by the agreement stated in your letter. (Very stiff and unfriendly.) *Please* acknowledge. (This is a sharp command.) In reply to your letter dated 16 January, *please* be informed that your Medical History sheet was mailed to the Bureau of Medicine and Surgery on 1 Nov. 1950. (Yes, this is bureaucratic, stilted military style.)

Use "please" sparingly in your business letters. It still has its place—as witness my deliberate use of it previously. But keep this word in its place. Promiscuous use, abuse, and misuse of "please" have caused it to fall into disrepute.

> You may be sure that we will abide by our agreement. (Here "will" has been used because the writer means "promise," "determination."

> Won't you acknowledge this order immediately? (This softens a peremptory command or order. It is not so likely to offend as the original.)

> In reply to your letter of 16 January, your Medical History sheet was mailed to the Bureau of Medicine and Surgery on 1 November 1950. (This doesn't alter the military style of writing; it merely corrects and improves it.)

80. *position, in a position to*—Now, I haven't anything against the word "position," only against its implication when used in these sentences:

> We are not *in a position to* offer you this advice. (Be careful! Don't get yourself in an awkward "position"! You might fall on your face.)

> We are *in a position to* show you tachometers and to quote you prices, too.

Be frank and honest with your customer. Come right out and say "can't" or "cannot." Don't beat around the bush or try to hide a negative behind a lot of big words.

> We just can't offer you any advice now. (This comes to the point clearly, swiftly.)

> We can now show you tachometers and quote you prices.

(There is no doubt about what the writer means in this sentence, is there?)

81. *possession*—another good word gone wrong in this sentence:

We are glad to have the opportunity of placing this information in your *possession.* (What part of one's anatomy is his "possession"?)

Say your piece simply and naturally; then stop!

We are glad to send you this information. (There are only 8 words in this forceful, clear revision as compared with 14 words in the windy original.)

82. *postal card*—It used to be a slur on your reader to say that you received his "postal" or "postal card" inquiry. But that was before the price was raised to two cents.

I have your recent *postcard* and, as you requested, am enclosing literature concerning our refrigerants.

Since there is some embarrassment when a person, for some reason or other, has to make a request on a postal card, it would be most considerate of the person who answers his letter to ignore the fact that the request was made on a card. Just speak of his "request" or "inquiry."

Thank you for your recent request. Here is some literature on our refrigerants. I hope that it will be of much help to you in your studies at Cal Poly.

83. *present time, present writing*—trite and repetitious. "Present" includes "time."

At the *present time* we are unable to use your services.

At the *present writing,* we cannot see our way clear to make this investment.

Actually, both expressions mean "now."

We cannot make this investment now. *Or,* Just now we cannot make this investment.

84. *proposition*—perfectly correct when something has been proposed,
but quite incorrect or improper in this sense:

That little *proposition* we inspected yesterday is a bargain. Correct *only* if something has been proposed. Otherwise, be specific.

That little ranch-type home we inspected yesterday is a bargain.

85. *prox., proximo*—Latin for "next." Just think—at one time in the

dim long ago, letter-writers and stenographers had to learn such jaw-breakers as "inst.," "prox.," "ult."

Our terms are net 10th Prox. (A garbled form of shorthand.)

"Proximo" in business jargon means "next month." Why not be natural? You are trying to help your reader, not befuddle him.

All invoices are net the 10th of the following month. (Yes, this is longer, but it is clear and in contemporary English, not medieval Latin.)

86. *pursuant*—According to the *American College Dictionary,* this word means "proceeding comfortably; pursuing," among other definitions.

Pursuant to your request, we enclose herewith copy of General Catalog No. 46.

Again, and again, and again throughout this book I have kept hammering away at one idea: SAY WHAT YOU HAVE TO SAY SIMPLY, NATURALLY, and CONVERSATIONALLY —that is, interestingly.

As you requested, we are glad to enclose (or "to send you") a copy of our General Catalog No. 46.

87. *re*—Here is an abbreviation whose meaning has been lost. At least, there are so many different definitions that I'm sure nobody knows for sure just what "re" actually means. I don't.

Re Radiant Heater Tile Floors

In re your letter of January 15, would say we are definitely interested in your proposition.

What are we to say to each other *re* factory?

Avoid this juicy bit of business jargon. Be specific, as indicated in these revisions:

Subject: Radiant Heater Tile Floors

We are definitely interested in the proposal you made in your letter of January 15.

What are we to say to each other about that factory?

88. *received, in receipt of*—To say that you have received a person's letter is about the silliest thing you could say. Of course you have. How else could you answer it?

We *received* your card this morning and are now answering it. (Who's crazy now?)

We are *in receipt of* your inquiry dated Dec. 22. Start your

letter by saying something your reader would like to

hear. Thank him for his letter, etc. (See Sixth Day: "Get Off to a Flying Start.")

Thanks for your inquiry about .... (Be specific. If there is nothing significant about the time when the inquiry arrived, don't mention it.)

Your inquiry of December 22 is much appreciated. (At least, this will make him feel good for having written you.)

89. *recent date*—All business communications—letters, reports, memorandums, etc.—should be dated.

As requested in your postal card of *recent date,* we take pleasure in sending you herewith copy of our latest catalog.

If you don't know the date or don't have the letter handy, then simply say "your recent letter" or possibly "recently."

We are pleased to send you the catalog you recently requested.

90. *records, according to our records*—Be cautious about loosely referring to your records. All companies keep records. Yours are not unique. Moreover, it sounds as if you don't believe your reader.

According to our records, your account is 30 days overdue. (This sounds as if you are not quite sure whether it is overdue by 30 days.)

The best thing to do in this case is to omit "according to our records" entirely, and to start with what immediately follows:

Your account is thirty days overdue. (This is positive and sure. It certainly doesn't mince words or hide behind some fuzzy phraseology; yet it is courteous.)

91. *remain*—This is a weak, spineless ending.

With our best wishes for a joyous Christmas, we *remain* Quit remaining! Get an ending that really says something worth hearing.

Best wishes for a joyous Christmas!

92. *replying to your letter of, referring to yours of*—All participial openings (and closings, too) are weak and in very poor letter-writing practice. (See also Seventh and Eighth Days.)

Replying to your letter of the 10th, beg to state that we sincerely appreciate your addressing us. (Trite, old-fashioned, and weak.)

Referring to yours of the 6th, wish to say we very much appreciate your thoughtfulness in sending us under separate cover a supply of new catalogs.

The only thing to strengthen a weak participial closing is to make the phrase into a complete sentence, or eliminate it completely. Begin by getting off to a good start, and step on your brakes firmly but gently.

> Thank you for your letter of May 10. We sincerely appreciate your writing to us.

> It was certainly good of you to send us a supply of new catalogs mentioned in your letter of September 6.

93. *return mail*—What, pray, is "by return mail"? Does this mean grabbing the postman by his coat tails, dragging him into your office, and holding him there until you can dictate and sign a re ply, with which he can return to the post office? I don't know what else such an absurd statement could mean.

> Please answer by *return mail.*

There is no such thing as "by return mail." This is another pet expression that has mushroomed into popular use simply because letter-writers never considered the absurdity of the statement. Instead, either be specific—"by next Friday"—or use "promptly," "soon," "immediately," etc. Help your reader answer as you want him to in every way you can. Being specific is one very good way of helping.

> Please answer promptly. *Or,* Please answer by January 22. *Or,* Please answer by Friday of this week.

94. *same*—This adjective or pronoun is often misused, as in this vague bit of business jargon:

> We shall appreciate *same.*

> Please be assured that this office will notify you immediately upon receipt of *same.* (Just what does "same" refer to or mean?)

> Please note the base can be removed and you should have no difficulty in mounting same in the amplifier cabinets.

People often use "same" to keep from repeating something previously said. This is not too bad when you have the original letter. It is better, however, to eliminate this word from your business vocabulary. The pronouns "it" and "them" are better than "same."

> We shall appreciate it (or "them"). (Better still, use the noun for which "same" stands.)

> You may be sure that we shall notify you as soon as we receive your application for medical service. (I know what "same" means—you see, I read the rest of the letter!)

Since the base can be removed, you will have no difficulty in mounting it in the amplifier cabinets.

95. *satisfy*—There is an unpleasant overtone to this word when it is used in this way:

We hope that this information will *satisfy* you. (To me, that means that we hope you will be satisfied with what we have sent and not bother us any more.)

Customers want to be pleased, not just satisfied.

We hope that this information will be very helpful in your work.

96. *self-addressed*—There is no such thing as a self-addressed envelope.

Kindly send a *self-addressed,* stamped envelope for reply.

Eliminate "self" and this designation is O.K.

Please send an addressed, stamped envelope for reply.

97. *stated*—This is a rather pompous way of saying something.
You *stated* that you expected to be in Los Angeles in June. (This sounds as if you did not believe him, or as if he went back on his "statement.")

Instead, use words like "said," "mentioned," "remarked," or rewrite the phrase entirely.

You mentioned that you expected to be in Los Angeles this June. Will you?

I hope that you will be in Los Angeles this June, as you indicated.

98. *such*—Another overworked word. Quite a favorite of the business jargoneer.

Until *such* time as you are free to accept employment with us, we shall keep your application in our inactive file.

Often this word can be omitted, or the entire phrase "such time as."

Until you are free to accept employment with us, we shall keep your application in our inactive file.

99. *take pleasure in, take this opportunity to*—a bit trite. How can you "take" pleasure?

We *take pleasure in* enclosing herewith our catalog No. 46, which we trust you will find of interest and assistance. (A sentence filled with hackneyed words.)

We *take this opportunity to* wish you a very Merry Christmas.

Instead of "take pleasure in," use "are pleased"; omit "take this opportunity to" entirely.

> We are pleased to send you our Catalog No. 46, which we are sure will be of much help to you in your work at California State Polytechnic College.

> We wish you a very Merry Christmas. *Or,* A very Merry Christmas to you!

100. *thank you*—Everyone likes to be thanked, but it does seem to me that politeness or courtesy, like beauty, is more than skin deep. Merely tacking a cursory "Thank you" onto the end of a letter does not make that letter a friendly one. In fact, I think that these words have just the opposite effect; they sound like peremptory commands: "Now you do what I have asked you to, for I have condescended to thank you. So hop to it!"

> Last week I ordered six 81" x 108" percale sheets. To date I have heard nothing from you. Would appreciate your advising me as soon as possible. *Thank you.*

If you have not thanked your reader, why not add something to these two words in order to make them seem less curt and abrupt: "Thank you for all the time and trouble you have taken to get me this information." After all, it's the spirit of the letter, far more than the honeyed words that may be used, that determines its friendliness. You can't manufacture friendliness out of honeyed words. They will sound hollow and ring untrue. Real friendliness must flow from your heart:

> Last week I ordered six 81" x 108" percale sheets. I wonder whether you received my order. Would it be too much trouble to look into this matter and let me know what you find? Thanks for your trouble.

101. *thank you again*—Thanking the reader once is enough. If you thank people too often, they will begin to doubt your sincerity.

> *Thank you again* for all the trouble you have gone to in my behalf.

Whenever I see these words "Thank you again," I think of a Casper Milquetoast sort of person, who timorously goes about thanking to the right and to the left.

> I appreciate all the trouble you have gone to in my behalf.

102. *thank you in advance, thanking you in advance*—a very dubious way of putting your reader under obligation to you. By "thanking him in advance" you seem to force him to do what you wish, even if he doesn't want to do it. This is presumptuous.

Thank you in advance for your kind attention to this important matter. *Thanking you in advance* for your trouble, I beg to remain

In addition to being presumptuous, this closing is a lazy man's way out. He thinks that he's very smart by thanking the reader in advance so that when the reader does his bidding, he won't have to bother writing to thank him.

I'll appreciate anything you can send. This is important for me.

I hope this won't be too much trouble. Whatever you send will be sincerely appreciated.

103. *thank you kindly*—You wouldn't thank him gruffly, would you?

Thank you kindly for sending me this information. Omit the word "kindly" and you have a good sentence: Thank you for sending me this information.

104. *thanking you*—another of those weak, insipid participles. Elim inate them entirely.

Thanking you very kindly for your esteemed interest and *trusting* that we may hear further from you in the very near future, we beg to remain (It could be worse, but I doubt that. I don't recall having seen any ending that topped this one.)

There are such things as "perfect" participles in grammar, but in business letter-writing participles are perfectly insipid.

Thanks very much for your interest. If we can help you in any other way, just drop us a line. (Colloquial? Certainly it is. That's the essence of forceful business letter-writing—being natural, conversational, down-to-earth. Try it!)

105. *therein*—another sadly overworked word that should be eradi cated from the language.

This will acknowledge receipt of your letter dated August 22nd, 1947, and confirm reservation contained *therein* for you and your family, beginning August 28th. (Believe it or not, this came from the manager of a large metropolitan hotel.)

Just forget there ever was such a word as "therein." You'll never miss it.

Thank you for your letter of August 22 reserving a room for you and your family for August 28-31. We shall be very glad to have you, and will do everything we can to make your stay in Chicago a memorable one.

106. *this is to inform you that, this is in reply to*—formal, frigid, frightening sentence openings. They are like the knock of the Gestapo on my door at midnight.

> *This is to inform you that* we are happy to open an account in your name. (After scaring the wits out of me with their first six words, they tell me that they are happy!) *This is in reply to* your kind letter of October 14.

If you will start with whatever immediately follows "that," you probably will have an excellent opening—or sentence:

> We are happy to open an account in your name. (I believe they mean what they say. At least, they certainly sound sincere. I'll take their words at face value.) Thanks for your encouraging letter of October 14.

107. *trust*—Now don't misunderstand me and go away thinking that I don't trust people or believe in "trust." In a business letter, nonetheless, your use of the word "trust" can certainly be carried too far, as witness:

> We *trust* these bulletins may be of assistance to you. (Snooty, snobbish, supercilious, unsure.)
>
> We *trust* that same is satisfactory. (WOW!!! How bad can a sentence get? Don't ask me that. I've seen some beauties in my time—in fact, I have included quite a few of them in this book, as you probably have noticed.)
>
> We *trust* that our handling of these requests will meet with your full approval.

When used as it was in the three sentences just shown, "trust" is a threadbare word. It's stiff and stuffy, snooty and snobbish, supercilious and sanctimonious.

> We hope that these bulletins will be of much help to you in your studies.
>
> Is this satisfactory? *Or,* Are these satisfactory? (A question is a strong closing.) We are anxious to handle your requests.

108. *trusting, hoping, thanking, feeling*—These are "scared-rabbit" closings. Cy Frailey calls them weak, puny writing.

Once and for all, let's quit being scared rabbits and stand on our hind feet, like the men we are.

109. *undersigned, the undersigned*—another choice cliche, which should go the way of all flesh—*pronto!*

> *The undersigned* wishes to state that we take extreme pleas-

ure in accepting your esteemed order subject, of course, to the terms contained herein.

It is the sincere wish of the *undersigned* that ....

Don't be afraid to use "I" or "we" wherever they would be used in natural conversation. Don't resort to subterfuges in trying to avoid using these pronouns.

I am delighted to accept your order, subject to the terms stated.

I certainly wish that ....   *Or,* I certainly hope that....

110. *under separate cover, by separate cover*—If the material, book lets, or pamphlets are not enclosed, they obviously must be sent separately.

Under separate cover we are sending you copies of our latest bulletins.

I am also sending *by separate cover* samples of our standard colors.

If you *must* indicate that they are not enclosed, why not say that they are being sent separately? Or indicate the exact method of shipment: express, parcel post, etc. Or omit it entirely. This is probably the best solution.

We are sending you copies of our latest bulletins.

I am also sending, separately, samples of our standard colors.

111. *upon investigation we find that*—What a windup before letting go of the ball!

Upon investigation we find that your order will be shipped on January 15.

Start with whatever follows "that," and you probably will have a pretty good sentence.

Your order will be shipped on January 15.

112. *up to this writing*—wordy and pompous.

We have not heard from you *up to this writing.*

Why not omit entirely?

We have not heard from you.

113. *your valued wishes*—much too effusive and flattering. Sounds in sincere.

We take great pleasure in complying with *your valued wishes.*

Shades of the long dead past! Let it rest in peace—PLEASE! We are glad to handle this order as you indicated.

114. *in view of the fact that*—wordy, trite, illogical.

> *In view of the fact that* we will have only a limited quantity of this manual, we advise that you contact us in the very near future if you wish to obtain a copy.

Instead, use "since."

> Since we will have only a few of these manuals, let us know immediately if you want a copy.

115. *We*—Wherever you can, write your letters from your reader's (the YOU) point of view. This doesn't mean that you should twist your thoughts into pretzels just to avoid using a natural "we" or "I." Use good old horse sense and you will write much more successful letters. Here's what to avoid, however:

> *We* thank you for your inquiry. (Big WE, little you! Should be reversed.)
>
> *We would like to* thank you for your application. (Sounds as if you aren't going to thank him—you would only "like" to.) *We wish to acknowledge* your card dated April 17th, 1951. (Pompous and silly.)

I-trouble and We-writis are annoying and sometimes fatal diseases. Whenever I read a letter filled with WE's, I am reminded of a character in George Meredith's novel, *The Egoist.* As I recall the incident, the hero, Sir Willoughby Patterne, looked into his sweetheart's eyes, saw there the man he loved, and took him in his arms. In other words, he was like the man who said: "Of all my wife's relations, I like myself the best." A lot of egoists spend a lot of valuable time writing letters!

> Thanks for your inquiry.
>
> Thank you for your application.
>
> We appreciate (or "Thank you for") your inquiry of April 17.

116. *We are handing you*—I thought I had finished with this "hand" business, but not quite. Here's another of this breed.

> *We are handing you* our latest catalog on heat apparatus. (Sending, YES; handing, NO!)

Don't let your hands get out of hand. Or maybe I should say: Keep your "hands" to yourself.

> Here is our latest catalog on the heat apparatus that we manufacture.

117. *We are today in receipt of*—wordy and unnatural.

> *We are today in receipt of* your order for four dozen #253.

Be yourself—be natural.

Thank you for your order for four dozen #253. (What's significant about the "today"?)

118. *We regret to advise that*—negative, frightening, and wordy.

We regret to advise that our stock of #631 is depleted at the moment.

Accentuate the positive—eliminate the negative wherever you can.

Although we are temporarily out of #631, they should be in next week. . . .

119. *With your kind permission*—It was nice of you to ask permission, but I'll bet you didn't wait to get it.

With your kind permission, we are sending you samples of our latest prints.

I hope by this time that I have exploded the stuffed-shirt balloon. After all, the only thing that makes a balloon go up is hot air. Save yours for the Fourth of July. Write just as simply and naturally as you can without making your writing childish. We are glad to send you samples of our latest prints.

120. *the writer*—This is certainly a case of false modesty and a subterfuge just as undesirable as "the undersigned," which we just discussed.

The writer wishes to say that your application will be placed in our active file for due consideration upon the occasion of an opening which would be commensurate with your training and ability.

If you will only let the rules of forceful conversation guide you, you won't have any trouble with your I's and WE's. Learn to write as you talk, and your letters will always be forceful, friendly, and natural.

Your application will be kept in our active files. We never know when there will be an opening for a young man with your training and ability. The next time we have such an opening, we'll get in touch with you.

121. *would say, would suggest, wish to say*—Clipped constructions are avoided by writers of successful business letters. This style was popular fifty to a hundred years ago, but it is not today.

Would say your order will be ready within a week. (Aren't you sure?)

Would suggest that you reinforce the partition with additional steel rods before cementing over.

Wish to say that we will be very happy to have you visit us the very next time you are in our neighborhood.

Subterfuge won't get you anywhere. Just omitting the I or WE subjects of verbs doesn't eliminate them. They are there, all right. By clipping them off you are merely making a second mistake—and two wrongs don't make a right.

Your order will be ready within a week. (See how much better this is than the stiff, clipped original?) Why not reinforce the partitions with additional steel rods before you cement them over? (A question is always good. It puts the reader legitimately "on the spot.") The next time you are out this way, drop in for a visit, won't you? (Friendly, colloquial, inviting in more ways than one. *That* is forceful writing.)

122. *do yeoman service*—Here is an old chestnut that continues to creep into business correspondence. At one time this was really an apt description; today, not one person in 10,000 really knows—or cares—what it means.

Jones certainly *did yeoman service* as chairman of the Ways and Means Committee.

Say what you mean, and mean what you say. If he was in the Navy, maybe he actually did yeoman service or duty.

Jones certainly worked hard as chairman of the Ways and Means Committee.

123. *yours truly*—another corner into which false modesty can chase the unsuspecting. At one time it was very popular to speak of yourself as "yours truly." But this expression went out of style when people stopped wearing frock coats and mutton chops.

Kindly sign and return these contracts to *yours truly* at your earliest convenience.

Please use common sense in trying to eliminate the I's and WE's from your business correspondence. Often the cure is worse than the disease itself. So it is with "yours truly" and other makeshift devices.

Please sign and return (to me) these contracts as soon as you can. *Or,* Will you please sign and return these contracts as soon as possible?

*   *   *   *

Well, there they are—123 trite expressions, which forceful business letter-writers try hard to avoid or eliminate from their letters today; more than 200 sentences containing one or more of these old-fashioned, hackneyed expressions. But for each trite sentence, there is at least one modern, up-to-date rewrite as we would speak it today.

Yes, this list is incomplete. But I had to stop somewhere, or else this Appendix would have dragged on interminably. Now why don't *you* go back through your files, look over your letters for the last month or two, and make a list of your own hackneyed, trite, moss-covered, moth-eaten expressions? As you make out your list, write down a snappy, modern revision, just as I have here.

What do *you* say?

INDEX

Also available from www.sunvillagepublications.com

BRAIN STORMING

The Dynamic Way To Create Successful New Ideas

Charles H. Clark

How To Write SUCCESSFUL BUSINESS LETTERS In Just 15 Days

John P. Riebel

CHALK TALK MADE EASY

A COMPLETE SELF-INSTRUCTION COURSE IN CRAYON AND BLACKBOARD DRAWING

BY WILLIAM ALLEN BIXLER "THE RILEY ARTIST"

USING CHARTS TO IMPROVE PROFITS

Ely Francis

How To Help Groups Make Decisions

Grace Loucks Elliott

HOW TO CREATE NEW IDEAS

A Comprehensive Course in The Art and Science of Creative Thinking

Jack W. Taylor

How To Plan Meetings

And Be A Successful Chairperson

Joseph G. Glass, PH.B., LL.B.

How To Run BETTER MEETINGS

Edward J. Hegarty

The Successful Sales Meetings Handbook

Bill N. Newman

www.ingramcontent.com/pod-product-compliance
Lightning Source LLC
Chambersburg PA
CBHW071400170526
45165CB00001B/120